Courts and Federalism

Law and Society Series
W. Wesley Pue, General Editor

The Law and Society Series explores law as a socially embedded phenomenon. It is premised on the understanding that the conventional division of law from society creates false dichotomies in thinking, scholarship, educational practice, and social life. Books in the series treat law and society as mutually constitutive and seek to bridge scholarship emerging from interdisciplinary engagement of law with disciplines such as politics, social theory, history, political economy, and gender studies.

A list of the titles in this series appears at the end of this book.

LAW AND
SOCIETY

Gerald Baier

Courts and Federalism: Judicial Doctrine in the United States, Australia, and Canada

UBCPress · Vancouver · Toronto

15 14 13 12 11 10 09 08 07 06   5 4 3 2 1

Printed in Canada on ancient-forest-free paper (100% post-consumer recycled) that is processed chlorine- and acid-free, with vegetable-based inks

Library and Archives Canada Cataloguing in Publication

Baier, Gerald, 1971-

Courts and federalism : judicial doctrine in the United States, Australia, and Canada / Gerald Baier.

(Law and society, ISSN 1496-4953)
Includes bibliographical references and index.
ISBN-13: 978-0-7748-1235-1 (bound); 978-0-7748-1236-8 (pbk.)
ISBN-10: 0-7748-1235-4 (bound); 0-7748-1236-2 (pbk.)

1. Judicial review – Canada. 2. Political questions and judicial power – Canada. 3. Judicial review – United States. 4. Political questions and judicial power – United States. 5. Judicial review – Australia. 6. Political questions and judicial power – Australia. I. Title. II. Series: Law and society series (Vancouver, B.C.)

K3175.B35 2006   347.71'012   C2005-907496-5

Canada

UBC Press gratefully acknowledges the financial support for our publishing program of the Government of Canada through the Book Publishing Industry Development Program (BPIDP), and of the Canada Council for the Arts, and the British Columbia Arts Council.

This book has been published with the help of a grant from the Canadian Federation for the Humanities and Social Sciences, through the Aid to Scholarly Publications Programme, using funds provided by the Social Sciences and Humanities Research Council of Canada, and with the help of the K.D. Srivastava Fund.

UBC Press
The University of British Columbia
2029 West Mall
Vancouver, BC V6T 1Z2
604-822-5959 / Fax: 604-822-6083
www.ubcpress.ca

For Kirsten

Contents

Acknowledgments

I am most fortunate to have had encouragement and advice from a number of teachers and colleagues as this project developed. Peter Aucoin, Herman Bakvis, R. Kenneth Carty, Paul Groarke, Samuel LaSelva, Patrick Malcolmson, Richard Myers, Wesley Pue, and Peter H. Russell all merit special recognition for their contributions or simply for their examples of engaged teaching and inquiry. Jennifer Smith is owed particular thanks for wise advice as well as critical and challenging viewpoints. My intellectual debts to her are considerable and will take a long career of honest, diligent, and rigorous scholarship to repay.

For financial assistance during initial research, I am grateful to Dalhousie University and the Killam Scholarship Trust and for a SSHRCC Postdoctoral Fellowship held at the University of Toronto. I also benefited from a SSHRCC strategic grant under the Federalism and Federations program. Kelly Hogan and Erin Crandall provided research support, and both were regularly one step ahead of the researcher.

Initial research on the Australian parts of the study was undertaken at the Centre for Public Policy, University of Melbourne. Its director at the time, Brian Galligan, was a most welcoming host. The American material was greatly improved by interactions with participants of the Federalism and the Courts conference held at the University of Georgia, Athens, in February 2001. I also derived considerable benefit from being a fellow at the Supreme Court Historical Society's Summer Institute in 2002. The seminar's coordinators, Vicki C. Jackson, Charles McCurdy, and Harry Scheiber, and the other fellows made a substantial contribution to my overall understanding of the United States Supreme Court and its historical role in the federal system.

Randy Schmidt and Darcy Cullen at UBC Press shepherded the project through the editorial and production processes with admirable skill and enthusiasm. I am grateful to the anonymous reviewers of the manuscript, whose suggestions were most helpful in improving the final product.

My largest debt is to Kirsten Craven, who has been my best critic, champion, and friend for the past decade and a half.

Acknowledgments

Courts and Federalism

Introduction

Ignoring Judicial Review

It is said that familiarity breeds contempt. If that is true, then one of the most familiar topics to students of Canadian federalism, judging by the scorn piled upon it, must be the judicial interpretation of the federal division of powers. Despite its apparent relevance for an understanding of federalism, the study of judicial review is seen as a tired, dull, or at best misleading exercise for political science. This book seeks to revive the study of judicial review as a structural element of Canadian and comparative federalism. To do so, it employs evidence from the practice of judicial review in Australia and the United States as well as Canada to demonstrate the relevance of judge-made law to federalism.

While lawyers and legal academics stay conversant with developments in the constitutional law of Canadian federalism, the same developments seem to have almost wholly escaped the attention or concern of political scientists. Developments in the interpretation of rights certainly have not. While the *Charter of Rights and Freedoms* is little more than twenty years old, it has spawned a boom of constitutional scholarship by political scientists. Observers vigorously attend to and analyze in detail the Supreme Court's decisions and doctrinal approaches to various rights. Given the impact that the Charter has had on our understanding of rights and the way that political conflicts have been diverted to the courts, Charter politics unquestionably merits this attention. But so too does the division of powers. Only the Charter is currently getting its due. Judicial review of the division of powers remains a topic of neglect despite its genuine importance to the study of Canadian government.

The explanation for this shortfall is unclear. The lack of attention paid to federal judicial review generally is not indicative of a lack of developments. The Supreme Court may decide two or three major cases on federalism in any given year. Currently, the cumulative impact of those decisions can be seen only in the work of scholars of public policy as they follow particular policy sectors. Such studies frequently make note of developments in the interpretation of the division of powers and the impacts on the sector that result. Environmental protection, to name just one example, is a policy area routinely influenced by the judiciary's interpretation of the division of powers. François Rocher and Miriam Smith note that "the difference between formal jurisdiction (as laid out in sections 91 and 92 of the *Constitution Act, 1867*) and the working reality of Canadian federalism" is best highlighted by a closer look at specific policy fields.[1] The process of untangling is more dependent upon judicial review in some fields than in others. But clearly the division of powers is still relevant. It is just uncommon for it to be approached as a subject in its own right.[2]

If the lack of attention cannot be credited to a lack of activity, what other reasons might explain it? The prime suspects appear to be an excess of skepticism about the impact of judicial review and an even greater excess of "realism" about how courts come to their decisions.

The Judicial Committee of the Privy Council (JCPC), Canada's final court of appeal until 1949, betrayed a preference for the provinces in constitutional litigation. Many observers believed that this preference set a course for decentralized Canadian federalism. Alan Cairns challenged this accepted wisdom. "It is impossible," he wrote, "to believe that a few elderly men in London deciding two or three constitutional cases a year precipitated, sustained and caused the development of Canada in a federalist direction that the country would not otherwise have taken."[3] If hindsight suggested a less prominent role, the committee was still seen as a prime motivator of federalism by its contemporaries. After the JCPC rejected federal laws designed to alleviate some of the effects of the Great Depression, F.R. Scott wrote that the impact of the Judicial Committee would "have grave and far reaching consequences. It is probably not too much to say that they have created for Canadians a constitutional situation scarcely less critical than that which led to Confederation itself."[4] At the very least, it may be said that the committee's decisions reinforced and encouraged the development of Canadian federalism in a decentralized direction. The JCPC's impact led observers to the reasonable belief at the time that judicial review was critical to understanding Canadian federalism. These points have been reiterated in a comprehensive account by John Saywell of the JCPC and its influence on Canadian federalism.[5]

The JCPC's era is long past in more ways than one. The Supreme Court of Canada replaced the JCPC as Canada's court of final resort in 1949. More importantly, judicial review seems to be of less immediate impact in establishing the tone of federalism. Changes in the federal system have also changed the way that political scientists understand Canadian federalism. An unprecedented level of intergovernmental cooperation that began in the late 1950s has blurred the lines of distinction between governments and their responsibilities ever since. Those lines were ones that the courts were tasked to patrol.

As Canadian governments have become increasingly comfortable with blurry lines, their desire to clarify responsibilities in court has waned. Negotiation, not litigation, is the preferred means to resolve jurisdictional conflicts in Canadian federalism today. Both levels of government reasonably expect to maximize their goals by negotiating with each other rather than submitting to the zero-sum game of litigation. So much of what actually affects the character of the federal system goes on outside the purview of the judiciary that the decisions of the court seem to be a poor guide to the state of intergovernmental relations at any given time.

Accompanying this decrease of influence (or perhaps inducing it) has been a decrease of faith in the decision-making methods used by courts. The style of judicial decisions on federalism has generally been formal, phrased in legal maxims and categories, not much attuned to the overt policy context of jurisdictional disputes. With governments doing more cooperating and compromising, the formalism of the court seems to be outdated at best and frustrating at worst. This "trap of formalism" further prevented political scientists from accurately demonstrating the effects and significance of judicial power. Peter Russell noted in 1986 that "few ... authors have attempted to construct a general theory of judicial review or of judicial decision making by appellate judges."[6] Russell credits James Mallory's *Social Credit and the Federal Power* for creating a new understanding of judicial decisions as an important dependent variable interacting with other political forces to shape the Canadian federation.[7] By making judicial decisions a dependent variable, Mallory moved from an understanding of decisions as "self-evident or self-enforcing logical deductions"[8] to a product of judicial choices informed by ideology or simple policy preferences. Mallory claimed that the "judges could not separate themselves completely from their own personalities,"[9] a position in keeping with the emerging judicial behaviour or attitudinal model.[10] The attitudinal model, which posits that judicial policy preferences dictate the direction of judicial decisions, is a predominant paradigm in political science approaches to judicial power. With the attitudinal model, observers have come to disassociate the reasoning in decisions from their political impact. Judges are presumed to be policy maximizers, unconstrained by the strictures of the law. Hence, the "bottom line," rather than the thinking of the Supreme Court, is the only reliable information that one can take from judicial review for political analysis.

Attitudinalists, like legal realists before them, begin with the assumption that judges are making conscious, political decisions in the way that they interpret the constitution or any other law. Constitutional adjudication cannot really be believed to be "a series of logical inferences from abstract legal categories."[11] Political scientists who think otherwise, it is alleged, are nothing more than "little law professors" bandying about an "arcane lawyer-babble of case names."[12] For attitudinalists, the only way to properly study the courts as an agent of politics is to try to isolate and measure the political qualities of the judicial branch. Political outcomes are better explained by the behavioural and attitudinal characteristics of judges than by the post hoc justifications found in judicial decisions. Researchers explore questions such as who appointed the justices? What kinds of policy preferences have those justices articulated in their pre-judicial careers? What process does a judicial panel use to come up with its decisions? What influence do clerks have on their justices? But most dominant has been the development of large-scale databases with judicial votes coded on the basis of the ideological preferences represented by preferred outcomes.[13] These results are then subjected to sophisticated statistical analysis for evidence of patterns in judicial preferences and ideology. External actors are also looked at in political terms. The adjudication strategies of governments and repeat litigants are probed. The arguments that governments are willing to make and the kinds of results that they pursue in court can vary and may not always make sense on the surface, but they represent the "politics" of judicial review. "Overcoming legal formalism," as Russell described it, has led to more systematic study of institutional variables but less concern for the explanations that courts advance in defence of their own decisions.

Approach of the Book

Perhaps it is not surprising that Canadian political science has lost interest in federal judicial review. A narrowly focused study of the judicial interpretation of constitutional law is a practice whose time has passed. There are too many possible influences on the state of Canadian federalism to rely on a single institutional variable when describing its development. Judicial review is, however, still a variable that deserves some attention. If there is an obvious need to study judicial review, what do we do about the problem of studying it? How do we take judicial review seriously yet avoid the trap of a sterile and narrow formalism? One must begin by acknowledging that the approaches of legal realists and attitudinalists do not tell the whole story. Those scholars make a genuine effort to take the law seriously as a political phenomenon, but they plainly disregard the most obvious evidence available – the recorded arguments of the courts that they are studying. Any revival in the study of federal judicial review in Canada must start by paying more solemn heed to written judicial reasoning.

The study of law and courts is increasingly moving towards a "post-behaviouralist" approach. While attitudinal studies of courts and their decision making remain a prominent part of how the discipline of political science approaches judicial power, other scholars of public law see more relevance in continuing to look at the reasoning of courts and the normative implications of those decisions. Under the rubric of "historical institutionalism" or "new institutionalism," this approach continues to pay attention to the traditional doctrinal history typical in an earlier generation of public law scholarship but does so in a way more cognizant of the overall effect of judicial power. As a method, it is unwilling to be naïve about the reality of judicial power but also unwilling to be reductionist about the role that judicial thinking plays in the development of constitutions and politics. Judicial reasoning remains front and centre in the new institutional approach to courts.

Comparative experience demonstrates the virtue of this choice. Australia and the United States have been chosen as sources of comparison for this study. The reasons for choosing them are numerous. The obvious advantages to a comparativist are the common-law tradition and the written federal constitutions that both countries share with Canada. There are also reasonable similarities in the structure and operation of all three high courts. Most important, as the book demonstrates, there is a relative commonality of approach to the task of federalism adjudication. This similarity allows one to draw reasonably generalizable conclusions about the place of law and courts in federations.

The United States has clear and immediate relevance to students of the judicial review of federalism. The original problems of federal constitutional interpretation were first raised and addressed by Americans. Many of the judicial and scholarly approaches that have been adopted in Canada and Australia owe their origins to American practice. Doubts about the certainty and virtue of the law also have American origins. The skepticism so common among observers of twentieth-century jurisprudence derives in large part from American thinking about the limits of the law. Even more importantly, the present-day Supreme Court of the United States has made federalism jurisprudence newly relevant by engaging in a relatively polarized debate over the meaning of federalism and the proper role of a high court in a federal system. The stakes raised for the political system by judicial review are high enough to merit attention, attention not just to the bottom line of the Supreme Court's rulings but also to the manner in which the justices get to their decisions. Institutional variables, including the conditioning effects of legalism, are recognized in the present American literature as important explanatory variables in a nuanced account of judicial review.

Contemporary Australian jurisprudence is less dramatically engaged in debates about the fundamentals of federalism. Historically, the approach of the Australian High Court to federalism has been rigidly legalistic. That formality has come somewhat under fire, but its resilience despite the questions raised by legal realism is interesting in itself. The staying power of legalistic constitutional interpretation makes judicial reasoning as relevant as ever in Australia.

A survey of judicial review in all three federations reveals considerable evidence that the reasoning of courts can be taken more seriously in the study of federalism. The problems encountered in constitutional interpretation obviously differ from country to country, but the general approach to adjudicating federalism disputes that all three countries share suggests an important lesson for students of federalism and the law.

This is a book about both law and politics. While many deny there is any difference between those two worlds, new accounts of law and politics characterize judicial processes as unique from the kinds of trade-offs and choices that we expect from legislative and executive institutions. Having such a conception of the law may seem to be a liability when making a critical study of judicial review. It is perhaps naïve to try to deny the obvious politics at work in the judiciary. The great contribution of legal realism and critical legal theory, after all, has been to teach observers of constitutional law that judicial choices are policy choices. Apparently, there is no standard or set of standards within the law that can remove discretion from the hands of judicial decision makers. Can one see any more in judicial review than simple politics dressed up in the language of law?

For federalism, this is a particularly critical question. The workaday cases on the federal division of powers reviewed here hint that the choices made by judges might not be wholly political. When high courts are thrust into a political spotlight, as the Supreme Court of Canada was in the *Secession* and *Patriation* references or the Supreme Court of the United States in *Bush v. Gore*, politics seems to be inevitable. But in the admittedly more mundane and slow evolution of a constitutional division of powers, there appears to be at least one element of judicial decision making that works differently. The effort to construct tests and rules or doctrines, while done in the name of certainty and formalized judicial practice, may not actually achieve it. But the effort does go some of the distance. Doctrine conditions the approach of legal actors to the problems before them. While I most certainly defend a particular (and debatable) conception of the law, I do so in the interest of "getting to" how the courts affect federalism. The book is concerned less with answering questions about the philosophical nature of law than with understanding the place of judicial review in federalism.

The outline of the book is as follows. The chapter immediately following will present a more detailed case for studying doctrine in judicial review. The case draws mainly from Canadian literature on judicial review. It also calls on new developments in the study of the American Supreme Court.

This theoretical foundation establishes the approach that will be taken in the chapters that follow. Before turning to contemporary evidence, a quick survey is made in Chapter 2 of the constitutional landscape and the previous effects of judicial review in all three of the federations. This chapter is necessary background for a clear understanding of the historical state of the judicial review of federalism.

Thereafter commences the core of the book, three chapters looking at the development of federalism doctrines within the three Anglo-American federations over roughly the last thirty years of the twentieth century and the opening years of the twenty-first. The United States is surveyed first, as it perhaps most starkly demonstrates the way that doctrine and political preferences can be confused and how the law shapes federalism decisions. The American court also demonstrates most strongly the potential influence of a high court on the long-term evolution of a federal system. A chapter on Australia follows. There too one finds evidence that a doctrinal approach to the study of federal judicial review is one that accurately reflects the decision-making process at hand and gives a clear indication of the kind of influence that judicial review may have on the evolution of a federation. Finally, the work of the Canadian Supreme Court is studied for recent evidence of doctrine and its application. The applicability of the doctrinal approach is re-evaluated in a final chapter drawing on the evidence presented in Chapters 2 through 5. Particular attention is paid to the alternatives to judicial review. The conclusion suggests some of the implications that the understanding presented here has for the study of both Canada and comparable federations.

1
Judicial Doctrine as an Independent Variable in Federalism

Law, Doctrine, and Federalism

Federalism is legalism. At the core of a functioning federation is an uncommon respect for the rule of law. The formidable British constitutional scholar A.V. Dicey criticized federalism mercilessly for just that feature. He saw in federalism too much of a reliance upon law to settle political and social problems. Particularly troubling for Dicey was the amount of power that federal systems appeared to grant courts. "Federalism" he wrote, "substitutes litigation for legislation, and none but a law-fearing people will be inclined to regard the decision of a suit as equivalent to the enactment of a law."[1] Compared to more flexible and pragmatic sources of legitimacy and authority, such as parliamentary sovereignty, Dicey found that the privileging of constitutional law that accompanied federation could be rigid and uncompromising – even conservative.

Ironically, perhaps, it is the British constitution and the hegemony of the Dicey-led explanation of parliamentary sovereignty that are now accused of excessive conservatism. The "narrow, legalistic interpretation of what constitutes 'federal'" inherited from Dicey is, according to Michael Burgess, partly to blame for the blindness to other constitutional possibilities currently suffered by Europhobic Britons.[2] What Dicey saw as faults – rigidity and inflexible certitude – were exactly what the architects of most federal systems were looking to build into their institutions. They wanted reliable and predictable rules that would allow competing values and communities to coexist. Whether or not courts were meant to enforce the rules by invalidating legislation that they found to be in conflict with constitutional principle was admittedly less clear.

The constitutional designers of the federations surveyed here did have a high degree of faith in the law as an instrument of governing. They believed that legalism and a respect for rules were what would prevent federations, and societies in general, from succumbing to the whims of raw power. The law was intended to serve as a conceptual fence, conserving communities and assigning them an autonomy that logic, evolution, and even the founders' intent might otherwise have treated less kindly. Dicey recognized a federation as a unique paradox: its inhabitants "must desire union, and must not desire unity."[3] Regional particularities are preserved and differences are allowed to coexist through the legal forms provided by federal constitutions, even in the face of forces such as cultural homogenization, security threats, and market logic. With the benefit of hindsight, it is clear that legalism is also capable of distorting the unregulated natural order to the point of promoting the slightly perverse or arcane. But odd or eccentric holdovers such as the American states of Wyoming (population 494,423) and California (population 34,501,130) having equal senatorial representation are nothing more than proof that constitutional design and constitutional law count in federations. Law was not just respected because it would keep the national government in check. The American federalism that was born in the Philadelphia convention had as much concern for remedies of law against state courts as it did for securing union for security and expansionist purposes.[4]

Dicey might well have exaggerated federalism's rigidity. It is clear that constitutions need to be able to evolve or the institutions that they create risk becoming irrelevant or counterproductive. Martha Fletcher has called this evolutionary need the "problem of adjustment." The disconnect is caused by the fact that "even the most carefully drawn [constitutional] language is subject to multiple interpretations, and ... the context in which the arrangements operate changes over time."[5] William Livingston claimed that the ever-evolving societal bases of federalism (what he termed "diversities") would always ensure that institutions (or "instrumentalities" in his vocabulary) remained out of step.[6] In the three federations discussed here, eighteenth- and nineteenth-century constitutions are still the core documents regulating governmental practice in highly developed twenty-first-century societies. The solutions to the problem of adjustment are many. Most obviously, there are provisions in all federal constitutions for formal amendment of constitutional arrangements.

But federal constitutions are notoriously immune to major formal change. Dicey ascribed this apparent weakness to the problem of a "slumbering sovereign," namely popular sovereignty. He contrasted the American process of constitutional change with the "ever-wakeful" English Parliament. For Dicey, "a monarch who slumbers for years is like a monarch who does not exist. A federal constitution is capable of change, but for all that a federal constitution is apt to be unchangeable."[7] The Australian constitutional scholar Geoffrey Sawer once referred to that nation as the "frozen continent" given the inability of constitutional reformers to secure the necessary popular consent to effect almost any constitutional change. Canadians who lived through the constitutional odyssey of the 1980s and 1990s could also serve as witnesses to Dicey's charges. Given the challenges of formal constitutional amendment, other mechanisms of evolution are usually required. Less formal arrangements can be used to accommodate change as the need arises. In Canada, these kinds of agreements, under the rubric of "cooperative" or "executive" federalism, proliferated in the last half of the twentieth century, so much so that they are, to many, the defining feature of Canadian federalism. Intergovernmental cooperation tends to overshadow the solution to the problem of adjustment discussed here and the one that most bothered Dicey – judicial review and interpretation of a constitution.

The task most commonly associated with a high court in a federation is the supervision and interpretation of federal arrangements. Courts complete this task in two ways, either by directly altering the division of powers through the simple resolution of jurisdictional disputes or by altering, in that process, the vocabulary and habits of federalism. The task of dispute resolution is familiar enough. When presented with disputes over jurisdiction, high courts must elaborate on the generalities of the constitution to assign jurisdiction to the appropriate legislature. In division-of-powers cases, high courts must routinely decide whether legislation is constitutional by determining if the subject is legitimately one for the federal government or the unit governments. With minor variations, this is the principal task of judicial review in most federations. In making such judgments, courts either lend legal legitimacy to or reject and thus effectively delegitimize the practical arrangements presented to them by particular legislation. Courts, as agents, do not initiate changes in a federation so much as legitimate those that come about when legislatures push the envelope of their respective powers. When courts endorse or reject these changes, the evolution taking place in practice becomes more formalized.

Perhaps the more persistent method by which courts introduce constitutional change is by altering the vocabulary of federalism. The process of adjudication makes it abundantly clear that constitutional language is never precise enough to cover all eventualities. That is why adjudication cannot be contracted out to a suitably programmed judicial supercomputer. But federalism is supposed to be legalism! It should be as certain and reliable as any algorithm. Constitutions, which are presumed to be the main source of this certainty and legitimacy, are unquestionably the work of human hands and demonstrate an inability over time to keep pace with the naturally evolving order or to anticipate the changes that occur in a society and demand the engagement of the state. Federalism and the law are meant to introduce certainty, but constitutional language is often intentionally imprecise or quickly becomes outdated. Provisions are vague enough that contending societal forces and battling governments certainly cannot agree on equally acceptable definitions of key terms or provisions. This is the paradox of federal legalism that judicial review attempts to overcome. A large part of the judicial task is struggling with the meanings and intentions of words. Judges in the common-law tradition are aided in this task by the time-honoured methods of their profession. They construct rules and limitations on meaning and elaborate otherwise imprecise concepts through the creation of doctrine. Judicial doctrine effectively creates the parameters of constitutional language and evolution.

More importantly, a robust and vigorous tradition of judicial doctrine is essential to the maintenance of federal legalism and federalism itself. Judicial review of constitutional arrangements is a bare necessity that enables federations to evolve. In order for judicial review to serve its purpose, doctrine requires some pride of place. Doctrine is the engine that drives judicial review yet sustains the practice of legalism. Unfortunately for the general observer and perhaps fortunately for legal academics, historians, and political scientists, doctrine is complicated, occasionally unclear, and always variable. That is not to say that doctrine is completely unintelligible or uncertain. It is easy to observe, and in that sense it is a tempting source of raw material for the social scientist. Doctrine, like the positive law that it supplements, is meant to be consistent and clear. However, there are no guarantees that it will be consistent or consistently applied. As a matter of fact, the capacity of doctrine to adequately operationalize legalism is an issue of perennial debate in the legal academy. Doctrine itself becomes the disputed variable between advocates of a legalist, formal approach to constitutional review and those less inclined to accept that there is any such thing as certainty in constitutional law.

In this chapter, a role for judicial doctrine as an independent variable in the evolution and maintenance of constitutional federalism is claimed. The chapter offers a definition of judicial doctrine. In legal and constitutional literature, the definition of doctrine usually varies according to the user's normative evaluation of law as a social and political force. In order to construct a working conception of doctrine, the chapter will try to avoid such overt judgment and instead posit a minimalist definition. This definition will be followed by an examination of what some constitutional theorists may be said to add to that minimalist definition. All will be shown to be unsatisfying variants. A more compelling account of how doctrine operates in federal jurisprudence is found in "new institutionalist" accounts of judicial power. These accounts add a structuring role to the minimalist definition of doctrine. In this view, doctrine has something of a life of its own. It is seen as a compelling influence on those most susceptible to its influence – the judiciary. With such a conception in mind, the role of doctrine as an independent variable in the evolution and maintenance of federalism becomes clearer.

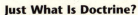

Just What Is Doctrine?

David Beatty describes the task of constitutional interpretation as follows: "The courts, when faced with a text that was written in broad and sweeping terms, have, over time (and, as with any human institution, not without some difficulties along the way), been able to develop a set of *mediating principles* that allow them to differentiate fairly and impartially between the laws that are constitutional and those that are not" (emphasis added).[8]

This description of the process is as good a point as any upon which to start a discussion of judicial doctrine. What Beatty calls "mediating principles" are, in effect, doctrines. Charles Fried similarly describes constitutional doctrines as "rules and principles of constitutional law ... that are capable of statement and generally guide the decisions of courts, the conduct of government officials and the arguments of counsel."[9] A bare-bones definition of doctrine should probably add little or nothing more. Beatty's implication that these mediating principles are by their nature fair or impartial must be considered more critically. That Beatty includes such adjectives in his description is symptomatic of the most exuberant type of legalism and a regular target for critics of judicial review.

What form do these mediating principles take? For a Canadian or Commonwealth audience familiar with those unwritten constitutional rules known as conventions, there might seem to be a parallel. Yet doctrine is entirely distinguishable from constitutional conventions. The latter are notably not enforced by the courts but instead are political in nature. According to the accepted definition, they are simply "considered binding by and upon those who operate the constitution"[10] – in other words, mostly by politicians and office holders. In that sense, conventions are an aid to practice rather than determination. Doctrine on the other hand is enforceable by the courts. It is, in fact, law. Doctrine finds its concrete expression in judicial decisions and is supplemented and elaborated in academic analysis. Judges will refer to previous cases on similar matters, to the techniques used therein, or to constitutional scholarship when making their decisions. In practice, doctrine is largely this distillation of ideas and approaches into what amounts to a series of techniques and rules for dealing with new fact situations. Doctrine often takes the form of tests or standards that can be applied to the contested law or action before the court. Sometimes a doctrine is expressed simply as a definition, of either a prohibited or a permitted state of affairs. The concept of precedent or *stare decisis*, a fundamental aspect of the ever-evolving common law, is something of a metadoctrine in itself. Like all doctrines, it can theoretically be disregarded. Hence, high courts occasionally defy precedent. They do so because, in addition to the doctrine of *stare decisis* to which courts regularly submit, doctrines exist that counsel the courts to refuse to be bound by their own precedents when they believe them to be in error. When courts refuse to be instructed by precedent, they usually do so with substantial justification and an alternative line of reasoning that often draws on competing precedents and judicial opinions and dissents. The latter, which Fried labels "doctrine in a minor key," provide "room for distinguishing, narrowing, and abandoning precedent altogether."[11] While dispensing with precedent should not be routine, it is not irregular, particularly when constitutional matters are involved. Peter Hogg, for one, argues that "in constitutional cases the [Supreme] Court should be more willing to overrule prior decisions than in other kinds of cases."[12]

But as Beatty's description shows, doctrine tends to do double duty in many definitions. More than a mere aid, for some, it serves not only as a tool but also as the source of the certainty and legitimacy of the law. This school is generally described as legal formalism or legal positivism. This is a highly normative position, one challenged rather mercilessly in the twentieth century by legal realists. On these lines, not only do judicial principles help to decide cases, but they also help to decide them correctly or objectively. In fact, it is argued, legal principles should dictate the correct answer to any legal problem. Doctrine, in this positivist way of thinking, enables "fair and impartial" differentiation between constitutional and unconstitutional laws. In other words, doctrine not only structures the options for resolution of legal disputes but also holds within it the objective and value-free (or non-political) protection of constitutional values – a.k.a. the "right" answer.

A minimalist definition of doctrine must exclude such a normative claim. The more modest replacement for the modifiers "fair and impartial" should be "consistent." Consistency is a much less normative trait. A rule or doctrine can be consistently fair or unfair, consistently good or bad. To suggest that by their nature rules are fair is to make a normative claim on behalf of the rules or, in this case, the law. At its most basic, doctrine provides a degree of continuity, of likelihood of results. This does not automatically translate into results that are fair or impartial, not certain – just reasonably foreseeable results. Adding objectivity or impartiality as inherent traits suggests that doctrine reflects an even greater degree of certainty, that there are right and wrong answers to questions of law, federal or otherwise. A minimalist definition must refrain from such assumptions.

In its minimalist form, then, doctrine is a set of standards, maxims, tests, and approaches to the interpretation of the law that is used to regularize law's application and make it more routine and predictable. Objectivity or fairness is not a trait inherent to doctrine; it is only something claimed on its behalf by positivist adherents. Scholarly writing on doctrine and its place in judicial reasoning goes some way to structuring a discussion of the alternatives to the minimalist definition. Perhaps the most elemental debate in the study of judicial decision making is between those who believe wholeheartedly in the capacity of the law to provide objectivity and certainty – the "legal model" – and those who are much more skeptical about such possibilities – the "instrumental model." This conflict is well represented in Canadian debates by the writings of David Beatty, on the one hand, and Patrick Monahan and Paul Weiler, on the other. A similar dichotomy can be found in the Australian literature about High Court interpretation. The "literalist" school advocates a limited, formal approach to the understanding of the constitution's provisions, but as in Canada and the United States there is a much more skeptical school of thought that distrusts the dichotomy made between political and legal decision making.[13] The Canadian debate will remain the focus here. For positivists like Beatty, law has an objective character by definition. Monahan and Weiler are much more cautious about the potential of law to be apolitical. Monahan, for example, does not deny law its place in federalism, but he does have grave doubts about the ability of judges to adjudicate impartially on policy issues.

Doctrine as Certainty

David Beatty, as we have seen, is not satisfied with a minimalist definition of doctrine. The same might be said of many observers. Both critics and champions of doctrine tend to presume objective, neutral certainty as either a necessary or a claimed characteristic for the law. For Beatty, doctrine's primary virtue is its capacity to help courts settle on the correct and principled solutions to constitutional problems. In this view, it is possible to write the rules and develop fair and apolitical ways of applying them, in which event legal conflicts, federal or otherwise, will be more easily resolved. If the law does not work properly at present, it is because of poor judicial application. If judges give in to the temptation to deviate from the prescribed standards and practices of law, that is not the law's fault. It is the job of observers in the legal academy and elsewhere, in this vision, to offer prescriptions to jurists to ensure that the law lives up to the just standards that it is meant to embody.

Beatty has set out the core of his position in *Constitutional Law in Theory and Practice*. He seeks to direct the treatise specifically to "all of my colleagues who, for one reason or another, and in different ways and degrees, have abandoned the notion that there is an independent, objective and determinate idea that makes the concept of law intelligible."[14] Furthermore, he states, "this book is much more about the possibility and the perfectibility of the law than it is about unremitting triumphs and unalloyed success." This is so for the simple fact that "how the courts have actually decided cases is not uniformly flattering and supportive of the virtue of law."[15] "The virtue of law" is a telling phrase. It demonstrates Beatty's belief that there is nothing wrong with the constitution or the notion of law (either as written or as an institution) and that failings in the Canadian or any other constitutional order are instead the result of poor practice by judges.

What are they doing wrong? Regarding the division of powers, Beatty claims that the courts have made a basic mistake in not living up to the set of principles derived over time to maintain federalism. In other words, they have not followed their own doctrinal instruction. According to Beatty, doctrines emerge naturally in the quest for realizing law's intrinsic fairness and will serve the development of constitutional law well, but only if they are properly applied by judges. In current and recent Canadian jurisprudence, Beatty contends that the Supreme Court is failing to apply its own doctrines properly.[16]

What are those principles, and from where are they derived? In division-of-powers cases, Beatty argues that the external aids of precedent and definition can provide only some of the direction that courts need when deciding which level of government is responsible for a particular subject. Assigning powers on the basis of common definitions and the respective assigned jurisdictions of either level of government is difficult. Beatty finds that a simple literal or dictionary-style approach is too general to fulfill the need for concrete guidance demanded by the judicial task. For Beatty, the internal logic of the constitution is a much more appealing guide. In looking to such a source, he is not seeking the mind-set of the founders to determine what particular constitutional phrases meant at the time of Confederation so that those definitions can be applied to current issues. Rather, he tries to reduce the constitution to its most basic elements and then construct answers to new questions from those certitudes. He takes as irreducible a commitment to federalism and to democracy.[17] These values serve as Cartesian certainties upon which more specific principles can be built or developed. A commitment to federalism implies a commitment to the federal principle, which in turn is operationalized as two practical values to guide the courts. These practical values are the operative, doctrinal elements – culled from the Supreme Court's jurisprudence – that he believes will offer certainty and guidance to judicial decision makers. In the case of the division of powers, they are "mutual modification" and "concurrency."

Beatty proposes the doctrine of mutual modification as a variant of the requirement that Canadian courts adjudicating the division of powers must choose between one of two lists of legislative authority. Canada is relatively unique among federations in its practice of listing the powers of both the national and the unit legislatures.[18] When choosing a category in which to place a subject matter, the courts must weigh the placing of a subject in one category against the effect that doing so will have on other categories. Mutual modification is the recognition that including a matter in the domain of one level of government effectively limits the sphere available to the other. An example may better illustrate this point. If the court is faced with a broad subject matter such as commercial fishing, it must make trade-offs between the federal power over seacoasts and fisheries and the provincial power over property and civil rights that could conceivably cover the processing and marketing of the fish. Modifying one heading with inclusion modifies the other by exclusion. Beatty argues that this is a principle and not just a simple effect in that the process structures the task of categorization. The court has the benefit of an alternative in every case. If something appears to be a matter for the federal power of trade and commerce, the court can also ask if it is not a matter dealing with property and civil rights in the provinces. With two competing lists of powers, there is always an alternative available when structuring the decision. In this way, the lists not only set out the powers of the two levels of government but also act as defences against the encroachment of the other level. Thus, Beatty argues, by way of the mutual modification principle, the Supreme Court has restricted the federal treaty-making power to respect the jurisdictions of the provinces and has been able to set limits on the seemingly all-encompassing powers of property and civil rights at the provincial level or peace, order, and good government at the federal level. Defining provincial and federal powers in relation to each other and in relation to the capacities of each level, both literal and constitutional, creates a balance between the two, preventing the federal nature of the division of powers from being weakened over time.

Beatty's second animating principle is concurrency. It commands the courts to remember that political life cannot be hived off into "watertight compartments." Overlap, Beatty argues, will occur any time two governments are operating in the same territory. When the courts allow concurrency in some form, but apply restraints where necessary, they enable both levels of government to maximize their sovereignty. Beatty calls this a logical rather than a literal reading of the constitution. Doctrines that recognize the need for overlap and seek to minimize the deleterious impact of it are at odds with the clean compartments set out in the constitution. However, Beatty recognizes this as a place where the law can provide a more subtle understanding of social change and maintain its place in federal arrangements.

Beatty has much to say about recent developments in Canadian federalism jurisprudence, all of which is better considered in a later chapter. For the time being, it is worth reiterating what he considers to be the place of doctrine in a properly constituted federalism. For him, doctrine is the legitimate expression of the law's place in federalism. It also assures that the basic principles of the constitution are followed. Where Beatty perceives the legal side of federalism to falter is in the judiciary's application of doctrine. Recognizing this weakness might be the one thing to rescue Beatty from complete naïveté. Judges have been inconsistent in applying the principles that he recommends, a fact that is simple to prove. Indeed, Beatty himself gives accounts of several cases in which the courts have failed to adequately address the principles that he identifies. Some would interpret this failure as a clear indication of the impossibility of an objective judicial review. However, Beatty regards it as an indication of something wholly different. That judges sometimes or even regularly fail to uphold doctrinal standards and principles is, oddly enough for Beatty, proof of the general objectiveness of the standards. The fact that one can identify deviations from good practice proves the possibility of a better method. Those cases that depart from the use of proper standards are the exceptions that prove the rule.

There are two points on which one may take issue with Beatty's presentation of the process of constitutional adjudication. The first point of contention is his method. Beatty's description of the judicial process suffers from an unexamined presumption that objectivity and certainty are inherent in law. Political scientists, perhaps more attuned to questioning the normative presumptions of actors, have probably erred in the opposite direction, categorizing nearly all judicial behaviour as instrumental in its use of the law. Beatty's description of the process of adjudication is inaccurate in presuming that judges, when properly applying the law and applying doctrine, are always deciding objectively. Beatty injects a normative trait into the very definition of doctrine by adding fairness and impartiality to the minimalist definition of "mediating principles." Not only is doctrine a set of mediating principles for Beatty, but it is also a set of standards, objective and fair within themselves, that demonstrate the difference between constitutional and unconstitutional laws. According to this line of thinking, the very act of creating mediating principles extends the natural certainty of the law. The presumption that the law is by its very nature objective is a critical leap that Beatty offers little incentive for the reader to make. It is a presumption on his part that cannot or should not be easily shared.

The second point of contention is that Beatty's normative argument suffers from his presumption of law's perfectibility. The constitutional values that Beatty identifies as universal come from his own reading of what federalism or other values mean. One might as easily suggest that the constitutional commitment to federalism implies a preference for national over provincial power. Empirical evidence from different federations shows that different sorts of values can be emphasized in federal systems depending on the preferences of governments and electors. As only one example, the degree of regional or unit equality varies substantially from federation to federation.[19] Likewise, financial redistribution in the form of equalization programs in Canada and Australia ensures that citizens of all provinces or states receive comparable levels of public services despite varying economic capacities. The American federal system does much less to ensure this sort of equality, at least on a regionally redistributive basis.[20] Yet Beatty seems to suggest that a commitment to federalism implies a commitment to universal principles that courts can then uphold. Indeed, he expends some effort to make comparisons to demonstrate that some of the basic principles that he singles out in the Canadian case can be found in other jurisdictions. The problem with this kind of argument is that, in an effort to give objective status to the law, Beatty must suggest that the law and hence the concepts grounding federalism are apolitical and universal.

Doctrine as Politics

David Beatty represents a more recent incarnation of what is essentially the oldest position on the place of doctrine and law in federalism. His approach to judicial review does not differ markedly from the original judicial guardians of the Canadian constitution, the Law Lords of the Privy Council. He may believe that their reasoning was flawed or that their application of doctrine was biased and inconsistent, but his justification for the role of judicial review is the same as any that they articulated. For Beatty, judicial review is beyond politics because law is a perfectible instrument. The polar argument is equally adamant that the courts are unable to provide the federal system with this level of neutral arbitration. As early as the 1930s, Canadian scholars began to question the ability of courts to find any doctrines that would save them from misinterpreting federalism. Sterile and inward looking, the law of federalism was detached from the social forces over which it held tremendous influence. Even so, critics of the Supreme Court and of the JCPC largely took issue not so much with the role of the tribunal as with the results of its jurisprudence. Thus, a generation of critics – F.R. Scott, Bora Laskin, and W.R. Lederman prominent among them – dissected the reasoning of the court and concluded that it promoted an unrealistic and inappropriate (usually decentralized) conception of Canadian federalism. This placed a great deal of the blame for the problems of Canadian federalism on the heads of misinformed judicial decision makers.[21] Eventually, these critics began to doubt the capacity of the law alone to solve the problems that they perceived in the Canadian state. By 1967 and the publication of G.P. Browne's *The Judicial Committee and the British North America Act*, the disenchantment of the critics was clearly complete. Browne offered a prescriptive account of the missteps taken by the JCPC and how alternative reasoning could have resulted in more appropriate outcomes. Bora Laskin, one of the most prominent of the critics of the JCPC, in a scathing review of the book, suggested that the kind of formalist analysis of the assumptions and logic of the *BNA Act* that Browne conducted would have been better left a private exercise.[22] Dissatisfied with the direction that the scholarly dialogue was taking, critics such as Laskin began to see past the perceived doctrinal mistakes to suggest that there was a more basic flaw with the power of judicial review. Eventually, the very concept of judicial power was directly challenged. In 1974, Paul Weiler offered a foundational critique of Canada's high court that questioned the very role of the judiciary in federalism.[23]

After a thorough examination of the law of Canadian federalism in the post-1949 period (the period in which the Supreme Court of Canada was the final court of appeal), Weiler claimed that he had a hard time finding the sorts of principled reasoning and justification required of the court by its own apparent standards of law. In his view, the judicial task is to provide simple adjudication of disputes and the adoption of general policies for the law. In the latter role, the best aid to a court is the formation and maintenance of legal principles. Principles allow the courts to make choices by giving them a frame of reference that connects legal rules to the facts before them. Legal principles can be sifted out of the past jurisprudence of a court and the internal logic of its decisions, but they can also be contested – there is no one certain or right answer. In sum, Weiler argued, "legal argument in terms of principle is not only a necessary avenue towards a better quality of legal *justice*, it is the primary source of the stability and predictability of a legal *order*."[24] While the law is not perfectible and objective in this version, the margin of policy making required by a degree of principled argumentation from judges is enough to ensure that the judicial branch does not slide into subjectivity.

That said, Weiler argued that the judges of the Supreme Court held "an outmoded and unduly narrow conception of the role of law in courts."[25] He saw little more than politics at work in the deliberations of the court. And a dishonest politics at that, for the court's deliberations were accompanied by an almost devout commitment to the mythology that politics was nowhere involved. The result was a jurisprudence markedly weaker than if political decision making was frankly admitted. The court and its judges, Weiler contended, clung to an idealist vision of judicial review in order to cover up their own political decision making. In the United States, where the political tenor of the court's work has been conceded to a greater extent, that court lived up to its self-imposed standards better. In Weiler's opinion, by setting an impossible task as a guardian of pure law, the Canadian court not only failed to achieve its goal but also perverted its potential contribution to the system. The court encouraged a way of thinking that was no longer of net benefit. It did more harm than good.

For Weiler, this was particularly true in the field of federalism. The Canadian constitutional system, to his mind, sorely lagged behind the society that it was meant to serve. Weiler attributed this disconnect to the failure of the Supreme Court to make necessary changes to the constitutional order. This conservatism he attributed to the judiciary's "hidebound legalism." Weiler's preference was for the politicking to be out in the open and the umpire of federalism to be more of an arbiter of negotiated disputes instead of an oracle purporting to provide a singular truth. As an alternative, he proposed a model of federal judicial review much more akin to labour arbitration than anything then in practice. The judicial authority in Weiler's thinking should act as more of a conciliator, forcing both sides to articulate their demands and then impose a compromise rather than handing down zero-sum commands.

Patrick Monahan disagrees more fundamentally with the Beatty position. Weiler basically articulated an ideal vision of the law akin to Beatty's. Since the Supreme Court failed to live up to Weiler's standard, he recommended a different approach to the task altogether rather than rely on the hope that the mere law might get greater respect from its practitioners. The more practical and efficient alternative for Weiler was to abandon all pretence to legalism in the adjudication of federalism disputes. Weiler's was not a blanket criticism of the law as a social construct but simply a critique of the judiciary's inability to live up to the demands of constitutional law. Monahan's view of the law is much less optimistic. Monahan argues that doctrine is in decline and that we must "complete the inconclusive rebellion against the formalist impulse." According to Monahan, it is wrong to think of doctrine as a vehicle for certainty and objectivity. He calls the adherence to this way of thinking "'constitutionalism' – the notion that a legally enforceable document should define the society's federal institutions and establish standards for their evaluation."[26] Monahan agrees with the minimalist definition of doctrine. However, he also fails to see any particular value obtained by judicial doctrine that could not come from plain old political debate.

The doctrine of which Monahan speaks derisively is the same one that Beatty seeks to revive. Monahan finds it something of an oddity that the doctrinal impulse is far from gone in Canadian federalism jurisprudence. Formalism has been under siege in the Anglo-American legal world since the dawn of the twentieth century. The critics of legal positivism in the United States have almost entirely overwhelmed the "jurisprudentially inclined." As Howard Gillman notes, "decades of social science research ... ha[ve] demonstrated ... that ideological and political considerations drive decision making. This research has been so completely internalized by many political scientists that it is considered the common sense of the discipline."[27] Quite legitimately, then, Monahan wonders why the Canadian court clings to doctrine. A desire for certainty and the appearance of neutral judicial decision making seem to be the main reasons why formalism remains despite the advances in understanding touted by legal theorists. Beatty regards attempts to codify federalism principles as the worthy search for certainty and objectivity that should occupy the court.

Monahan pays a similar amount of attention to court-articulated principles of Canadian federalism. However, he makes a special effort to recognize that equally compelling counterprinciples exist, ones that can be defended with the same degree of certainty. Monahan seeks not to raise the counterprinciples as replacements but to wholly remove the mystique from the very notion of principle. For every element of certainty that one might discover in the constitution's commitment to democracy and federalism, Monahan claims to be able to identify and defend an equally compelling and entirely contrary element. Neither view, he argues, is less arbitrary than the other. It is impossible, therefore, to draw any meaningful distinction between doctrinal and political discourse. The construct that Beatty defends cannot, in Monahan's opinion, be upheld.

Despite the best efforts of the Supreme Court to construct rules that remove political discretion from its decision making, results appear to rely upon what Monahan calls "background understandings" of federalism and its purposes. These background understandings are what make legal doctrine political. "Ultimately," Monahan claims, "the constitutional adjudicator is being called upon to make some accommodation between the competing social visions that underlie Canadian federalism. Political choices on these issues are the true 'stuff' of constitutional adjudication."[28] While doctrine seems to provide a non-political account of federalism based on principle, it actually provides more than one "principled" explanation for a variety of tenable political viewpoints. In that sense, the law offers nothing more certain than what could easily be labelled a simple political choice, albeit in this case one dressed up with judicial finery. For Monahan, it doesn't matter how thin the corridor for decision is. As long as judges have a choice between doctrines to justify their political preference, they are still making a political calculation. He suggests that there is an "essential continuity between legal and political reasoning."[29] There are no grounds upon which distinctions can be fruitfully drawn between these presumably different approaches.

Monahan's solution to this surfeit of contingency is to revel in it rather than lament it. He proposes that "federalism disputes to both federal and provincial legislation should be resolved through political processes. The claim is simply that federalism issues are inescapably political and there is no plausible reason for removing them from the political arena."[30] However, the courts show no signs of reneging on their role in federalism. Despite the best efforts of Canada's federal government and provinces to modify the federal system outside the strictures of constitutional law, the law reasserts itself whenever it has the opportunity.[31] By altering the federation without changing the constitution, contemporary federal and provincial governments are attempting to place federalism entirely within the realm of politics. Despite these trends, Monahan argues, "at the most general level, the challenge facing Canadian federalism is to revive flexibility and innovation in political life. The task is to make politics something more than a constricted consideration of marginal adjustments to an established system of prerogatives."[32] It is not clear that leaving federalism entirely to the political arena is conducive to enhanced debate and an appropriate degree of accountability. By abandoning legalism, the guarantees of federalism that benefit the weakest or poorest positioned may also be abandoned, and those actors may be left to the whims of a rawer sort of power, one less patient with legal niceties, traditional prerogatives, and altruism.

To demonstrate where a theory like Monahan's leaves those seeking to explain judicial review, consider another highly critical account of federal high courts. Political scientist André Bzdera argues that there is no feasible political theory of judicial review in federations other than one that recognizes the role of high courts as centralizing agents. With nothing to guide them but their political preferences, judges will inevitably be kindest to those who put them in office. Bzdera calls upon less than systematic evidence from a number of federations to suggest that the main effect of the judicial review of federalism is to legitimize and strengthen the central state in preference to its units. This he cites as a "failure of modern judicial review in the federal state."[33] The claim pivotal to Bzdera's conclusion is that, since high court judges are appointed by the central government, the incentives and culture of high court judging reinforce the legitimation of central government expansion.[34] Bzdera allows that some high court judges do favour the units in a federation and that there are decisions that go against the wishes of central governments. However, he claims that the net effect of federal judicial review is the eventual centralization of power.

Most constitutional scholars in Canada suggest that the court is, on the whole, more balanced in its approach to federalism. Bzdera calls this the "pendulum" theory of judicial review – for every swing to the benefit of the central government that a court takes, it appears to take an equivalent swing to the favour of the provinces. To Bzdera's thinking, this pendulum theory is inaccurate, for it takes too little account of the structural conditions of the court's place in Canadian federalism, particularly "the political importance of the judicial selection process on the policy output of the high court."[35] Additionally, the pendulum theory is said to suffer from a shortage of international comparisons. On the basis of that evidence, Bzdera suggests that our understanding of federal judicial review needs to be reevaluated. He goes so far as to claim that the political theory of federalism itself must be altered to take into account the inescapable reality that federal high courts favour their centralist counterparts. He writes that "there appear to be no exceptions to the centralist theory of the judicial function."[36] This centralist bias upsets the traditional theory of sovereignty implicit in a federal arrangement.

The primary failing of Bzdera's method is the lack of any attempt to take seriously the output of courts. If the so-called pendulum watchers are blind to the obvious evidence that federal high courts are puppets of the central government, Bzdera is equally blind to the contrary evidence contained in the reasoning of high court decisions. Perhaps a considered reading of cases is not something he wishes to do. But what he writes off as the "positivist vision of the judicial function"[37] proves to be much more influential in determining trends in interpretation than are the methods of appointment and the sinister co-opting of judicial elites into a central government consensus.

Doctrine as Autonomy

Is there any understanding of doctrine that might be useful to constitutional scholars? Beatty's faith in the law may strike a reader as too evangelical, and Monahan's reliance on politics seems to lead to shallow claims that threaten any distinction between judicial and political institutions. Is there a compromise position that gives doctrine and judicial review a place in federalism that is not naïve about the law but does not remove some of the certainty and procedural protections of legalism? In what way can a minimalist conception of doctrine aid such a theory of judicial review? Recent scholarship on the history of the American Supreme Court suggests another way in which doctrine might be conceived. Barry Cushman's account of doctrinal developments in the New Deal period suggests that it is possible to be neutral about doctrine and study it as a variable like any other in the decision-making process undertaken by judges. Doctrine is worth studying not because it holds all the right answers but because it is a formative force on the answers, a force that gains its legitimacy from tradition and formal methods. Doctrine serves as a set of mediating principles that, while not indifferent, are central to the determination of judicial outcomes.

Strictly political accounts of judicial review, like that proffered by Monahan or by conventional histories of the American New Deal, have a low opinion of doctrine. It is merely a front for other forces. According to the standard realist account, the New Deal court is supposed to have reversed its initial opposition to the constitutionality of the progressive reforms of the Roosevelt administration only after its institutional integrity was threatened by the president's plan to add extra judges to the court and then "pack" those vacancies with more sympathetic jurists. By this telling, it was the self-preservation instincts of the justices, rather than any convincing legal precedent, that brought them around to support the New Deal legislative agenda. The episode is best explained by politics, not by law. Cushman calls this account "superstructural." Doctrine, in such an account, like false columns in neoclassical architecture, is irrelevant to the real stability of the decision-making structure. Stately columns, like judicial rhetoric, are impressive, but much more mundane materials are doing the work of holding the building up. By this account, "when a judge reviews the constitutionality of a given piece of legislation, he first decides whether it embraces a political, social or economic policy with which he concurs. Having made this essentially political determination, he then instructs his law clerk to go out and find the precedents that will support the result he desires."[38] The judge is a political actor like any other, except that she is momentarily inconvenienced by the method of her profession to unearth some "technical mumbo-jumbo" to justify her decision. Lorne Sossin, drawing on his personal experience as a clerk to the Supreme Court of Canada, suggests that the interaction between clerk and judge is never so simple. He claims that judicial decision making, even with the aid of clerks, still operates very much within the realm of "legal reasoning."[39]

Technical mumbo-jumbo is the derisive term for what has thus far been called doctrine. Drawing from the work of other legal scholars, Cushman contends that legal forms and practices (i.e., doctrine) may have a degree of relative autonomy. They may indeed have agency. Quoting legal theorist Robert Gordon, he claims that legal forms and practices "can't be explained completely by reference to external political/social/economic factors. *To some extent they are independent variables* in social experience and therefore require study elaborating their peculiar internal structures" (emphasis added).[40] Cushman's purpose in endorsing this definition is to provide a different account of how the American Supreme Court played out its role in the New Deal era. To do this, Cushman takes doctrine seriously as a variable in the legal and political order of the New Deal. By doing so, he is able to explain much of the change that has otherwise been ascribed to the overt influence of Roosevelt's court-packing plan. Cushman studies in detail the methods that the court used and how they compare with pre-New Deal doctrines. By doing so, he is able to establish the importance of those doctrines and emphasize the role of the New Deal advocates in Roosevelt's second term who narrowed issues for the court and turned around the unfavourable outcomes experienced in the early days of the administration. To approach the period any other way, he argues, "is to deny the constitutional jurisprudence of the period any status as a mode of intellectual discourse having its own internal dynamic. It is to dismiss the efforts of the lawyers defending the constitutionality of New Deal initiatives as irrelevant and redundant ... and to suggest that sophisticated legal thinkers casually discard a jurisprudential worldview formed over the course of a long lifetime simply because it becomes momentarily politically inconvenient."[41]

The empirical content of Cushman's argument is more relevant to the specific discussion of the New Deal period in the next chapter. More important to the argument here is his conception of doctrine. Cushman gives real intellectual substance to judicial doctrine and accepts it on its own terms. Why? Because it acts as a serious restraint on the way that judges conceive their role and carry out their task. Judges are schooled in the law. All high court judges have practised it for many years. They respect doctrine as an aid to decision making, not because it is objective or because it provides a nice cover for their personal preferences, but because it is a part of the trained method of legal reasoning. Cushman's description of legal history is telling: "Legal history is not simply political history, or social history, or economic history; legal history is also intellectual history. Judges are participants not merely in a political system, but in an intellectual tradition in which they have been trained and immersed, a tradition that has provided them with the conceptual equipment through which they understand legal disputes. To reduce constitutional jurisprudence to a political football, to relegate law to the status of dependent variable, is to deny that judges deciding cases experience legal ideas as constraints on their own political preferences."[42]

Certainly judges have predispositions, but that does not mean that we ought to conflate doctrine with political discourse. Predispositions are one variable, doctrine another. Other variables might include the circumstances of the case, the climate of opinion at the time the case is heard, or the strength of presentation by those at the bar in a particular case. All of these add up to influences on the way that cases are decided. Institutionalist reactions to rational choice literature on US Supreme Court decision making suggest much the same thing. A leading proponent of the new institutionalism, Howard Gillman, for example, is ready to admit that there is always a "possibility that people use their institutional positions to promote extra-institutional or personal agendas," but he adds that "it is also assumed that actors like Supreme Court justices may sometimes view themselves as stewards of institutional missions, and that this sense of identity generates motivations of duty and professional responsibility."[43] In the context of a court, this means placing some premium on legal reasoning. And unlike some of the other less tangible inputs, the product of legal reasoning – doctrine – stands apart from the circumstances of a case before the courts.

These sentiments are echoed elsewhere in the new institutionalist literature on courts. Rogers Smith argues that "political scientists should recognize the centrality of legal and political institutions as independent forces in the decision-making process of judges." In addition to whatever ideological baggage a judge might carry, these institutions and forms "have a life of their own and an influence on the self-conception of judges and other actors who occupy roles defined by them in ways that give those persons distinctively 'institutional' perspectives and values."[44] Even if legal principles are ultimately contingent on judicial attitudes and interpretations, the form that they must take has an influence on outcomes that is not easily overcome. Smith argues that attitudes alone will not explain the judicial process. Instead, it must be acknowledged that "judicial values and attitudes are shaped by judges' distinct professional roles, their sense of obligation, and salient institutional perspectives."[45]

Developing this formulation further, Mark Richards and Herbert Kritzer focus on law as the primary institutional variable. They argue that "the central role of law in Supreme Court decision making is not to be found in precedents that predict how justices will vote in future cases. Rather, law at the Supreme Court level is to be found in the structures the justices create to guide future decision making: their own, that of lower courts, and that of non-judicial political actors."[46] Richards and Kritzer operationalize these structures in the idea of jurisprudential regimes. The concept refers to "a key precedent or set of related precedents ... that structures the way in which the Supreme Court justices evaluate key elements of cases in arriving at decisions in a particular legal area." Their formulation is much like the definition of doctrine proposed here. Like the minimalist definition, their conception is not overly theorized. In fact, they look upon the idea as almost a matter of practicality. "Justices need something like jurisprudential regimes to overcome what might otherwise be major co-ordination problems if each justice simply sought to advance his or her own policy preferences. Thus, law can be thought of as serving this co-ordination function."[47] Richards and Kritzer, like many of the new institutionalists, do not propose the jurisprudential regime as a one-dimensional view of how judges make decisions. They count the jurisprudential regime as simply one among many sources of judicial decision making, perhaps not even the most important. While their tests of this theory are more quantified than any offered in this book, the method used here is in keeping with their general thinking.

The study of judicial doctrine can be viewed as an intellectual pursuit in its own right. The study of doctrine is not unlike the study of any other intellectual history. There are core ideas, leading personalities, innovators, and disciples. At the outset of this chapter, I suggested that courts alter federations by changing the vocabulary of federalism. Altering doctrine over time changes the basic way in which we engage with the concept of federalism. It changes federalism's vocabulary and consequently the structure of federations.

Doctrine must not be understood as a tool of objectivity and certainty or as a wholly political, post hoc justification for policy preferences. Doctrine is neither certain nor political. But it is distinctly legal in character. Contrary to the claims of Monahan and others, there is a difference between the legal and the political. Legal decision making is constrained by very different forces than its political counterpart, and those restraints have a very real effect on the outcome of those conflicts. Legal reasoning and decision making are bound by the strictures of the courtroom and the formality (however contrived) of the conflict. As a means of resolving disputes about federalism, legal reasoning is called upon for specific purposes and offers specific benefits to a federal system. In approaching doctrine, one must learn to be more indifferent about its application. That is the true test of having a better understanding of the concept. One must not expect such noble things from doctrine and then be disappointed when it does not appear to work in the way that one hoped it would. Criticizing the court for departing from the "proper" interpretation commanded by doctrine risks a slide to a positivist quest for (an elusive) certainty.

There are constraints in doctrine of a degree unlike any other. The legal character of doctrine is crucial. The discipline of thinking required to make a legal argument and to render a legal decision is a critical degree removed from plain political decision making. This is true even if a judge or a number of judges are cavalier about the formalism of the law. Formalism is a natural default position for a court to take, and over time it is a more credible determinant of outcomes than any isolated policy choices are likely to be. Additionally, doctrine is a reminder that federalism is a legal as well as a political order. Legality can be distinguished from certainty without becoming political.

Canada's preeminent constitutional law scholar, Peter Hogg, seems to be in relative accord with this approach. In an elegant footnote to his discussion of the role of the courts in federalism, he describes the difference between political and judicial decision making: "I do not acknowledge that judges make political decisions similar to those made by politicians. To me, the element of political choice in a [judicial] decision is *reduced to a very narrow compass by the substantive constraints of the language of the constitutional text and decided cases,* and by the procedural constraints of the litigation process. A much wider choice of outcomes and reasoning is open to politicians" (emphasis added).[48] While judges make decisions of political consequence, for Hogg that does not translate into political decision making.[49]

The intention of this chapter has been to divorce doctrine from some of the normative and pejorative uses made of it. Doctrine is neither a surrogate for certainty in constitutional judgment nor a thin veil for political decision making. It is a variable that stands alone, separate from these descriptions. It is an independent variable that shapes outcomes. But more importantly, it is a variable critical to a properly functioning federalism. Federalism thrives upon a healthy tension between the strictures of law and the flexibility and innovation of politics. The continuity of the law is a staple of federalism, not because the law in itself is good, but because the rule of law protects elements of the federal system that would otherwise quickly be lost to regularizing pressures. Economic logic and universalizing social forces can make quick work of federal diversity. The law is one of the prime protectors of that diversity. Doctrine is what helps the law to stay consistent without losing its formality, without descending into politics itself. It is only upon those grounds that judicial review can be considered legitimate.

At the same time, doctrine is not even close to being a prescription for all that ails a federal system or the task of judicial review. It is neither a solution nor a problem; it is simply a fact of federalism. To the scholar's benefit, it is one of the more easily approached variables in a federation. The current state of the Canadian court's doctrine is plain for everyone to see, yet it goes virtually unconsidered by most political scientists. It is a variable worthy of independent study for the main reason that courts continue to resort to the habits of doctrine regardless of the favour in which it is held by any particular theory or theorist.

2
A Brief History of Federalism Doctrine in Practice

All three federations discussed here have a notable tradition of courts interpreting and patrolling the constitutional structure of their federal system. This tradition has provided the raw material for constitutional scholars to chronicle the dynamic between the courts and federal constitutions of these states. With all due respect, when one looks at the current literature on these seemingly enduring themes, it appears as though the field's glory days are sadly over. Not only is there less attention paid to these matters, as the previous chapter has shown, but observers have argued that the formal legal and political analysis of federalism is an unwise or misplaced use of scholarly energy.

The previous chapter sought to explain why ignoring the content of contemporary judicial review provides an impoverished account of federalism. Later chapters will show that a shift has taken place in the constitutional interpretation of federalism of all three nations in the past twenty years. Landmark decisions have revived federalism as a matter of debate in high courts. In fact, developments in all three federations show that judicial doctrines of federalism are a very real and critical determinant of the character of a federation, as indeed they have always been. Doctrines of the courts were often viewed in the past as among the most important determinants of federal evolution, and they were subsequently studied in some detail. Today's courts are both aware of this previous evolution and well attuned to it. Understanding the approaches of their predecessors is important to studying the present courts. The stable of doctrines previously used by the courts provides the practical and theoretical foundation upon which present doctrines are constructed.

This chapter begins with a quick review of the way in which power was divided between governments in the three federations at their founding. That discussion is followed by a brief comparative sketch of their high courts' historical approach to division-of-powers questions. The overview is intended to provide background for the detailed discussions of contemporary judicial decisions in later chapters as well as to show the place of doctrine and its logic as a variable in federal evolution.

The Constitutional Frameworks

The United States is the first modern federation. K.C. Wheare, perhaps the most celebrated observer of federal government, when articulating his seminal "federal principle," wrote that the "federal principle has come to mean what it does because the United States has come to be what it is."[1] There was something of a fundamental innovation in the founding of the United States. The Founding Fathers undertook no less than a revolutionary approach to constitutionalism, an approach to which the founding generations of other states have looked when pondering new constitutional arrangements. The American founders redefined conceptions of liberty and government for generations to come. They introduced the modern practice of a permanent and written constitution. Americans also changed the definition of federalism. The ancient and accepted definition of federal government was much more confederal (in effect decentralized) than what was to emerge from the Philadelphia meetings of the constitutional convention. Martin Diamond believes that Americans, though not the first federalists, certainly altered the concept in a significant way. A close reading of the *Federalist Papers,* the primary record of the political philosophy of the founding, suggests that the Americans were engaged in nothing less than a reinvention of what it meant to be federal. Unlike preceding federations, the American system surrendered power and real sovereignty, through the mechanism of divided popular rule, to a national and ultimately competing loyalty.[2]

The American founding is well documented and requires little elaboration here. The thirteen original states whose delegates met in Philadelphia undertook a unique exercise in unity but created a federalism that by today's standards would still be considered reasonably decentralized. Key to their creation was the concept of enumerated powers. The American national government, unlike its state subunits, is one of enumerated and thereby limited powers. The constitution lists the powers assigned to the Congress in detail. The powers of the states are not similarly catalogued. This is the trademark of American federalism's logic. Under the first, post-revolutionary constitution, the *Articles of Confederation,* the states maintained almost all sovereignty, and what passed for a national government could act only with the explicit authorization of the individual state sovereigns. The states reluctantly gave up some of this sovereignty to the national government with the second and present constitution.[3] Anything not covered in the inventory of Article 1(8) was retained by the states. The *Articles of Confederation* had assumed the primal sovereignty of the states, and the new constitution carried on that belief. Under the Tenth Amendment, all powers not delegated to the national government are retained by the states or the people of the states. This so-called residual power ensured that matters not foreseen by the founders that did not meet the descriptions found in Article 1(8) would remain the responsibility of the states. Theoretically, at least, the bulk of legislative responsibility would fall to the subnational units.

In a government of enumerated powers, the matters assigned to a level of government are important resources, particularly in cases of intergovernmental conflict. By that count, the American federal government fared better than its predecessor under the *Articles of Confederation* but was still by no means dominant in relation to the states. The sixteen grants of power assigned to Congress by section 8 have had to evolve into the significant powers that they are today. Some have attained their present prominence through circumstance; others have required the determination of the national political process and the indulgence of the judicial branch to become more consequential. For example, the military powers given to the federal government have obviously grown exponentially with the rise of the United States as a major military force. The definition of the military power has not changed, but circumstances have just made it a much more elaborate (if not actually more significant) set of responsibilities than it was when the constitution was first written. In contrast, the most important domestic power assigned to the federal government currently is interstate commerce. It was and is potentially very expansive but has required generous judicial interpretation to reach its present wide scope.

The Canadian founders, nearly a century later, were working in the shadow of an American Civil War that gave that nation's federal structure a measure of infamy. Regardless, while still enamoured of parliamentary government, the Fathers of Confederation were convinced of the need for a federal arrangement in British North America.[4] The unification of Upper and Lower Canada was unable to secure political stability. Additionally, the Maritime provinces harboured doubts about a legislative union. Some form of decentralization that would accommodate the wishes for self-rule of French Canada and the Maritime provinces was clearly needed. Too much power in the hands of unit governments, however, was also out of favour. An approach entirely different from the American one was taken when dividing governmental responsibilities in the Canadian constitution. The Canadians drew two lists of legislative powers, one for the national government and one for the provinces, rather than enumerate just one level and depend upon residual sovereignty to define the rest. Section 91 of the *British North America (later Constitution) Act* of 1867 assigns a general power to make laws for the "peace, order and good government of Canada" (or POGG) to Parliament as well as a list of twenty-nine specific powers on which it may legislate. Then, instead of leaving the rest to the provinces, sixteen specific heads of power were enumerated and assigned to the provincial legislatures under section 92

– including quite general categories such as property and civil rights and matters of a "merely local and private nature in the provinces." Section 93 recognizes that each province will have exclusive lawmaking authority for education within and for the province. The residual power, in contrast to the American scheme, was left to the federal government.[5]

Historically, scholars have suggested that the Canadian constitution was meant to be centralized. As evidence, they point to (among others) the POGG clause, the federal appointment of the lieutenant governor (the representative of the Crown and the holder of the Crown's discretionary powers for the provinces), the powers of reservation and disallowance (whereby a lieutenant governor may temporarily withhold assent or the federal Parliament may overturn a duly enacted provincial statute), and the lowly status of the legislative responsibilities accorded to the provinces. In addition, they found no shortage of arguments in the debates preceding Confederation that the new Canada should resemble a legislative union more than the American federal system.[6] Canada's first prime minister, Sir John A. Macdonald, was known to prefer a unitary over a federal state, at least in theory. That said, critics of this historical interpretation have tried to demonstrate exactly the opposite intention. The selection of phrases such as "property and civil rights," which had a fairly expansive meaning,[7] and the compromises attendant on the federal settlement are thrown back at the centralists as proof.[8] Nevertheless, the constitution clearly has a capacity for central government dominance. In fact, Canada was able to become deeply involved in two world wars, with the central government taking unprecedented control over nearly all aspects of Canadian life, without truly compromising or subverting the constitutional structure. At the same time, the document has proven sufficiently ambiguous to allow the practice of a more decentralized federalism when conditions are right.[9]

The Australian founders, like the Canadians before them, were keen observers of other federations when setting about to transform their own loose association of colonies into a more unified whole. As latecomers to federalism, they had the benefit of the experience of two cousins having gone before them. The Australians found much to recommend the US constitution. While they remained great fans of parliamentary responsible government, the Australian founders were less enamoured of the Canadian approach to federalism and the division of powers. The Canadian constitution was certainly the most prominent marriage of federalism and parliamentary government available for emulation, but it was determinedly overlooked by the Australians. The Canadian constitution offended antipodean sensibilities in at least two ways. First, the overt federal sway over provincial affairs represented in the appointment and presumable control of lieutenant governors, as well as the provisions for reservation and disallowance, would not do. Second, the subject matters assigned to the provinces were seen as too inconsequential, giving the units a lesser status in the division of powers.[10] The American constitution was at least superficially more "federal" and thus more appealing to the no-nonsense founders.

The Australians paid particular attention to James Lord Bryce, whose *American Commonwealth* was standard reading for admirers of American federalism at the time. Under the sway of Bryce, and given their own seminal brand of states' rights, the Australian delegates opted for a Commonwealth (national) government of enumerated powers with the residue ascending to the states. A Canadian observer of the Australian constitution, accustomed to finding two lists of powers, will search in vain for a list of state powers comparable to the enumeration in section 92 of the *Constitution Act, 1867*. As in the American document, there is no list. The states – as the semi-sovereign colonies that they were – carried out regular functions before federation, and they continued those jobs after federation. The nominal purpose of federating was simply to promote standards in areas of common concern. The rest was left to the states. Therefore, the new Commonwealth government was accorded some responsibilities in section 51 of the *Commonwealth of Australia Constitution Act* and expected to act within the confines of those enumerated powers as essentially a servant of the states. Section 107, much like the American Tenth Amendment, secures the residual power to the states. Specifically, it preserves for a state those powers that it had as a colony, "unless it is by this Constitution exclusively invested in the Parliament of the Commonwealth or withdrawn from the Parliament of the State."[11]

American Federalism in the Courts

The history of division-of-powers jurisprudence in the United States is closely tied to the fate of Congress's commerce power. The constitution provides in Article 1, section 8, that "Congress shall have the power ... to regulate Commerce with foreign nations, and among the several states."[12] Among the enumerated powers of Congress and hence the national government, this is the closest thing to a plenary power. That it has become so is due almost solely to the interpretation of the Supreme Court. It has been very much the case that the federal government's regulation of commerce is synonymous with its overall degree of regulation. With notable exceptions, apart from the imagination of Congress, there has been little limit on commerce clause activity. In those periods of American history when the court has found reason to be restrictive about Congress's power over commerce, as in the aftermath of the *Lochner* decision, the nation has experienced relatively small government. When the court has been more responsive to commerce claims, Congress has been secure in taking a much more active role. Present-day interpretation of the commerce clause continues to be at the crux of federal legislature's interventionism and is examined more closely in Chapter 4. What follows is a Cook's tour of the major developments in federalism jurisprudence up until the past thirty years.

The post-Philadelphia generation of American governing elites remained heavily populated with the fathers of the nation. Successful in their founding enterprise, many went on to man the institutions that they had created, armed with the distinct nationalist vision of the new republic that they had helped bring to life. Not surprisingly, many in the first generation of American national politicians sought to aggrandize and empower their new creation, to the obvious detriment of the powers of the states.

The newly minted Supreme Court did not distinguish itself particularly well in this campaign for the new nation. Instead, it lived up to Alexander Hamilton's characterization of it as the "least dangerous" branch.[13] Historically speaking, the tenures of the first three chief justices were both undistinguished and uneventful, a point proven by the difficulty that administrations had in even recruiting and holding onto personnel for the court. John Jay, the first chief justice and *Federalist* coauthor, resigned to pursue the governorship of New York. John Rutledge, whose interim appointment failed to receive the approval of Congress, followed Jay. The third chief justice, Oliver Ellsworth, the man responsible for the *Judiciary Act* that created the court, held the job for four years, but ill health shortened his stay in office. While the judicial careers of these men were unremarkable and left the court largely in the shadows, the man who would next take their office led a quiet revolt that forever changed the court's standing in American politics.

John Marshall was sworn in as chief justice in 1801. His tenure left an indelible mark on the relationship between the Supreme Court and the other branches of government. In the bluntest sense, the Supreme Court became a "player" under Marshall, claiming for itself the power to interpret authoritatively the constitution. The most famous decision to come from his pen was *Marbury v. Madison,* in which he claimed for the court that very power. While legal theorists and political scientists still debate the soundness of his reasoning and the appropriateness of his claim, it was at that point that the court established its de facto legitimacy in this endeavour – legitimacy enough to weather the challenges to its authority as the principal interpreter of constitutionality.[14]

On matters of federalism and commerce, one decision stands out in the Marshall era. In *Gibbons v. Ogden,* the court gave its first consideration to the scope of the commerce power and extended it along nationalist lines. The majority opinion by Chief Justice Marshall also provided the grounds for future reasoning on commerce. The court was asked to decide whether the extension of a monopoly over steamboat service by the State of New

York could exclude those wishing to operate service between states (in this case between New York and New Jersey). Gibbons was authorized by Congress to run interstate service, while the holders of the monopoly granted by the State of New York licensed Ogden. The true question at hand was which law prevailed. The answer was equally simple. For the court, "the acts of New York must yield to the law of Congress." However, Marshall also took the opportunity, partly in response to the arguments of counsel, to discourse on the scope of commerce. Marshall did not grant that a power over commerce was "complete and entire," as the famed advocate Daniel Webster had argued before him. Rather, the chief justice characterized the grant as divisible – much as commerce among foreign nations could stand alone, so could commerce among states. He owned that even commerce among states existed to some extent as an internal matter, yet Congress could regulate commerce within states. But Marshall made a now famous disclaimer: "It is not intended to say that these words comprehend that commerce which is *completely internal,* which is carried on between man and man in a State ... and which does not extend to or affect other States" (emphasis added). Thus, "the completely internal commerce of a State ... may be considered as reserved for the State itself."[15] This dictum would be incorporated in later doctrine as a distinction between inter- and intrastate commerce.

Following the long tenure of John Marshall that ended with his death in 1835, Roger Taney was appointed chief justice. Taney was not known to share the nationalist sentiments of his predecessor and in some measure pushed the country to instability by aiding the states' rights cause in the South. Taney oversaw a most turbulent period in the court's history, represented well by its decision in *Dred Scott v. Sanford.* Scott, a slave, had accompanied his Missouri owner, an itinerant army surgeon, to free states over the course of his service. After returning to Missouri, Scott instituted a suit for freedom against his owner's widow. It was an established principle of Missouri law that, "having sojourned in a free state or territory, that slave was entitled to freedom by virtue of residence in the free state."[16] The Missouri Supreme Court rejected Scott's claim. Scott's lawyers then filed a federal suit that ended up in the Supreme Court. That court's decision ruled Scott still a slave. The court, in effect, nullified the Missouri Compromise, which had confined the practice of slavery to the old states of the South and kept newly formed states in the West slave free. This decision had no small part in heightening tensions in the run-up to the Civil War. By invalidating the Missouri Compromise, the court demonstrated the difficulty of settling the slavery issue. Motivated by the irreconcilability of slavery with the emerging national consensus, the southern states seceded from the union four years later. *Dred Scott* was taken as a prime indication that compromise on the issue of slavery was unworkable.

Felix Frankfurter, looking back on the commerce clause from the vantage point of 1937, characterized Taney's approach to the power as a counterpoint to the Marshall doctrines. In particular, Taney challenged the notion that there was a "dormant" commerce clause, a principle that Marshall took as orthodoxy. The notion of a dormant clause is meant to suggest that even unexercised congressional power over commerce carves a space out of state jurisdiction from which the states must refrain from acting. Taney agreed that when active commerce regulation takes place, conflicting state laws must concede to the power of Congress, but Taney would not accept that the states were unable to exercise commerce-related powers simply because the constitution assigned such a heading to Congress.[17]

The American Civil War was many things. It was a struggle over the appropriate moral vision of a nation; it was a quarrel between old and new, North and South, industry and agriculture, conservatism and progress. It was also a fight over federalism. Just as the earliest years of the republic and the formative debates that preceded it were about articulating a political theory for the nation, the Civil War and the reconstruction period were very much about redefining the political philosophy of the republic. Much as the court had acted as a provocateur (perhaps unintentionally) before the war, it also had a hand in shaping the nation in its reconstruction.

The South's defeat and the illegitimacy of the claim to states' rights may have seemed to put to rest any doubt about the status of national power in the United States. The Supreme Court, however, did not necessarily agree. The period following the war is marked by a distinct hostility to the extension of federal power. The Republican Congress, which assumed the task of reconstruction, immediately pursued the passage of the Fourteenth Amendment. The amendment includes an affirmation of citizenship for all those born or naturalized in the United States. It also includes the provision that "no State shall make or enforce any law which shall abridge the privileges or immunities of citizens of the United States; nor shall any State deprive any person of life, liberty, or property without due process of law; nor deny to any person within its jurisdiction the equal protection of the laws."[18] The amendment gave primacy to national citizenship over state citizenship for the first time.[19] While the federalist era had a strong nationalist inclination, the postwar Republican regime had an even more heightened sense of the need for a strong federal government. The court's response to the Fourteenth Amendment and the attempt to expand national power on those grounds is typical of its style of jurisprudence.

Courts

The *Slaughter-House* cases are generally cited as the prototype of the court's work in this period.[20] Bruce Ackerman paints a more sympathetic picture of the court by emphasizing the severity of the challenges that it faced. He believes that the court was forced to synthesize pre- and post-Civil War constitutionalism and that such a task necessitated some ugly compromises and difficult decisions. To make a workable whole out of the concepts inherent in *Dred Scott* and the Fourteenth Amendment required the court to walk a fine line. The *Slaughter-House* cases did exactly that. The court refused to extend the provisions of the Fourteenth Amendment to invalidate discriminatory state legislation. The cases at hand challenged the Louisiana legislature's grant of a monopoly over butchering in New Orleans to one central slaughterhouse. Butchers excluded from the monopoly or unwilling to work in the central facility protested on the ground that their equality of citizenship, guaranteed by the Fourteenth Amendment, was compromised. The court, replying in the negative, interpreted the Fourteenth Amendment to be strictly about race and not a guarantee of other kinds of equality. While it could be seen to be moving forward the postwar consensus on the racial front, the court was permitting state-ordered discrimination on other grounds by excluding appeals to other forms of inequality. In the court's words, "we doubt very much whether any action of a state not directed by way of discrimination against the Negroes as a class, or on account of their race, will ever be held to come within the purview of this provision."[21]

The jurisprudence of this period develops two concepts essential to later commerce doctrine. The first development is that the court found in *Hammer v. Dagenhart* that to manufacture is not necessarily to engage in commerce. The case itself concerned the constitutionality of a congressional law banning the transportation of goods in interstate commerce that were the products of child labour. The defendant was charged under the legislation for shipping goods produced by child labour in his North Carolina cotton mill. The defendant challenged the ability of Congress to make laws regulating intrastate activities (the milling) under the auspices of an interstate power (trading outside the state). The process of manufacturing was argued to be an activity exempt from Congressional oversight. While the products of the mill may have been destined for use in interstate commerce, it was argued that their manufacture was an activity that took place wholly within the boundaries of a state. The court acknowledged that commerce "succeeds to manufacture" but accepted the argument that the process of manufacture could be isolated from the trade and transportation of goods, more properly understood to be interstate commerce. The scope of the commerce power was subsequently limited so as not to apply to activities that were demonstrated to occur wholly within a state. By divorcing manufactures from interstate commerce, even though the products were destined for interstate trade, the court limited Congress's ability to police the national economy and particularly impaired its ability to impose national labour standards.

The second important development in this period is that the court picks up the metaphor of commerce as a "stream." As early as 1871 with *Daniel Ball* and into 1905 with *Swift*,[22] the court characterized commerce as a stream or flow of activity, which involves various stages. Products enter (and presumably exit) the stream of commerce at different points; the metaphor was meant to help determine the scope of congressional power. Before a product enters the stream, it is excluded from regulation. Once it is in the stream, it can be regulated. Which activities and stages of manufacture and trade were in the stream and which were not became critical to future determinations of the scope of Congress's power.

The New Deal period would bring federalism and the commerce clause to the centre of national political debate once again. At no point in American history has a conflict between the Supreme Court and the two other branches of American government been so plain, and the consequences so high, as during the first two terms of Franklin Roosevelt's presidency. President Roosevelt and the New Deal Congress believed that they had a clear mandate to effect considerable change in the American way of life. They were met with an obstructionist court that held up the progress of the expansionist program of the era.

The opening shots in the battle over the New Deal came in the lower federal courts, which issued injunctions at an astonishing rate, effectively stalling the application of federal regulations without actually resolving questions of constitutionality. The administration itself was reluctant to bring test cases to the courts for fear of losing. Industrial opponents of regulation who had cleverly launched "friendly" lawsuits against firms for obeying New Deal legislation brought the bulk of the litigation. These suits were usually filed by the firm's own shareholders. This prevented the government from even having an opportunity to defend its laws, as the case was usually a private one between the firm and its "disgruntled" shareholders. In such cases, with both parties really seeking the same outcome, vigorous defences of the legislation were noticeably absent.[23] When it went to the Supreme Court, the government fared little better than in the lower courts. In the "hot oil" case, the court dealt the first major blow to the legislative program of the New Deal, invalidating portions of the *National Recovery Act (NRA)* – a centrepiece of the administration's agenda.[24] This initial defeat was followed by a brief reprieve in the "gold clause" cases, which upheld the administration's plan for monetary policy, allowing federal debts to be paid in deflated dollars rather than remain redeemable in gold.[25] This ruling forestalled an increase in the value of government debts at a time when it could least be afforded. Shortly thereafter, in true roller-coaster fashion, the court then invalidated the *Railway Pension Act*, altering for the worse the financial well-being of a million rail workers and their families.[26] That case in particular seemed to foreshadow a negative ruling on the broader social security projects of the federal government then wending their way to the court.

The darkest day of the New Deal in the Supreme Court would come three weeks after the railway pension case on 27 May 1935, a day otherwise known to New Dealers as Black Monday. While previous decisions had held out some hope for a reversal of New Deal fortunes, with close and seemingly ideological divisions on the court, the trio of decisions released on this fateful day were all unanimous. The most important of the three decisions, *Schecter Poultry*, invalidated the whole of the *National Industrial Recovery Act (NIRA)*.[27] The act provided for minimum wages and maximum hours of work. The Schecter corporation, charged with violating the act, slaughtered poultry destined for local retail sale from farms in New York State and Pennsylvania in its Brooklyn slaughterhouse. The slaughtered chickens were not sold through interstate commerce but did arrive for their demise through the stream of commerce. The question for the court was whether or not that stream ended at the slaughterhouse door. The court agreed that it in fact did and that there was no interstate element relevant to the slaughter of the chickens. Congress had thus invaded the reserved power of the states to control working hours and wages.

In the early days of the court's conflict with the New Deal, partisans of the administration ridiculed the older, conservative members of the court who were hostile to the administration's efforts as "the four horsemen,"[28] a menacing holdover from a previous, less progressive era. But on Black Monday, the whole court, including the judges whom the partisans thought were more sympathetic to their project, rejected New Deal legislation. Justice Brandeis, one of the three reputedly liberal justices, not only agreed with his colleagues but also made a point of demonstrating his displeasure to a confidant of the president in the court's robe room following announcement of the decision. Arthur Schlesinger recounts Brandeis giving this message to be passed on to Roosevelt: "This is the end of this business of centralization and I want you to go back and tell the president that we're not going to let this government centralise everything. It's come to an end. As for your young men, you call them together and tell them to get out of Washington – tell them to go home, back to the States."[29]

The anger that the court experienced in return was substantial. Speaking to reporters in the Oval Office, President Roosevelt, with a copy of the *Schecter* decision sitting on his desk, decried the court for returning the country and constitution back to the "horse and buggy era."[30]

While Justice Brandeis may have been frank in the robe room about the consequences of the decision, the formal reasoning of the court was, predictably, much more muted. The court relied less upon a dislike of centralization than on a commitment to a limited textual view of the provisions of the constitution. The court was unwilling to widen the stream of commerce and steadfastly refused to bring the context of the Depression into its reasoning. "It is not the province of the Court," it argued, "to consider the economic advantages or disadvantages of such a centralized system. It is sufficient to say that the federal constitution does not provide for it."[31] Felix

Frankfurter, writing in the *Harvard Law Review* with Henry Hart, viewed this as abhorrent behaviour since the court's relationship with Congress had historically been much more accommodating and flexible. The warning against legislative activism they believed to be implicit in the tone of the decision was particularly disturbing. "Against such advisory pronouncements," they wrote, "the constitutional theory and practice of a century and a half unite in protest."[32]

The court's unanimity in opposition to the New Deal was short-lived. By the fall of 1935, the conservative faction and the contending liberal group of three had begun to polarize. Caught between these two sides were Chief Justice Charles Hughes and Associate Justice Owen Roberts. On a nine-person court so divided, the direction of their sympathies was crucial to outcomes. Immediately after *Schecter,* the two swing votes continued to reject New Deal legislation. Thus, 1936 saw more rejections of federal power under the commerce clause. The court continued to define the power narrowly and excluded most of the activities that Congress sought to regulate. *Carter Coal,* decided in that year, did for the beginning of the stream of commerce what *Schecter* had done for its terminus. The court rejected the constitutionality of labour standards applied to the coal-mining industry on the ground that the production of coal was outside the scope of interstate commerce. The manufacture and sale of coal were to be looked upon as two separate and distinct activities, and during production coal was not yet in the stream of commerce. Drawing directly from *Schecter,* the court ruled that "in the *Schecter* case the flow [of commerce] had ceased. Here it had not begun. The difference is not one of substance. The applicable principle is the same."[33]

Other congressional powers were also narrowly interpreted. *U.S. v. Butler* did to the *Agricultural Adjustment Act (AAA),* another cornerstone of the reform package, what *Schecter* had done to the *NIRA*. In the *Butler* decision, the court refused to accept the justification for intervention in agriculture under Congress's spending power. The whole New Deal agricultural policy was thrown out with the decision. This decision had a significant negative effect on the reputation of the court. Roosevelt, who had harboured hostility toward the court as far back as 1929, was now firmly convinced of the need for change.[34] The emerging split in the court confirmed his suspicions that a personnel change would result in the more favourable verdicts that he sought. Emboldened by a landslide victory in the 1936 elections, Roosevelt prepared a legislative package for altering the court and sought supporters in Congress to ensure that it would pass. The plan focused on changing the composition of the court by increasing its size to accommodate six more judges whom FDR himself would then appoint. Shortly after Roosevelt presented the court-packing plan to Congress, the famous "switch in time saved nine." The actual "switch" by Justice Roberts was in *West Coast Hotel v. Parrish,* which upheld the State of Washington's minimum wage law. The case was decided in chambers several weeks before the court-packing plan made its way to Congress. National regulation would not be upheld until later in the year with the more consequential *NLRB v. Jones and Laughlin Steel*. The timeline is important for those who suggest something other than political pressure changed the court's attitude.[35]

The National Labor Relations Board (NLRB) was an agency set up by the New Deal Congress to enforce labour standards in interstate industries. The NLRB was better prepared than many of its hastily constructed counterparts for a constitutional challenge to its authority. The board counted among its staff some of the more astute federal government lawyers of the time. Under their leadership and the pressure of the court-packing plan that was now making its way to Congress, the New Dealers won their first major battle in the Supreme Court.[36] *NLRB v. Jones and Laughlin Steel* was a clear about-face from the court. It expanded commerce along the lines first envisioned back in *Gibbons v. Ogden*.[37] Whereas *Schecter* and *Carter Coal* had blunted the stream of interstate commerce, the *NLRB* case took a more holistic view of how interstate commerce was being carried out and thus where national regulation was necessary or allowable. In *NLRB*, the court gave the first favourable consideration to the idea that labour practices had an "effect" on interstate commerce regardless of their local or intrastate nature or their status outside the stream of commerce. Even indirect effects on interstate commerce, argued the five-to-four majority, could be regulated by Congress. This significantly expanded the scope for congressional oversight. Chief Justice Hughes, for one, had noticeably come around to the view that outcomes and political backgrounds needed to be considered. Compared to the tone in *Schecter*, he rejected the idea that "we are asked to shut our eyes to the plainest facts of our national life and to deal with the question of direct and indirect effects in an intellectual vacuum."[38] Rather, the court considered the effects of not regulating wages and working hours in the steel industry generally and found that, by allowing differing practices among the several states, interstate commerce would be adversely affected.

NLRB inaugurated the so-called constitutional revolution of 1937. From this point on, the commerce power provided justification for countless regulatory forays by Congress. The self-styled conservative historian Forrest McDonald writes that the court, "in sum, had stepped out of the way and it would stay out of the way for more than a generation. The only remaining restraints upon Congress and the President were democracy and bureaucracy – neither of which is to be found in the constitution."[39] If the revolution was a travesty of constitutionalism for conservatives, the general consensus among court watchers was quite the opposite. Most of the legal academy was supportive of the New Deal from the start. More importantly, it supported a change in reasoning about commerce that allowed its expansion along the lines of necessity rather than some narrow, originalist interpretation. By expanding the doctrine of commerce to include activities that affected interstate commerce indirectly, the door was opened for Congress to expand the regulatory state.

An alteration in personnel and approach was completed and the revolution finally confirmed four years later in *United States v. Darby,* which overruled the extreme laissez-faireism of *Hammer v. Dagenhart.* From that point on, judicial deference to the various schemes of Congress continued, as did the consequent, rapid expansion of the national governmental apparatus. It was only to be checked marginally by the court in 1976 with *National League of Cities v. Usery.* The expanded commerce clause became the main justification for national governmental activity and remained unchallenged by the court for nearly fifty years. The logic of this expansive doctrine was pushed to its limit in *Garcia v. San Antonio Metropolitan Transit Authority. Garcia* is a turning point in the development of recent federalism doctrine, and that case will open Chapter 4.

Australian Federalism in the Courts

In none of the federations studied here has one single case marked such a dramatic reversal of judicial doctrine as the *Engineers*[40] case did in Australia. That 1920 case marked a complete turnaround by the Australian High Court on the interpretation of federalism. In both Canada and the United States, change has been much more incremental. While the constitutional revolution of *NLRB v. Jones* in the United States may be cited as a definitive turning point in the modern era of American constitutional law, it only confirmed an alteration already well afoot in the court's thinking. Another important feature of Australian jurisprudence is that it has been much more unidirectional. Federalism interpretation experienced one dramatic push with *Engineers* and has only recently acquired the subtlety that creates any degree of balance.

The immediate post-federation period was filled with constitutional developments. The High Court was set up without much delay following the creation of the Commonwealth. While the federation conferences agreed on the need for such a court in a properly constituted federation, it took two years to settle on its legal form and to pass the enabling legislation through the first Parliament. Prominent constitution makers were recruited to the initial three-justice panel, and they immediately set about emulating their colleagues in other federations. They met with some popular resistance for such pretensions. Only the eminent status of those initially appointed to the court kept it in good stead. Public opinion in the states was cautious about judicial review as the court, not surprisingly, was perceived to be a nationalizing force. Unlike in the early American court, there was no shortage of work for the justices, who were also burdened with duties on other judicial and quasi-judicial panels and heard their cases in the various state capitals rather than in one central location. Unlike in Canada, appeals to the Judicial Committee of the Privy Council (JCPC) were not ones of unrestricted right. Such appeals were known as *inter se* ("as of grace") and required the grant of a certificate by the High Court itself. The first draft of the Australian constitution provided for no appeals to the JCPC. This was a matter of some contestation with the Colonial Office; the *inter se* mechanism was a compromise, albeit one that nearly achieved the same result for the Australians. Only a small fraction of the court's work was granted permission to be appealed to the JCPC.[41] Brian Galligan, in a comprehensive history of the High Court, states that these early years produced an "even-handed" jurisprudence that relied "more heavily on the sagacity and authority of the justices than on logical consistency or a literal construing of the constitution's text."[42]

Some important interpretive movements were made in this early period. Preeminent among them was the establishment of the doctrine of implied immunity. Essentially, the doctrine dictated that neither level of government, coordinately sovereign as they were, could be subjected to the will of the other. This doctrine had little to do with determining the substantive meanings of the items in a list of powers. The coordinate vision of federalism (which K.C. Wheare advocated as the ideal expression of the "federal principle"[43]) was swallowed whole by the first generation of Australian constitutionalists. What they admired in the American model was the sovereignty of the units and the federal government from one another. Accordingly, the court became a vigilant patrolman on the border between federal and state power, keeping both sides in their respective realms and encouraging a forceful separation of functions and application of law.

Implied immunity, when put into practice, extended quite far. Commonwealth government employees, for example, were relieved from having to pay state income taxes. *D'Emden v. Pedder,*[44] decided only a year after the court began hearing cases, found the state government practice of imposing a stamp duty on the salaries of federal employees unconstitutional. With American precedents at its side, *McCulloch v. Maryland*[45] foremost among them, the court ruled that the nature of the federal system required governments to be immune from such interference in their activities, unless expressly authorized by the constitution. The court believed the stamp duty to be unjustified in this regard and disallowed it, giving the Commonwealth an early endorsement of its supremacy.

Following that principle, the court applied the doctrine in the opposite direction by ruling that state-controlled railways were equally immune from the interference of Commonwealth laws. In the *Railway Servants* case, the High Court exempted state railway employees from Commonwealth labour arbitration laws. Parenthetically, state regulation of the railways is one of the most questionable accomplishments of Australian federalism. Unlike Canada, which federated in part on the promise of a national rail system, the Australian rail infrastructure predated federation and thus lacked any degree of standardization. The legacy was a system that required passengers to change trains on interstate journeys as track gauges from state to state were incompatible. In addition to varying infrastructures, the employees of these state enterprises were subject to different labour laws. The Commonwealth government tried to create a standard labour regime through a common court of arbitration. In this effort, it was no more successful than the wide-bodied trains of Victoria were at traversing the narrow-gauge rail lines of South Australia.[46] Again the court made pointed reference to American precedent, reinforcing its support for the concept of coordinate federalism. The majority quoted from the American case of *Collector v. Day* that, "in respect of the reserved powers, the State is as sovereign and independent as the general government."[47] The inclusion of *Collector v. Day* in the *ratio* of the case signalled zero tolerance for any government interference in the jurisdiction of another. The doctrine of implied immunity was invoked in six cases up until 1919. All involved taxation or industrial arbitration issues.[48]

The *Railway Servants* case also strengthened the other significant doctrine of the founders' court, that of reserved powers. Leslie Zines describes the doctrine as a product of the interpretive problem caused by comparisons to the Canadian constitution, which is unique among the three countries examined here for its enumeration of the powers of both the federal and the unit governments. In the Canadian case, the residual or reserve power is theoretically left to the federal government. Interpreters of the Canadian constitution have to determine which exclusive power a particular governmental activity falls under. Is the requirement of a business licence (to borrow Zines's example) a matter of "trade and commerce" and thus federal responsibility, or is it a matter of property and civil rights and thus provincial responsibility?[49] The residual power is less relevant a category when two lists provide so many possible homes. By contrast, the only positive grants in the Australian constitution are those given to the Commonwealth government. The High Court saw the need to give some shape or character to the reserved powers in order to determine if a matter is better left to the states. In *Railway Servants,* the court found that, to give real teeth to the reserved powers of the states, the reserve had to be assumed to be the predominant grant of power, and the enumerated fields needed to be read narrowly. The doctrine of reserved powers essentially gave the benefit of the doubt to the states by explicitly limiting the extent to which Commonwealth powers could expand.

The court's apparent motivation for being sensitive to state concerns for nearly two decades after federation was its own sense of self-preservation.

Being pragmatic, rather than dogmatic, was the safest way for the High Court to ensure that the states did not lose their faith in this strange new central government institution. The introduction of judicial review through Canada's Supreme Court eight years after Confederation meant that the federal government was less likely to invoke the powers of reservation and disallowance. The Supreme Court had instant legitimacy in the eyes of the provinces because even a federally appointed court appeared to be more neutral on questions of provincial law than the federal cabinet.[50] The Australian court had no similar grounds by which it could be automatically trusted, so it had some reason to curry the states' support. The court was not completely averse to ruling in the Commonwealth's favour, however.

Several cases over the course of the First World War gave an expansive scope to the Commonwealth's powers. The court did not abandon the twin doctrines of implied immunity and reserved power to make such grants. Rather, the court found that the defence power of the Commonwealth, enumerated in section 51, was ample justification for some of the centralization necessary to make a contribution to the war effort. The leading case in this period, *Farey v. Burvett,*[51] allowed the fixing of bread prices in the State of Victoria as an exercise of the Commonwealth's defence power. Foreshadowing the technique that would change the court's approach to federalism, Justice Isaacs wrote that, "if the measure questioned may conceivably in such circumstances even incidentally aid the effectuation of the power of defence, the Court must hold its hand and leave the rest to the judgement and wisdom and discretion of the Parliament."[52] What might have been interpreted as patriotism and general support for the war effort was in fact the thin end of the wedge for a greatly expanded interpretation of Commonwealth powers.

Amalgamated Society of Engineers v. Adelaide Steamship Co. Ltd. (the *Engineers* case) turned the first twenty years of constitutional interpretation directly on its head. The court explicitly overruled the state-favouring doctrines of implied immunity and reserved powers and set a course for the centralization of Australian federalism. *Engineers* has a modest pedigree, considering that it is one of the most influential cases in Australian constitutional history. The court was asked to decide whether the labour arbitration provisions assigned to the Commonwealth by section 51(xxxv) of the constitution were applicable to state enterprises. A negative reply seemed to be certain as the High Court had already found in the *Railway Servants* case that state railways were exempt. In this case, Western Australia's state-operated engineering and sawmilling works had come into an industrial dispute with the national union representing its workers. Even the union believed the hearing to be something of a lost cause and accordingly engaged the services of one of the Victoria bar's more junior and inexperienced members. Little did they know a legend was in the making. Robert Menzies, later a long-serving prime minister, was retained as the barrister. Menzies, a mere twenty-five years old (an age that today finds most practitioners drafting memos, not appearing before the country's highest court), was given the brief at the last minute and came to the court equipped with what he later admitted was a young man's brashness. The story runs that in his argument before the court there came a point in his line of reasoning where he began to strain logic. Unimpressed with his attempt at an alternative characterization of the state enterprises as trading rather than governmental activities, one of the justices remarked that the young lawyer's theory was a lot of nonsense. Menzies brazenly agreed but denied responsibility for having to be so obtuse. Instead, he blamed earlier decisions for forcing him into a logical morass. He claimed that he could make a logical case only if he was granted standing to challenge those prior decisions.

Suitably chastened, the court granted him just that opportunity, and Menzies successfully convinced the court to alter its approach to the constitution and to federalism. He modestly notes that it was not only his courtroom skill that turned the tide. Despite the court having just previously endorsed some of the old doctrines,[53] he was young enough not only to be bold with his betters but also to have fresh memories of his instruction in law school. His tutelage prepared him well enough to know that those who formed the majority in those previous decisions were no longer with the court. The justices still present, he hoped, "might be willing to seize upon the opportunity to re-open the whole matter, overruling the *Railway Servant's Case* in the process."[54] That they did.

The *Engineers* case was especially innovative not only because it overturned the old doctrines of immunity or reserved powers but also because it endorsed a different way of looking at the Commonwealth powers in section 51. The rule that emerged is best stated this way: the specific grant must be defined before the residue can take any shape. This gave the Commonwealth a definitive upper hand in the process of interpretation. As long as the court was prepared to read the explicit provisions of Commonwealth power in section 51 with even a minimum of generosity, there was a good likelihood that an activity could find some place within those grounds of competence before even being considered for assignment to the residue. While the Australian court avoided the trade-offs between mutually exclusive categories that preoccupied Canadian interpreters, such a convenience probably worked to the detriment of the states in securing their reserve jurisdiction.

Galligan calls the majority decision a "powerful polemic, but a logical muddle."[55] Similarly, Zines notes that "it is written with more fervour than clarity."[56] The logical mess, it seems, was a necessity for securing the agreement of a majority of the court. Isaacs, who wrote the decision, held nothing back in his criticism of recently deceased colleague Samuel Griffith, who was a major force on the court in its pre-*Engineers* years (and subsequently a hero of observers who favour a states' rights approach). Isaacs and Griffith had serious disagreements about the course of federalism, and now Isaacs was able to advance forcefully his views on interpretation. "There can be no doubt," claims one observer, "that Isaacs dipped his pen in vitriol before drafting the judgement."[57] Yet the legacy of the decision defies such a characterization. It is more simply known for its endorsement of a particular brand of literalist reasoning, which – logical or not, reasoned or not – would come to dominate constitutional interpretation in the years to follow. The decision rejected the use of American precedent, readily accepted in the High Court's early decisions, in favour of an idealized form of British legal reasoning. Consequences were deemed irrelevant. Coming to a decision neutrally was what counted.

The preferred technique of the *Engineers* court was to read the section 51 powers literally. So if, as in this case, the Commonwealth was granted the power to settle industrial disputes extending beyond the state boundaries, that grant had to be interpreted as all-encompassing. Exceptions are not implied by the literal grant rule. In fact, the power is basically understood to be unlimited. The reserved powers and implied immunity doctrines were limits allegedly read into the Commonwealth's powers by the court, based upon the constitution's commitment to federalism. Here "a proclaimed neutral technique produced an expansion of national powers at the expense of the states."[58] This literalist technique removed the need for more particular doctrines, such as reserved powers or implied immunity, in effect becoming something of a superdoctrine in itself. Literalism meant that, if the activity in dispute seemed to fit under the auspices of one of the grants assigned to the Commonwealth, then the Commonwealth was entitled to it. The advantage in disputes rested with the Commonwealth, for only it had a list of enumerated powers to work from. Only when the court was unconvinced by counsel stretching the boundaries of a Commonwealth category to absurd lengths would the Commonwealth lose.

Like the American court after the New Deal revolution, the Australian High Court has barely looked back since the *Engineers* case. The concept of reserved powers previously endorsed by the court was undoubtedly "exploded and unambiguously rejected"[59] and would not be revived. The default method of constitutional interpretation has been to expand routinely the reach of Commonwealth power through the generous interpretation of the section 51 headings. That said, Australian federalism has not been the one-way train that was the American commerce clause. There have been important qualifications of both the *Engineers* doctrine and its reasoning. Hence, there is a more tempered quality to the decisions of the High Court. The balance is particularly evident when one considers the centralist ambitions of the Commonwealth government at various points in the twentieth century.

Brian Galligan claims that the Australian High Court, despite the semblance of legal impartiality, is a consummate political actor. It has encouraged a remarkable degree of stability in Australian politics by keeping tight control over the pressure release valve of constitutional conflict and making changes through judicial interpretation. The basic struggle of Australian political life, in Galligan's thinking, has been between the democratic-socialist Labor Party and a strong corporate-liberal culture opposed to most if not all of the Labor Party's policies. This conflict plays itself out in the politics of federalism. Labor has consistently sought to use the national government to exercise authority over the economy and life of Australian citizens, while its opponents have worked equally hard to remove the Commonwealth government from regulatory roles and to decentralize power and decision making to the states. Labor's program historically even went so far as to include the explicit goal of dismantling federalism, despite the party occasionally holding power in the states.[60] More practically, Labor has sought the piecemeal constitutional change necessary for greater centralization. Given that they have been frustrated by negative referendum results in almost all these efforts at formal constitutional change, Labor governments have sought to push the limits of the Commonwealth's constitutionally assigned powers, doing through evolution what they have been unable to do through formal alteration. On many occasions, the ambitious centralists have been granted leeway by a generous High Court, thereby forestalling the more radical changes that some Labor partisans would have preferred.

In the post-*Engineers* period, the tone of interpretation has been captured in the manner with which the court approached Commonwealth powers. Literalism was the legacy of *Engineers* as theory. In practice, this meant that the characterization of the section 51 powers assigned to the Commonwealth was the prime determinant of that Parliament's scope for action. For example, if power over taxation was broadly construed, then the Commonwealth would gain considerable financial power relative to the states. Similarly, if the Commonwealth-assigned trade and commerce power was widely interpreted (much like commerce was in the US), then the states would have less of an opportunity to impose (or not impose) regulations on commercial activity. The post-*Engineers* period, up until the startling expansionist decision in the *Tasmanian Dam* case in 1983,[61] witnessed a slow accretion of power into the hands of the Commonwealth legislature courtesy of a generous judicial characterization of its assigned subject matters.

This expansion can be characterized as careful and slow only when contrasted with the ambitious program of the Labor Party. Former Labor Prime Minister Gough Whitlam summed up the theme of fifty years of "constitutionalism as struggle" in the title of a famous paper, "Labor versus the Constitution."[62] Galligan argues that the most intense conflicts of this sort occurred pre-1950. Commonwealth expansionism was not limited to Labor Party dogma. After his prodigal career as a barrister, Robert Menzies oversaw a long period of Liberal Party government as prime minister. He too was a central expansionist, simply not as fervent a one as his colleagues in opposition. Galligan calls Menzies a proponent of "centralising federalism" in contrast to the "socialising centralism" of the Labor Party.[63] Apart from arguing the *Engineers* case, Menzies influenced constitutional interpretation through his appointment of Owen Dixon as chief justice in 1952 and the appointment of many like-minded colleagues on the court. Menzies trained in the law as Dixon's junior, and Dixon remained for Menzies the ideal judge, articulating the constitutional principles that Menzies tried to put into practice from the other side of the bench.[64] Justice Dixon's tenure on the court was the judicial embodiment of Menzies' balanced approach to federalism.

The most significant expansion of Commonwealth power in the immediate wake of the *Engineers* decision came in the form of a wartime income tax. The Commonwealth government, through a system of uniform taxation, had centralized the collection of income taxes and took on the task of thereafter redistributing revenues to the states. Both the states and the Commonwealth are entitled by the constitution to impose taxation, but much like in Canada the rates imposed by the Commonwealth made further taxation by the states politically untenable. The redistributive elements of the Commonwealth program were only in effect for those states that committed to the uniform collection scheme. That process was justified as a necessary measure for emergency wartime fiscal management. Prior to implementing the system, the federal government could not get enough tax room, particularly in the poorer states, which had higher rates, to secure the money that it needed for the war effort. If the Commonwealth took sole responsibility for the collection of taxes and redistributed amounts equivalent to what the states would have otherwise collected on their own, it would avoid the problems anticipated in the poorer states, such as Queensland. While other centralist initiatives had been approved during the war, including schemes as crucial as central banking and as mundane as drinking hours, the *Uniform Tax* decision was the first to extend such powers for reasons other than the ongoing war. The court, with Dixon absent in America as a wartime diplomatic representative, found that the Commonwealth's power in section 51(ii) to impose taxation justified the scheme. It allowed the Commonwealth to tempt or entice the states into a scheme of uniform taxation. This was further legitimated by the section 96 provision that allowed the Commonwealth government to make grants to the states under whatever terms and conditions it thought were justified. Section 96 could not compel cooperation, but it could encourage and reward it. The provisions of the *Uniform Taxation Act* were deemed to be non-compelling as states could essentially opt out. In a noted turn of phrase, Chief Justice Latham wrote for the court that "the States were being tempted to cease levying income tax, but temptation did not amount to compulsion."[65] Doing away with the uniform rates after the war would have devastated some states' finances or led to the reintroduction of unreasonably high tax rates. The Commonwealth had many of the states in an impossible situation, thereby securing to itself a monopoly on the taxation of income. This in turn gave it a considerable ability to influence state governments through the power of the purse.

The court made much of its inability, under strict tenets of literalism, to consider or to prevent undue outcomes for the politics of federalism. If the effect of a decision was to emasculate the power of the states, that was a matter to be resolved by the political branch of government. Menzies, for one, claims to have offered to alter the form of fiscal federalism during his term as prime minister. However, he found that state leaders could never agree to a revision. Only those states that stood to gain from regained control were ever eager. Those states that received redistribution were loath to open up the system for tinkering. In short, Menzies saw no proposal from a state that he could accept without being unfair to some states or without placing an unreasonable compensatory burden on the Commonwealth government.[66] Leslie Zines quotes Chief Justice Latham on the possibility that the court's decision in the *Uniform Tax* case may have meant the end of political independence for the states, now dependent on the Commonwealth's money: "The determination of the propriety of any such policy must rest with the Commonwealth parliament and ultimately with the people. The remedy for alleged abuse of power or for the use of power to promote what are thought to be improper objects is to be found in the political arena and not in the courts."[67]

The court backed away from centralization in 1945 with the *Pharmaceutical Benefits* case,[68] in which it invalidated a Labor government strategy to provide for the semblance of a national health plan. On a similar note, it modified the then discredited implied immunities doctrine in the *State Banking* case of 1947.[69] The Labor government, when it created the central Commonwealth bank, sought to ensure that all government business, both from the Commonwealth and from the states, would be transacted through it, giving the Commonwealth government some significant leverage in the financial industry. The legislation, challenged by the City of Melbourne, compelled states and municipalities to do their banking with the central bank rather than with banks of their own choosing. Melbourne was an important banking centre, and the several private banks on hand to offer their services argued that the advantage given to the central bank was unfair. The court found that a Commonwealth bank was within the scope of the section

51 power for banking. It did not find that the states and local councils, as state agencies, could be compelled to do their business with the bank.

Justice Owen Dixon wrote one of the majority opinions for the court. He was not as hidebound by the principles of *Engineers* as were some of his colleagues. Dixon had maintained the court's line on the reserved power doctrine of *Engineers* and was the proudest defender of the "strict and complete legalism" that it had advocated. However, he steered the court in a different direction on implications and immunity. As a component of his legacy, this strain is often pointed out as a heresy.[70] Specifically, he believed that the Commonwealth government should not be able to bind the state governments in their policy choices. This belief gave positive substance to section 107 of the constitution, which was set up to save the pre-federation powers of the states but was of little consequence once the old reserved powers doctrine had been overruled. For Dixon, the existence of a federal system meant that some effort had to be made to ensure that the states would not be rendered irrelevant by a domineering central government. Thus, he argued, "the federal system itself is the foundation of the restraint upon the use of the power to control the States."[71] By discriminating against the states in their choice of banker, the Commonwealth legislation violated the basic immunity that the federal system required.

Another immunities case effectively restricted Commonwealth power the same year. In *Uther,* the states were empowered to preempt the Commonwealth's right to priority of debt repayment.[72] The implied immunity that was revived to benefit the states in the *State Banking* case was not reciprocated to exempt the Commonwealth from state laws that changed the right of priority of payment. Under common law, the Commonwealth had enjoyed the right to first repayment of outstanding debts from bankrupt companies. Dixon dissented from the *Uther* majority's decision and had his objections confirmed by the majority of the court in the *Cigamatic* case of 1962.[73] The latter is generally regarded as the definitive statement on what exceptions can be made to a general immunity rule. Specifically, the Commonwealth does enjoy some priority where the Crown's prerogative is concerned.

The period after 1950 has been characterized as a much less dramatic time for constitutional interpretation. The High Court's balanced centralism was always a pressure release for the more overt centralism coming from the political process, particularly during periods of Labor Party rule. The fate of the Commonwealth's "corporations power" is a good example of the cautious but incremental centralism of the period. *Strickland v. Rocla Concrete Pipes Ltd.*[74] was the first significant decision in the post-*Engineers* era to address the Commonwealth's power over foreign and trading corporations granted by section 51(xx). The case concerned the validity of

Commonwealth legislation to monitor restrictive trade practices by those corporations that fell under the definition of foreign and trading corporations. Prior to *Concrete Pipes,* the court's reading of the section could be found only in the case of *Huddart, Parker and Co. Pty. Ltd. v. Moorhead.*[75] That case rejected the constitutionality of the Commonwealth's Australian *Industries Preservation Act, 1906,* an earlier form of anti-trust legislation. The kind of commercial activity that the act sought to control was considered within the reserved powers that the states retained after federation. The Commonwealth, chastened by the *Huddart* decision, kept itself at bay for more than sixty years.

Justice Isaacs, the main author and force behind the *Engineers* decision, had dissented from the narrow interpretation of the corporations power made by a reserved powers majority in *Huddart.* Despite the unambiguous "explosion" of the reserved power in *Engineers,* the Commonwealth made no foray into corporations regulation until the 1960s. With *Concrete Pipes,* the court overruled *Huddart* along *Engineers* principles. By doing so, the court reaffirmed the primacy of its literalist approach with an explicit affirmation of *Engineers* and provided a potentially broad but still cautiously expanded avenue for Commonwealth power.

As a matter of interpretation, *Concrete Pipes* is notable for the point of view taken by the High Court on reserved powers. When speaking of the *Huddart* case, Chief Justice Barwick, in the lead judgment, wrote that "it is plain enough from a reading of the reasons given by the majority ... that the influence of the then current reserved powers doctrine was so strong that the court was driven to emasculate the legislative power given by section 51(xx)."[76] Such an interpretation would not be allowed to stand. Reserved powers would not be a limit on the corporations power in 1971. With the nasty business of overruling the *Huddart* court out of the way, Barwick proceeded to the task of determining what limitations were necessary to make the corporations power viable. He did not find that just any legislation related to trading, or foreign corporations would qualify under the power. If the Commonwealth were to be granted a power to make laws for trading corporations, it would not represent a general grant over commercial and corporate activity. Rather, Barwick noted that the legislation at hand was justified because the sections "were regulating and controlling the trading activities of trading corporations."[77] Trading was the operative word. Production and other facets of commerce were not included, but a literal reading of the power gave the Commonwealth considerable room to expand its activities in the area of trade. On a cautious note, Barwick articulated a need to evaluate legislation on a case-by-case basis to ensure that the corporations power was not used overbroadly – "the decision as to the validity of particular laws yet to be enacted must remain for the Court when called upon to pass upon them."[78] Still, the Commonwealth could take this decision as a clear indication that trade practices legislation, particularly as it applied to the trusts and monopolies of foreign or trading corporations, was permissible. The range of those interests to which the law was applicable and those activities that could be deemed trading would expand in later cases.[79]

The Commonwealth power for external affairs was another heading broadly interpreted by the High Court in this period. In fact, the logic of expanding central power was eventually pushed to its limits by an external affairs case, *Tasmanian Dam*, in 1983. That case accorded greatly increased jurisdiction to the Commonwealth for domestic policy making based upon treaty commitments made in the name of external affairs. It will be the starting point for Chapter 4, which examines the recent federalism decisions of the High Court.

Canadian Federalism in the Courts

The Canadian constitution's development has occurred, like Australia's, on a relatively short timeline but, unlike Australia's, without a clearly demarcated revolution of constitutional interpretation. Nonetheless, it is useful to divide the judicial development of Canadian federalism into eras. The main variable distinguishing these periods is the place of the Supreme Court of Canada, first as a junior to the Judicial Committee of the Privy Council (JCPC) until 1949 and then as the sole high court for Canada for the years after. The decisions of the imperial court had, on average, the effect of decentralizing Canadian federalism. That influence has since been tempered by the decisions of the domestic court.

If the American legal and political academy had the New Deal court to alert it to the extent of judicial power, the JCPC stirred the souls of the Canadian legal academy in much the same way. The JCPC's supremacy in constitutional matters for eighty-two years generated an intense bitterness among those who thought that the true constitution was being distorted. By the 1930s, in the shadow of the American conflicts described above, the stewing conflict finally came to the boil. The vitriol felt by Canada's legal academics toward the interpretation of federalism by the JCPC in the 1930s and 1940s was barely surpassed by the American critics of the "four horsemen."[80] As Alan Cairns has masterfully demonstrated, there were flaws in the logic of these critics, and they were noticeably blinded by their own normative social-democratic, central government bias. However, the critics are a useful starting point for exploring the evolution of the *British North America (BNA) Act, 1867* (later *Constitution Act, 1867*), during those years in which it remained in the care of the JCPC.

Three issues are of primary importance for federalism in the interpretation of the *Constitution Act, 1867*. First, the preamble to section 91, the POGG clause, granted the power to implement laws for the general welfare of the country to Parliament. Second, the provincial legislatures were granted the general power over property and civil rights in the provinces. And third, the federal Parliament was given power over trade and commerce. The interpretation of these three provisions has determined, in large part, the degree of centralization or decentralization in Canadian federalism, at least from the standpoint of formal jurisdiction. The JCPC largely interpreted the POGG and trade and commerce powers narrowly and the property and civil rights power expansively. The committee clearly favoured the provinces by doing so. Its interpretation is generally regarded as being in conflict with the apparent intentions of the Fathers of Confederation, who sought to create a centralized union of the provinces.

Bora Laskin, one of the more eminent constitutional scholars and jurists of the twentieth century, called POGG "the favourite whipping boy of constitutional commentators."[81] Critics pointed to the misinterpretation of POGG as the primary culprit for Canadian federalism's misdirection. Similarly, the clause is seen as an ever-present threat to the stability of provincial autonomy by those more sympathetic to decentralization. Laskin was no less guilty than any of his colleagues of pinning big hopes on POGG. Theoretically, POGG can be interpreted in one of two ways. According to more centralist assumptions, it should be interpreted as a general grant of power, the enumerated powers in section 91 serving only as examples of how that general power may be exercised. The Privy Council supported such a vision of POGG for a short period following Confederation. In a series of decisions, the committee endorsed what has become known as a "two compartment" theory of federal jurisdiction. POGG, along with the enumerated examples in section 91, comprises the federal compartment, while the section 92 list for the provinces comprises the other.[82] Alternatively, POGG was interpreted as part of a three-compartment interpretation of the constitution. In that case, the section 91 list and the section 92 list comprised the main compartments for the federal and provincial governments respectively, and POGG existed as an extraordinary power. It is, in effect, a third compartment to be used by the federal government in extraordinary circumstances, which the court can only review on a case-by-case basis.[83]

Extraordinary circumstances, in the collective mind of the JCPC, basically came to mean emergencies. Justifications based upon the POGG power were available to the federal government, but only in those instances when it could be proven that, for the sake of a national emergency, provincial autonomy had to be overridden. The *Board of Commerce* case in 1922 provided the committee with its first opportunity to define the emergency power.[84] Led by Viscount Haldane, the JCPC balked at the broad powers incorporated in the federal anti-profiteering legislation before the committee. There were not sufficiently compelling circumstances to justify federal intervention, but the court hinted that more dire circumstances might still qualify. A year later in the *Fort Frances* case,[85] the committee found such circumstances. However, the JCPC narrowed the scope of emergency two years later in *Toronto Electric Commissioners v. Snider*.[86] *Snider* provided grist for the satirical mill of critics, as Viscount Haldane reinterpreted the two-compartment decision some years before in *Russell* as a result of the committee's impression that the government supposed drunkenness (the upheld legislation imposed a temperance regime) had reached "emergency" proportions in the dominion.

The JCPC briefly indicated that potential justification for federal legislation under POGG outside emergencies might exist in *Re: Regulation and Control of Aeronautics in Canada*.[87] The committee upheld legislation creating a national regime for the control of aeronautics under the auspices of section 132 of the *Constitution Act, 1867,* which dealt with the implementation of empire treaties. Writing for the committee, Lord Sankey indicated that aeronautics might also be a matter of national interest to be dealt with under the POGG power of the federal government. The committee gave further encouragement to centralists in the *Radio* reference of the same year,[88] which gave treaty implementation power to Parliament without reliance on the empire treaties clause. The potential opened for central government activity by this decision encouraged the government of R.B. Bennett to proceed with some confidence in committing Canada to international treaties on labour standards and other social welfare issues. POGG did not fare as well as was hoped when further cases were put before the committee. The JCPC did not admit any emergency as justification for the so-called Bennett New Deal legislation that had been passed to cope with the vagaries of the Great Depression. The JCPC heard a group of cases related to these provisions in a single package. They were originally referred to the Supreme Court of Canada in November of 1935 by the Mackenzie King government, which had replaced the Bennett administration that October. The JCPC ruled on the cases in the early months of 1937.[89] Five of the eight legislated reform measures presented to the JCPC were rejected as *ultra vires* the federal government. The decisions enraged critics of the committee, so much so that the *Canadian Bar Review* for June 1937 was devoted solely to a series of chastising articles on the decisions. In addition to rejecting the existence of an emergency, the committee rejected the argument introduced by counsel for the federal government and later Prime Minister Louis St. Laurent that unemployment insurance was a matter of national concern and thus fell under the rubric of POGG without any reference to emergency.[90]

The JCPC's intractability spurred a successful effort to amend the constitution so that the federal government could have power over unemployment insurance[91] and further spurred a movement for halting appeals to the Privy Council. That the federal government had to rely upon arguments establishing an emergency before it could exercise POGG powers made a mockery of the centralist belief that POGG was a comprehensive residuary power. F.R. Scott, with his tongue firmly in cheek, gave faint praise to the JCPC for its interpretation of emergency: "Canadians know they can at least engage in wars without constitutional difficulties."[92] Despite the setback in the Bennett New Deal cases, the POGG category was provisionally expanded by the JCPC in its last days to include matters of national dimensions. One of the last major cases to be heard by the committee opened up space for POGG that did not depend upon the existence of an emergency. In the *Canada Temperance Federation* case, the JCPC, through Viscount Simon, refuted much of its POGG jurisprudence (including the emergency explanation for *Russell*) and gave credence to a national concern "branch" for POGG.

The JCPC's hostility to federal expansion was matched by its generosity toward the provinces. The committee expanded property and civil rights almost in direct proportion to its restrictions on POGG. The JCPC interpreted property and civil rights as a positive grant and accordingly increased the jurisdiction of provinces. In this way, property and civil rights played see-saw with the federally enumerated power over trade and commerce. What did not qualify as a matter of trade and commerce (and thus accrue to the federal government) was likely to qualify as a matter under property and civil rights. The first case to consider either power demonstrates this tug-of-war best. In *Citizens Insurance Co. v. Parsons,*[93] the JCPC found that the national regulation of fire insurance was not within the scope of trade and commerce but within the scope of property and civil rights. The court went further and suggested that the power over trade and commerce was effectively limited to the regulation of trade with other nations, interprovincial trade, and "the general regulation of trade affecting the whole Dominion."[94] By 1916, the latter category was narrowly interpreted in the *Insurance* reference as "essentially an auxiliary power incapable of serving on its own as a primary source of legislative capacity."[95] By similar means, the power over industrial disputes was placed in the property and civil rights bag,[96] and the previously mentioned nation-wide unemployment insurance scheme was denied federal justification.[97] Property and civil rights effectively became the residual power that POGG never was.

Once matters were solely in the hands of Canada's own court, the balance of power between the federal and provincial governments began to shift slightly. The Supreme Court took full advantage of the national concern possibilities of POGG first offered in *Canada Temperance* and began to define a broader scope for the power. This approach expanded POGG to include national control of aeronautics (in *Johannesson,* 1952), atomic energy (in *Pronto Uranium Mines,* 1956), a national capital region (in *Munro,* 1966), and seabed natural resources (in *Offshore Minerals,* 1967).[98] However, this generous view of POGG did not amount to a Canadian revolution of

American proportions. The Supreme Court did not shift dramatically to a centralized vision of federalism. To the contrary, it simply mimicked a particular approach of the JCPC. William Lederman argued that the Canadian court failed to be truly activist and instead opted for the "ready-made" and pursued what he called the "Watson-Simon" view. Lord Watson was responsible for the JCPC's three-compartment theory. Lederman overlooks Watson's restrictive trade and commerce interpretation in order to suggest that his was a very measured view of both provincial and federal power. It amounts to a lot of "on one hand, but on the other hand." Witness Watson's optimism in *Local Prohibition:*

> Their Lordships do not doubt that some matters, in their origin local and provincial, might attain such dimensions as to affect the body politic of the Dominion, and to justify the Canadian Parliament in passing laws for their regulation or abolition in the interest of the Dominion. But great caution must be observed in distinguishing between that which is local and provincial, and therefore within the jurisdiction of the provincial legislatures, and that which has ceased to be merely local or provincial, and has become a matter of national concern, in such sense as to bring it within the jurisdiction of the Parliament of Canada.[99]

Lord Simon was an equally measured creator of doctrine. He was responsible for the late moderation of the JCPC in the *Canada Temperance Federation* case. The "Watson-Simon" view approached the general power cautiously but was willing to extend it beyond the impractical realm of emergency.

The expansionist POGG strides of the post-JCPC era were made with considerable moderation. Small liberties were taken by the fully autonomous court. It stemmed the tide of aggressive Haldane-style decentralism, but the essence of the court's approach to federalism remained the same. The court did not feel an obligation to modernize the constitution through centralization, as so many of the commentators in the law journals had urged. The change in the court of last resort amounted to little more than a change of venue. The Canadian jurists in whom Laskin had a measure of hope continued to fire the "canons of construction"[100] forged and mastered by the Privy Council.

The Supreme Court has, however, had the opportunity to rule on questions that the law lords of the Privy Council did not. The delegation of power between governments through intergovernmental agreements has required the court to think carefully about the structure of cooperative federalism, something that the JCPC never had to oversee. The ability of the provinces and federal government to skirt the requirements of the division of powers by assigning or delegating responsibilities to one another is a major element of cooperative federalism. Since constitutional change is by no means easy to achieve, incremental change in the form of bilateral and multilateral agreements has often been seen as a means to dispel conflict and to manage the federation efficiently and effectively. The Supreme Court has not looked kindly on some of the more overt attempts to circumvent the requirements of the constitution and has effectively forestalled the use of a certain class of such agreements. But the court has demonstrated a capacity for balance here as well. While the justices forbade the cooperative scheme of the Nova Scotia and federal governments in the 1951 interdelegation case,[101] they permitted a slightly different form of delegation to pass a year later. In *PEI Potato Marketing Board v. H.B. Willis,*[102] the federal government was permitted to delegate responsibility to an administrative board created by the provincial legislature in preference to the legislature itself. The court has kept direct delegation at bay but has opened up considerable room for cooperative federalism through the *PEI Potato Marketing* case.

To the presumable chagrin of Scott and Laskin, a generous interpretation of POGG never developed in their lifetimes, even in spite of Laskin's own best attempts from the bench as chief justice. With Laskin as chief justice, Peter Hogg could still write in 1979 that "there is no basis for the claim that the court has been biased in favour of the federal interest in constitutional litigation."[103] The provincial autonomists on the bench, such as Jean Beetz, from Quebec, were able to maintain the tradition of provincialism begun in the chambers of Westminster with the JCPC.[104] Hogg concluded that the court favoured the provinces in fields such as taxation, the administration of justice (including the growth and development of quasi-judicial administrative agencies), civil liberties (in their pre-Charter form), and federal paramountcy. Small gains for the federal government in fields such as cable television regulation or aeronautics did not offset these general trends. The continued reluctance to expand POGG or trade and commerce has kept the post-1949 Supreme Court in line with its imperial predecessor. Peter Russell agreed a few years later, emphasizing the "uncanny balance" between results favourable to federal and provincial governments.[105]

The period from 1949 until the 1970s has not been generally regarded as the finest in Canadian jurisprudence. Many observers have been critical of the approach and methods of the Supreme Court. Alan Cairns, in his apologia for the Privy Council, also took the opportunity to criticize the Canadian court. He found that, in the years since it gained final authority, it had failed to live up to the standards of moderation and thoughtfulness about federalism that the JCPC demonstrated. By indulging, however little, the long-standing domestic critique of the JCPC's federalism, the domestic court may have been engaged in a fool's errand. Cairns claimed that the critics of the committee were blinded by their own policy preferences to the detriment of their grasp on the reality of Canada's federal evolution. The kind of federalism that the critics wanted, and that they were partly successful in persuading the Canadian court to move toward, was not the kind of federalism operating on the ground.

Yet the Supreme Court has never been a radical agent. Any attempt to break the bounds of interpretation along the lines of a constitutional revolution has almost always remained on the margins of Canadian decisions. Canada has no *NLRB v. Jones.* The federal government could unquestionably expand its activities if it were handed an unambiguous endorsement of the national concern branch of the POGG power, but no court has had the courage, or the folly, to endorse it. While Laskin's position in *Reference Re: Anti-Inflation* was very permissive toward the federal power, he did not write for a majority of the court. That case is something of a turning point in the doctrine of Canadian federalism and will be used to start the more detailed examination of current decisions in Chapter 5.

Lest the focus here give the wrong impression, it is nowhere contended that judicially enforced changes to these constitutions are the sole force in their evolution. Judicial interpretation acts more commonly as a referee, vetoing some and approving other choices whose origins lie elsewhere. The assumed legitimacy of the exercise of judicial review gives it the power and authority to shape future behaviour. Sometimes a court's role is critical to the way that intergovernmental strategies develop. Sometimes it is not. In the American case, we saw the extremes of judicial relevance to the big picture of federal development. At times like the New Deal, judicial review was obviously central to the progress of critical events. At other times, a court can start to write itself into irrelevance – as did the post-New Deal court, by staying virtually out of the way of congressional and national government expansion.

What should be obvious from this brief review is that all three courts worked under certain assumptions when playing their roles in federal evolution. Originally, observers attached a great deal of weight to these judicial assumptions for the clear effect that they had on the behaviour and ambitions of governments. When the courts questioned their own assumptions, they usually had a larger impact on the constitution and the nation than when they routinely relied upon doctrines. At the same time, doctrines often led to courts operating in an unbalanced fashion, promoting the interests of one level of government over another. Default positions based upon past choices often magnified this effect over time. Default positions, to the parties concerned, seemed to be unfair. They predetermined outcomes. What is not clear, even from this modest examination, is that common doctrines operated necessarily as strict default positions. Who expected the American Supreme Court's reversal of its New Deal opposition? Certainly the NLRB lawyers believed that they had a case. Other doctrinal alternatives were available, and those alternatives allowed the Supreme Court to short-circuit its own obstinance. The cheeky young barrister Robert Menzies was surprised by his own success in reversing the first twenty years of Australian doctrine in the *Engineers* case, but his strategy was sound. He helped the court through a door that it had already opened itself.

What doctrine does is condition the approach that a court will take to problems. Doctrine is only one independent variable in a court's decision-making process. To dismiss doctrine because it does not definitively force particular outcomes misses its ultimate relevance. Of course, it does not tie the hand. However, it does condition the mind. The cases surveyed in this chapter and the means by which they were commonly decided are reflected in the recent doctrines of all three courts. By undermining the status of doctrine as an explanatory variable, some observers may have thrown themselves off the scent of a complete understanding of contemporary federalism. The significance of recent high court decisions on federalism has probably been too easily dismissed. It is the project of the next three chapters to try to reveal what doctrinal developments lurk in these recent pronouncements.

3
The US Supreme Court: Revived Federalism

Doctrine: Lost and Found

The United States Supreme Court is literally the benchmark for students of judicial federalism. The court was the first to establish the practice of judicial review of a constitution and has been a regular and active participant in the shaping of American federalism. This has put the court at the centre of many a political storm. It has weighed in during most periods of tumult in the republic's history, from the seminal conflicts of the federalist era to the immediate antebellum and the years of reconstruction following the Civil War. The court was perhaps never more at the epicentre of political conflict than during the Roosevelt New Deal. The most enduring by-product of that period for federalism was a court-sanctioned, central government expansion that lasted for more than sixty years. The court's implicit approval of congressional expansionism was such that by 1985, in its decision in *Garcia*, the court appeared to, at least unofficially, resign from the task of umpiring federalism conflicts.

Garcia pushed the logic of permissive post-New Deal federalism to an extreme, and in subsequent rulings the court has moved back from that brink. At times, it has done so with a vengeance. The Supreme Court has become much less willing to give up its supervisory role in the federation. Under the leadership of former Chief Justice William Rehnquist, the court went more than eleven years without a change of personnel. Death and retirement in 2005 brought this era of remarkable stability to an end, but that period gave the justices an opportunity to engage in a heated debate about the kind of federation envisioned by the constitution and the proper approach to take to the interpretation of its key provisions. The role of doctrine in this debate is undeniable. The seemingly polar positions that divided members of the Rehnquist court were based upon an understanding of the history of constitutionalism and interpretation and are backed up by a vocabulary of meaning and precedent found mostly in the case law of the past two centuries. Both visions relied upon these shared understandings to develop what

Kathleen Sullivan calls "structural default positions" capable of providing answers to the constitutional questions put before the court.[1] By this account, there was certainly agreement on the Rehnquist court about how constitutional controversies should be decided – by reference to the inherent principles of the constitution. The justices simply disagreed on the proper interpretation of the relevant background material. The responses of the court to federalism cases were closely divided, and there was considerable room between the two sides, indicating little chance of compromise. That one position never truly triumphed is largely a result of subtleties of interpretation that swung the voting patterns of Justices Anthony Kennedy and Sandra Day O'Connor.[2] Justice O'Connor's retirement may tilt future results on federalism in a more definitive direction.

The dispute among members of the Rehnquist court was particularly evident in its commerce clause jurisprudence. If peace, order, and good government form the bellwether of Canadian federalism, commerce is its American counterpart. Where goes commerce goes Congress. The commerce power is the largest single formal determinant of national power in American federalism. Through the commerce power, Congress has made numerous forays into what may at one time have been considered state responsibilities. Since most matters have at least a minimal connection to or effect on commerce, the subject matters available to Congress under this umbrella have been nearly unlimited. The reasoning of the *Garcia* majority seemed to affirm that lack of limits and took the logic one step further by articulating what has come to be known as a functionalist approach. Essentially, the majority argued that the place of law in American federalism was less critical than the efficient operation of the federal system in response to national needs and priorities. To this way of thinking, federalism frictions are best reduced not by the intervention of the law but by informal agreements and political bargaining, both intergovernmental and within the institutions of the central government (often referred to in Canada as intrastate federalism).[3] This is a position with which the Rehnquist court, despite its differences on the appropriate vision of American federalism, would unanimously take issue.

This chapter reviews the high points of federal judicial review in the United States from just before the court's landmark *Garcia* decision up until the end of its 2004 term. The American situation is surveyed here first because the current dispute on the court has encouraged an effective revival in federalism doctrine. It is the strongest case for the argument that formal doctrine is critical to a contemporary understanding of federalism. By making judicial reasoning about federalism so transparent, the court has required considerable thoughtfulness of itself. The judges have had to articulate what federalism means and how their vision is translated into practical doctrines that settle constitutional disputes. More important, the subtlety demonstrated by the court shows how effective doctrine is as a tool for settling jurisdictional disputes. Observers like to accord uncompromising positions to the judges, and their current techniques, at least on the surface, seem to encourage default positions. But doctrine, by allowing fine distinctions, is proving capable of an important degree of flexibility.

National League of Cities: Commerce Expansion Ended?

The origins of the court's current split can be traced back to former chief justice Rehnquist's early days as a Supreme Court appointee. William Rehnquist was elevated to the high bench in 1971 by President Richard Nixon and in short order began to exact a conservative, "states first" influence on federalism jurisprudence. Rehnquist scored an early triumph for this perspective in 1976 with *National League of Cities v. Usery*[4] (hereafter *NLC*), the first Supreme Court decision since the New Deal to overrule congressional excursions taken under the auspices of the commerce power. At issue in *NLC* was the permissible scope of the federal *Fair Labour Standards Act,* which had been amended to include employment standards for state and local government workers. The legislation had its origins in the New Deal, originally passed in 1938 following the court's famous change of heart in *NLRB v. Jones*. It was also the legislation challenged in the court by *U.S. v. Darby.*[5] By upholding the legislation in *Darby,* the court overturned *Hammer v. Dagenhart*[6] and symbolically put to rest its opposition to the New Deal. *Darby* heralded a decades-long indulgence by the court of congressional commerce clause expansion. By 1976, however, the sheen of the New Deal consensus on the court was starting to wear thin. The judicial branch had by no means become as actively hostile to the legislative program of the national government as it had been in the years preceding 1937. However, Rehnquist led the move to challenge the scope of "big government" at the federal level.

In *NLC,* Rehnquist wrote the opinion for the five-to-four majority of the court. He emphasized the effect that federal law mandating state behaviour would have on state sovereignty. The concept of state sovereignty he took infinitely more seriously than the central government expanders of the previous forty years or even his counterparts on the court. A year earlier, in *Fry v. United States,* the court had found that state sovereignty did not exempt state employees from the provisions of the *Economic Stabilization Act* of 1970, with Rehnquist as the only dissenter.[7] Post-New Deal decisions had paid almost no heed to arguments in favour of state sovereignty. Rehnquist took the founding era rather than the "revolution" of 1937 as his benchmark. The framers' intentions, he argued, should serve as a guide to the constitutionality of the legislation at hand. In defence of this method, he invoked the practice of "earlier decisions of this court recognizing the essential role of the States in our federal system of government."[8] As such, Rehnquist was clearly driven by his interpretation of constitutional principles (particularly those with a states' rights pedigree) rather than the details of commerce jurisprudence and doctrine or the undue effects of the legislation. As it was, many states and municipalities stood to incur massive cost increases if they were forced to comply with the minimum wage and overtime provisions of the act. Rehnquist detailed some of these effects, but he claimed, only to demonstrate the degree to which the amendments would interfere with state policy choices, not to suggest that adverse consequences disrupted the balance of the federal system.

Rehnquist acknowledged in his decision that the commerce power is plenary and subject only to the limits prescribed by the constitution. Those limits are generally understood to be the guarantees of individual rights provided by the constitution. His innovation was to interpret the federal nature of the constitution, realized through states' rights, as a comparable restraint upon congressional action. Rehnquist argued that the sovereignty of the states is an equally affirmative limit on the scope of the commerce clause. In much the same way as the right to a fair trial or the right to due process limits the applicability of the commerce power on individuals or corporations, state sovereignty should limit the scope of the commerce power as it applies to the states. Rehnquist did not provide a great deal of evidence to suggest that state sovereignty was something that the constitution's authors explicitly sought to protect. He relied instead upon the habit of the court to respect state sovereignty in the past. This was particularly true when Congress had attempted to regulate the states as states.

Much of the commerce clause expansion that typified the post-New Deal certainly offended what might be labelled state sovereignty but generally by means of preempting or overruling what was traditionally understood to be state jurisdiction. Commerce clause regulation frequently assumed tasks previously undertaken by the states or presumed to be within the ambit of the states. The commerce power has much less frequently been used by Congress to actually regulate the states themselves. By trying to set wage and overtime rates for local government employees, Congress was recognizing the states as major employers and setting out to regulate them in much the same way that it regulated industry. In court, the federal government argued that its regulation of states and local governments as employers was no more abusive of state jurisdiction than the preemption of state authority more typical of commerce clause expansion. Rehnquist rejected this argument as missing the point of state sovereignty. He ruled that to hive off jurisdiction is one thing – but to invade the sphere of the state government compromises its independence and autonomy. Thus, he noted that the court has "repeatedly recognized that there are attributes of sovereignty attaching to every state government which may not be impaired by Congress, not because Congress may lack an affirmative grant of legislative authority to reach the matter, but because the Constitution prohibits it from exercising the authority in that manner."[9] In other words, the commerce power may very well allow Congress to make laws regulating employment, but it does not permit Congress to tell the states how to conduct their own affairs. What qualifies as an undeniable attribute of state sovereignty is somewhat vague. For his part, Rehnquist suggested that "traditional state functions" needed to be left untouched by congressional regulation. At a minimum, Rehnquist believed that the hiring and remuneration of state employees was an "undoubted attribute of state sovereignty."[10]

The court's decision in *NLC* made federalism an effective limit on the commerce power. That the American system of government was intended to be federal was indication enough for Rehnquist that limits were implied on national power. While congressional regulation of the states was as unwelcome and as costly as similar regulations applied to private industry, the states had a different status and thus were exempt from such burdens. While a state could have an effect on the economy and the labour market, a state, he argued, was not "merely a factor in the 'shifting economic arrangements' of the private sector of the economy ... but is itself a coordinate element in the system established by the Framers for governing the Federal Union."[11] The gist of his reasoning was that the states have special status, even if the constitution did not explicitly grant them exemptions from federal law.[12]

NLC was a stunner. The court had not overruled a commerce-based regulation by Congress for nearly forty years. Rehnquist's credentials as an advocate of state autonomy were firmly cemented by his opinion. Jeff Powell credits Rehnquist for single-handedly discounting "conventional wisdom" and reintroducing "state sovereignty as a functioning legal limitation on the federal legislative power."[13] Herman Pritchett notes that *NLC* engendered a rash of cases at the lower court level challenging federal regulation of the states. Indeed, some forty-two challenges were initiated in the two years immediately following the *NLC* result.[14] That said, Rehnquist's doctrinal innovation was not to last. State sovereignty may have challenged conventional wisdom, but it was not to become conventional wisdom itself.

When the matter of federal regulation of the states was raised again in the Supreme Court, as it was in *Hodel v. Virginia Surface Mining* and *Equal Employment Opportunity Commission (EEOC) v. Wyoming,* Rehnquist's hoped-for trend never took flight.[15] The court did try to put flesh on the bones of his theory. Thurgood Marshall, working with a precedent that he was clearly uncomfortable with, articulated a four-step procedure in *Hodel* to try to codify what sorts of activities would be eligible for exemption from federal regulation. The test that he articulated required (1) that the federal statute at issue regulate the states as states; (2) that it "address matters that are indisputably 'attributes of state sovereignty'"; and (3) that a state's compliance must impair its ability to "structure integral operations in areas of traditional governmental functions." A footnote implied that extraordinary conditions could require the federal government to override the federalism limits. Thus, for the state to qualify for exemption, (4) the import of the federal interest (i.e., the degree of emergency) must not be great enough to justify state submission.[16] The presumption following *Hodel* was that all three enunciated criteria and the fourth implied condition would have to be met for state activities to merit exemption from federal commerce regulation.

Hodel is an excellent example of contorting an unwelcome precedent almost beyond recognition. Marshall accepted the criteria that existed prior to his decision but effectively piled them one atop the other, raising the bar and thereby lowering the likelihood of a successful future state claim to exemption.

Garcia: Functionalism Triumphant

The closeness of the result in *NLC* and the work that it had left undone ensured that it would not be the last word on state sovereignty. As a concept, state sovereignty was not faring well. In fact, it was taking a beating. *Hodel,* it turned out, was only a first jab. The central government boosters threw an uppercut with *EEOC v. Wyoming,* applying the *Hodel* modifications to uphold congressional regulation. The knockout punch for Rehnquist's revived state sovereignty came with *Garcia v. San Antonio Metropolitan Transit Authority. Garcia* would end up directly overturning *NLC* to provide a distinctly opposite interpretation of federalism, state sovereignty, and the place of the court in federalism disputes.

Garcia brought the much-amended and multifaceted *Fair Labor Standards Act* before the court again. The San Antonio Metropolitan Transit Authority (SAMTA), a local government body, argued that it was effectively a state agency and that the local government activities that it undertook qualified it for the *NLC* exemption. Joe Garcia, a transit employee seeking the protection of the federal legislation, challenged the exemption. The lower federal court exempted SAMTA on the basis of *NLC.* The Supreme Court heard the case to test the justification.

Few Supreme Court decisions had followed the *NLC* model, though many cases, as was *Garcia,* were successfully argued on *NLC* principles in the lower courts. When given the opportunity to reconsider *NLC* with reasonably similar circumstances, the Supreme Court did not just make the piecemeal modifications that it made in *Hodel* and the *EEOC* case. In 1976, the members of the court had definitely chosen sides. In *NLC,* Rehnquist was at the vanguard of a core of state-sympathetic justices. His colleague William Brennan wrote for the more federally inclined foursome. Justice Harry Blackmun joined the *NLC* majority with a rather qualified concurring opinion, tipping the otherwise evenly divided court to Rehnquist's state sovereignty

SPECIAL OFFER

WEDNESDAY DECEMBER 26 TO MONDAY DECEMBER 31, 2007

BEHR GOOD. BETTER. BEHR. CIL RL PAINT

$7 on 3.78L cans **or** $25 on 18.9L pails

by manufacturer mail-in rebate when you purchase any Behr®, CIL or Ralph Lauren interior paint*

79, 123, 194, 215, 384, 210, 393, 404, 408, 121, 153

*Offer starts Wednesday, December 26, 2007 where open. Some exceptions may apply. Offer valid on Behr® interior paint, interior primers or ceiling paint, Ralph Lauren interior paint or primer, CIL Smart and CIL Dulux® interior paint and primer paint at The Home Depot Canada. Not valid in combination with any other offer. Selection varies by store and quantities are limited. We reserve the right to limit quantities to the amount reasonable for homeowners and our regular contractor customers. Offer valid to Canadian residents only. No substitutions or rain checks. See Store Associate or Special Services Desk for details. PE906759

THE HOME DEPOT

How to receive your Mail-In Rebate

The rebate will be fulfilled via manufacturer mail-in.

1. **Purchase any Behr®, CIL and Ralph Lauren interior paint** at participating The Home Depot stores between December 26 to December 31, 2007.
2. **Complete this form** and mail along with **original UPC code(s) from packaging** (exceptions include installed and assembled product or merchandise not in an original carton) **or** a copy of the complete, validated **Special Services Customer Agreement** (if applicable). Please include a copy of the **original sales receipt** and circle the qualifying purchase(s).
3. **Mail** these items to the address on the right:

Mail to: Dept. 906759
Interior Paint Offer
P.O. Box 1069
Fonthill, ON L0S 1E0

Please Print

Name: ______ Phone: ______

Address: ______

City: ______ Province: ______ Postal Code: ______

6-Digit Sku: ______ UPC: ______

Offer expires December 31, 2007. Must be postmarked by January 31, 2008. Void where prohibited or restricted by law. Photocopies will be honoured. Home Depot of Canada, Inc. ("The Home Depot") assumes no liability for delayed, lost, misdirected, incomplete or postage due mail. Fraudulent submissions may result in criminal prosecution. The Home Depot reserves the right to request additional information regarding this claim. Materials received become the property of The Home Depot and will not be returned. Keep copies of all materials sent. Return of merchandise shall invalidate this offer. Please allow 8-10 weeks for delivery from receipt of submission. **Limit one (1) rebate per household or company. Multiple receipts are acceptable for this offer as long as they are mailed in one submission.**

What is your language preference? ☐ English ☐ French

☐ Check here to receive direct mail offers. Email: ______

☐ Check here to receive special offer emails. At The Home Depot, we respect privacy. For full details on our privacy and security policy, visit homedepot.ca

For inquiries regarding redemption, please call 1-866-883-2500, or visit homedepot.ca/rebatestatus

PE906759

argument. It was clear by 1985 that Blackmun had abandoned his indecision and qualification on these matters. Unfortunately for those advocating a renewed federalism, he chose the strong national government position and proceeded to preach it with the zeal of the newly baptized.

If the reason for finding against commerce regulation in *NLC* was the need to preserve traditional state functions, future jurisprudence and legislation needed to flesh out the definition of such functions to provide a boundary line over which federal activity could not cross. *Hodel* went some of the way toward providing such a technique but still left out any explicit definition of traditional state responsibilities. Writing for the majority against state sovereignty in *Garcia,* Blackmun found that the search for such a core of traditional responsibility conducted in the interim between *NLC* and *Garcia* had been unfruitful. Of the fifteen lower court decisions that Blackmun cited as relevant to this debate, five had exempted states or their agencies, while ten had not. Regardless of the results, Blackmun wrote, it was "difficult, if not impossible, to identify an organizing principle that places each of the cases in the first group on one side of a line and each of the cases in the second group on the other side."[17] The task of articulating such principles, deemed worth a try in 1976, was for Blackmun now shown to be misconceived. In his view, not only was the "traditional state function" approach unworkable, but it ultimately frustrated the principles of federalism that the *NLC* majority so proudly tried to protect.

Specifically, he found that the reliance on a historical approach was not as objective as may have been claimed. Moreover, the lack of flexibility in such a method left the states trapped in what amounted to historical straightjackets. This is the core of what has been called a "functionalist" approach. Federalism, Blackmun argued, requires flexibility more than it requires formalism. For a federation to endure and for the units in a federation to flourish, he claimed, they must be allowed to experiment and work outside the bounds of rigid structures. A judiciary patrolling the border between federal and state power is, on the whole, hostile to such flexibility. Blackmun encouraged the judiciary to thin out its patrols to allow governments to blur the lines.

The most significant doctrinal issue for Blackmun was whether SAMTA's activities qualified for exemption from the *Fair Labour Standards Act* under the third *Hodel* criteria. That is, did they constitute a traditional governmental function? A better definition of traditional state functions than that generalized in *Hodel* was crucial to determining if SAMTA qualified for the exemption. The challenge in *NLC* and *Hodel* had been to find historical justifications for these characterizations. According to Blackmun, those efforts had failed. New attempts, moreover, would offend federal theory. States, he argued, should be free to pursue uncommon or unorthodox approaches to problems of government. If they were hemmed in by the courts seeking to define them in terms of "traditional" functions, their room to manoeuvre was consequently limited. The way to identify the appropriate limits on Congress was not to search for subjective and arbitrary historical standards about proper functions for the states.

The big question was how the courts were to provide flexibility for evolving federal arrangements yet avoid judicial subjectivity. Blackmun argued that it could not be done and that subjectivity was inevitable. But what of constitutional legitimacy? Questions about federal balance, once assumed to be judicial, he claimed, should instead find their resolution in the political branches. The heart of Blackmun's reasoning and reply to the formal doctrine of *NLC* was to wholly disavow a role for the court in determining the limits that were appropriate. Where in the more political branches was the substitute? According to Blackmun, the constitution provided the answer in the way that it structured the federal government.

Blackmun suggested two ways in which state interests are protected through the institutions of national government: the electoral college and the Senate. To him, the latter was most important: "The principal and basic limit on the federal commerce power is that inherent in all congressional action – the built in restraints that our system provides through State participation in federal governmental action."[18] One house of Congress is made up of the nominal representatives of the states. Blackmun believed that such representation should ensure that the federal nature of the country is respected. Contrast this claim with Rehnquist's articulation of federal limits in the form of state sovereignty. Under Rehnquist's model, and even by the standards of *Hodel,* protection of state interests has to come after the legislation via the scrutiny of judicial review. According to *Garcia,* if the federal legislation at hand made it through the national political process, that meant that state cautions had already been properly observed. It therefore became unnecessary for the court to consider state sovereignty or any other federalism limit that might be argued to overrule congressional action.

The discussion of *Garcia* has thus far omitted any reference to the Tenth Amendment's reserved power provisions. Areas not deemed to fall within the scope of the constitutionally defined congressional powers usually find their home among the reserved powers. A generous interpretation of the Tenth Amendment's scope is essential to a strong state position like Rehnquist's as it helps to restrict an open-ended reading of congressional powers such as commerce. Conversely, when little effort is made to define the residue, many activities can be construed as belonging to Congress under the commerce clause. The emphasis on traditional state functions in *NLC* provided an opportunity for expanding, or at least limiting the erosion of, state power reserves. If subject matters could be characterized as historically within the realm of the states, then Congress is precluded by the Tenth Amendment from invading such a field. If a subject falls under a congressional heading such as commerce, then the amendment precludes the states from a legitimate prior claim – in effect the subject is a matter that the sovereign states gave up at the founding. The Tenth Amendment lost much of its strength via Supreme Court interpretation in the post-New Deal era. The willingness of the court to entertain virtually all excursions into commerce with a variety of doctrinal constructs detracted attention from the Tenth Amendment. The court has even referred to the amendment as little more than a truism.[19]

By pushing the logic of post-New Deal federalism as far as it did, *Garcia* gave truth to Justice Rehnquist's invective of some years earlier: "One of the greatest 'fictions' of our federal system is that Congress exercises only those powers delegated to it, while the remainder are reserved to the States or to the people ... Although it is clear that the people, through the States, *delegated* authority to Congress to regulate Commerce ... among the several states, ... one could easily get the sense from this court's opinions that the federal system exists only at the sufferance of Congress."[20]

Rehnquist argued that the "fiction" of delegated powers was created by the weak scrutiny applied to commerce regulation and the unwillingness of the court to advance or accept Tenth Amendment arguments. The logic of making Congress the site for the protection of state interests took the fiction perhaps a final step. Rehnquist most certainly disagreed that this was the right approach to federalism.

Giving its own watered-down version of an argument against the need for judicial review in federalism controversies, the *Garcia* majority argued that jurisdictional disputes are essentially a minefield of politics and subjectivity and hence are unsuited to settlement by an unelected and unaccountable judiciary. If states wanted to grieve jurisdictional encroachments by the national government, the place to go was the Senate, not the high court. That the Senate is an adequate safeguard of state interests has been highly contested. Justice Antonin Scalia argues that the change wrought by the Seventeenth Amendment (which provided for the direct election of senators by the residents of states rather than the senators being chosen by state governments) has neutered the effective representation of the states in the institutions of the federal government. Others argue that there are substantial "political safeguards" for the promotion of state interests and that the Supreme Court is an unreliable or unnecessary interloper in federal-state relations.[21] Regardless, coming from an institution so long situated at the heart of federalism, the *Garcia* decision was met with some astonishment by students of American constitutional law. The argument is reminiscent of those made by Paul Weiler and Patrick Monahan with regard to Canada.

While Rehnquist's opinion in *NLC* tried to revive the quest for limits on national power, it seemed to have the opposite effect. Instead of starting the ball rolling, it alerted the court to the seeming futility of such a project.

The quest for limits is a quest for formal doctrinal constructs. In *Garcia,* the majority ruled that these kinds of limits cannot be had without introducing subjectivity into the judicial process. The court may have masked its subjectivity up until that point by not limiting Congress. If a policy enjoyed the approval of the national political process, it suffered very little opposition from the Supreme Court. Up until *Garcia,* this latitude was unofficial. The court did not actually say that any foray by Congress into commerce regulation would meet with little scrutiny. The resignation by the court in *Garcia* seemed to open the floodgates of central expansion. Senators, not state politicians or the court, were the last protectors of states' rights, and they seemed to be a weak set of sentries. *Garcia* was an argument against doctrine in its purest form. However, with judges sympathetic to the states still on the court, it was not expected to be the last word.

New York: Federalism Salvaged

If *Garcia* laid down a gauntlet for advocates of states' rights, it was not immediately taken up. The decision did garner much attention from legal and other observers, many or most of whom decried its sloppy and unprincipled approach to federalism. Most believed that the court left too little jurisdiction to the states and absolved itself of too much responsibility in matters of federalism.[22] The court's close division and the apparent strength of the viewpoints held by justices such as Rehnquist ensured that a reconsideration of *Garcia* would come at some point in the future.

New York v. United States,[23] with Justice Rehnquist moved to the chief's chair, forestalled the death of court-interpreted federalism and began the current era of rejuvenated federalism on the court. *New York* did not match *Garcia* in tone or enthusiasm and did not overrule the *Garcia* precedent since it did not directly concern the same issues. Nevertheless, it did signal a desire to protect state interests over the promotion of national priorities as defined by Congress and carried out through the commerce clause. The two factions familiar to current observers of the Supreme Court started to take shape in *New York.* The two most conservative justices on the court, Antonin Scalia and Clarence Thomas, joined the chief justice in supporting the decision written by Sandra Day O'Connor. Justice Anthony Kennedy, who has provided the crucial swing vote in most current decisions, also joined the majority. Justice David Souter, who has since tended to side with the pro-federal government faction in the court, also joined. John Paul Stevens and Harry Blackmun joined Byron White in the partial dissent.

Congressional legislation mandating the methods of disposal for low-level radioactive waste was at issue in the case. At its core (and in the simplest terms), the legislation required states to comply with a timeline for bringing low-level radioactive waste disposal facilities on-line. Congress created the law at the urging of the National Governors Association in order to cope with the oversupply of low-level radioactive waste and the shortage of facilities for its processing and storage. To discourage the temptation to ship the waste to less populous states (South Carolina, Nevada, and Washington originally handled all the low-level radioactive waste in the country), the states were required to take responsibility for their own waste and to build, either by themselves or in cooperation with other states, facilities for its disposal.

Those states that did not comply with the legislation or were tardy in setting up their facilities faced a series of escalating disincentives. First was the forfeiture of a special surcharge that they were otherwise entitled to levy on waste producers, then increasingly more expensive rates for the exportation of their waste. Finally, and most severely, if facilities did not exist by 1996 (eleven years after the initial act was passed), the offending states had to take title to the waste, making the state, not the producer, responsible for its storage and disposal. Only by having a place for waste generators to dispose of their material before January 1996 could states avoid the prospect of being stuck with piles of low-level radioactive waste. If they did not have facilities available, the state assumed all responsibility for the eventual disposal and the costs incurred. Congress was, in effect, compelling state action through negative sanctions.

For the most part, the legislation and the strategy were successful. By the initial seven-year deadline imposed in the legislation, nine new regional facilities existed, encompassing forty-two states. Four other states had made sufficient arrangements to keep the surcharges levied under the act, and the three states that originally had facilities were still covered. Forty-nine states in effect had met the requirements. And then there was one. New York, coincidentally one of the largest producers of low-level radioactive waste, had begun arrangements to build a facility but ran into opposition from the two counties chosen as potential sites.

Faced with the looming negative incentives of the "take title" clause, New York and the counties concerned applied to the Supreme Court for relief. They did not challenge Congress's ability to regulate the field of radioactive waste. There was an evident element of interstate traffic in radioactive waste that both parties conceded Congress was entitled to oversee as commerce. The entire field of radioactive waste was also open to Congress through the supremacy clause. What the appellants did challenge was the ability of Congress to enlist the states, both through positive and negative incentives, as agencies of its policy. The court was not asked to decide any jurisdictional issues, but simply whether Congress had the authority to compel the states into action.

The court upheld the core of the legislation as a legitimate exercise of the commerce power and of the federal spending power; it took issue only with the "take title" provisions. The Tenth Amendment was invoked as a possible limit on the manner in which Congress exercised its powers. Most Tenth Amendment cases, as Justice O'Connor noted in her majority decision, turned on whether or not states could be regulated under the commerce clause by laws that were generally applied to private citizens and organizations. In this case, the law was designed to operate directly on the states alone. No pretence was made to make this a law about regulating producers of the waste. The burdens were placed directly on the shoulders of the states, and only indirectly did the law regulate the actual producers.

Congress has been allowed leeway to regulate state behaviour through its spending power. The Supreme Court found in *South Dakota v. Dole*[24] that the funding of certain projects or programs could be made contingent upon the states complying with some requirement within their jurisdictional field. In *Dole,* states were obliged to set minimum drinking ages in order to qualify for federal highway funding. The voluntary nature of the requirements saved such programs. Even if the conditions were indirectly or even unusually connected to the purpose for which money was intended, the court ruled that, if the conditions bore some relationship to the funding in question, they were to be generally permitted. South Dakota challenged the requirement that it set a minimum legal drinking age of twenty-one or give up 5 percent of its federal highway construction grant entitlement. The state argued that the spending power could not be used to invade the state's constitutional power over liquor sales. The court disagreed, characterizing the requirement as encouragement rather than coercion. A minimum drinking age was found to bear some relationship to highway safety. Many youths took advantage of their ability to drive to travel to jurisdictions with a lower drinking age. Since highway funds are allocated for the provision of safe roadways, the court ruled that there was a reasonable relationship between the condition and the funding. As the states technically remained in control, the coercion exercised by Congress was saved from the constitutional junk heap. The court required some minimum conditions: that spending serve the general welfare, that the conditioning of state behaviour was unambiguous, and that states entered knowingly into the conditions. Finally, conditions were considered illegitimate if there was little relation between the requirement for funds and the federal interest in national projects or programs. On this point, Justice O'Connor dissented – finding that the relationship between drinking age and highway safety was too tenuous to bear a justifiable connection.

In *New York,* although the incentives were monetary, the money involved came from levies charged against waste producers for the disposal of their detritus, not from otherwise expected federal funds. The legislation made it explicitly clear that federal funds from general revenue were not involved – in fact, it appeared to be a point of some pride for Congress. The federal government acted as a trustee, holding the fees charged for disposal until the states met the legislative conditions. The majority did not find this an invalid use of the spending power. While the money was kept out of general revenues, the levy was in the form of a tax, and it remained Congress's prerogative to commit those revenues to the purposes that it saw fit.

Where the court disagreed with the legislation was in the structuring of the "take title" provisions. O'Connor noted with some sarcasm that the states had the "choice" of accepting title to the waste or disposing of it according to Congress's wishes. This did not constitute choice in the manner suggested by the voluntary test in *Dole*. The federal government argued that the states had implied their consent by requesting that Congress pass the legislation. In the era of post-*Garcia* federalism, direct involvement of state governors was one step better than even the court expected. Prior to the legislation, the states producing the waste and those few states handling it no longer found themselves in a tolerable situation. Congress brokered a compromise that looked likely to solve the problem. Jurisdictional squabbles to be formally resolved in the courts appeared to be unnecessary. The Supreme Court, however, found that the legislation's success rested on an illegitimate foundation. The majority argued that it was not the states' privilege to give up their sovereignty, even by negotiation. State sovereignty, it claimed, is not solely about protecting the states to serve their own purposes. Rather, federalism, and the division of authority inherent in it, were designed for the protection of individuals.

The majority argued that exercises in cooperative federalism had to adhere to the rules of sovereignty. Otherwise, they reasoned, accountability was lost. In the State of New York, where there were clearly local objections, public officials at both the state and the national level seemed to be able to elude personal responsibility through a compromise between them. The commitments in an agreement like the one contested in *New York* give the impression that officials at both federal and state levels have no choice – they thereby sought to avoid the political consequences of unpalatable decisions when facing their constituencies (electoral or otherwise). To avoid creating such an accountability vacuum, the court ruled that congressional direction of the states as agencies, as in the take title provisions, was not permitted.

The result of *New York* was to rescue some status for the states. Jurisdictionally, it did not increase the reserved powers or restrain the scope of the commerce power. In that sense, it did little to weaken the centralism of *Garcia*. *New York* did not usher in a state-centred perspective, but it did prime judicial minds for one. The majority articulated the possibility of limits to functional federalism. Even though the states consented to the cooperative arrangement at issue, the court found that federalism had formal legal structures that must be enforced. These limits did not restrict the jurisdictional scope of commerce. The court's main contribution with *New York* was the revival of the court as an agent of federalism and the constitution. Doctrine on the court's historical understanding of the spending power helped O'Connor to clarify the issue in the case and to enforce the formal structures of accountability demanded by the law of the constitution.

These issues were raised again near the close of the court's 1999 term. Justice O'Connor joined with the traditionally nationalist judges in the majority of *Davis v. Monroe County School Board,*[25] which upheld the use of federal anti-discrimination law to hold school districts, which are effectively state instrumentalities, accountable for systemic student-on-student sexual harassment. States accepted federal education funding on conditions, including the application of federal sexual harassment guidelines. When the conditions are made explicit in legislation and clear to the states, Justice O'Connor is inclined, as we see, to accept such use of the federal spending power.

Lopez: Commerce Narrowed

1995 was a mixed year for the fate of American federalism at the Supreme Court. The most celebrated case of the year was *U.S. v. Lopez,*[26] which struck an almost unprecedented blow to the scope of the commerce clause. It was the first decision since the New Deal era to find an entire piece of commerce clause legislation unconstitutional. The law at issue was classic post-New Deal congressional handiwork. With a standard logic-straining justification under the commerce clause, Congress passed the *Gun Free School Zones Act.* The act established defined zones surrounding public schools and made it a criminal offence to possess a firearm within them. The intent of the legislation was clear enough: to promote public safety and provide the means to promote a gun-free environment in schools. Similar laws existed in various states, but public concern for the safety of school attendees in all states encouraged Congress's intervention. In one fell swoop, through its near-plenary power over commerce, congressional legislation could universalize protection for students, teachers, and staff in all the nation's public schools, at least as far as making illegal the possession of firearms on school grounds and surrounding areas.

Alfonso Lopez was charged under the act for possessing a firearm on school property. Hoping to circumvent the charge, he challenged Congress's jurisdiction to enact such a law. Congress passed the law as an exercise of the commerce power based on the supposed link between interstate commerce and schools. The case law to that point suggested there were three categories under which Congress may legislate in regard to commerce: the channels of interstate commerce; the instrumentalities, persons, or things of interstate commerce; and matters that had a "substantial relation" to interstate commerce. Of the three, the last was the most general and unspecified category, and the federal government sought to justify the regulation of gun-free school zones under it.

Chief Justice Rehnquist arose from relative slumber on federalism in the years after *NLC* to deliver the majority opinion for the court. He was joined by the same justices that joined O'Connor in the *New York* majority, with the exception of David Souter, who appeared by this point to be more closely aligned with the pro-federal government faction. While *New York* limited Congress on the margins of its authority, it did not actually challenge federal jurisdiction, just the way that Congress conducted itself with the states. The *Lopez* decision struck directly at the heart of federal legislative dominance by challenging Congress's seemingly infinite jurisdiction over commerce. That the law challenged in *New York* was ever passed was a testament to the confidence of Congress in federal-state relations. By limiting the ability of Congress to force the states' hands, the court did little to diminish the source of that confidence, an expansive commerce clause. The consequences for federal power would be much greater if the court were to focus on limiting this power.

The court's jurisprudence on what constituted a "substantial relation" to commerce was the primary issue in the decision and dissent. The federal government argued that the provision of education had a direct effect on commerce and thus justified Congress mandating the terms of school safety. Unsafe schools, the government argued, would affect the national economy in that the costs of violent crime are substantial, the willingness of persons to travel is reduced by the perception that areas are unsafe, and the educational process, which influences the productivity of the citizenry, is handicapped by a "threatening learning environment." Accepting such an argument, Rehnquist reasoned, placed within the ambit of Congress a seemingly unlimited field of jurisdiction. He would have none of it. To his mind, this "national productivity" reasoning for granting commerce clause jurisdiction seemed to be limitless. How could any activity not qualify as somehow impacting, however indirectly, on national productivity? Rehnquist argued that, "to uphold the Government's contentions here, we would have to pile inference upon inference in a manner that would bid fair to convert congressional authority under the Commerce Clause to a general police power."[27] For too long, in his opinion, such extensions of commerce had been allowed to progress under flimsy rationales. He did not actually contend that the court had been wrong in the past; rather, perhaps it had been misunderstood in its willingness to approve congressional forays into uncharted territory. Rehnquist noted several times in his opinion that the federal government possesses enumerated powers. Since the New Deal, congressional frontiersmen had not been encouraged by the court to respect any borders for federal power. Rehnquist reminded them that commerce does have finite limits.

Anthony Kennedy filed a concurring opinion along with Justice O'Connor. The bulk of the opinion was devoted to determining the locus of accountability and what should constitute "areas of traditional state concern," a concept reminiscent of *NLC*. O'Connor too had expressed similar accountability concerns in her *New York* opinion. Here her caution did not seem to be as necessary. The attempt to avoid ultimate responsibility, so clear in *New York*, was missing in this case, as both levels of government were tripping over each other to be the saviour of the schools. In the Kennedy opinion, it seems that duplication, thanks to the confusion it causes, is as much a vice as outright avoidance of responsibility. The Kennedy opinion also noted that the federal balance was best maintained by the judiciary – in the absence of other structural mechanisms. Kennedy hoped to ensure that political convenience did not result in the creation of less politically accountable arrangements. *Garcia*-style abdication by the court of its oversight was not repeated here. Kennedy ruled that, on occasions when Congress overstepped the already generous lines drawn around commerce, it would not be allowed by the court to further encroach upon state jurisdiction.

Justice Clarence Thomas also filed a lone concurring opinion that constitutes some of the most state-sympathetic judicial text in recent memory.[28] He was most adamant about registering his discontent with the way that the "substantial effects" doctrine aggregated powers through a class of subjects rather than through particular exercises in isolation. The general practice of the court had been to allow Congress substantial leeway by examining the activities it sought to regulate in context rather than on their own. The classic example was the post-New Deal case of *Wickard v. Filburn*.[29]

In that case, the defendant, Roscoe Filburn, was charged with growing wheat in excess of the quota allowed under the federal *Agricultural Adjustment Act*. The production of such crops was regulated by Congress in order to mete out some of the effects of the market and to avoid oversupply and subsequent low prices. In his defence, Filburn argued that he used the excess on his own farm. The excess wheat was not intended for sale and therefore did not enter the stream of commerce. The secretary of agriculture replied that, even by growing wheat for his own use, Filburn had a negative effect on the marketing system. While his farm's volume did not have the kind of impact on its own that Congress was worried about, the effect of many farmers growing overquota wheat to supply their own needs would eventually pervert both the system's intent and its effectiveness. The court upheld congressional authority to regulate wheat destined for farm use as well as that destined for market. The court literally aggregated the field of wheat! The court claimed that Congress could not effectively regulate those fields that it was responsible for if it could not be sure that activities on the margins did not subvert the greater whole. Cumulatively, the actions of someone like Filburn, while outside strict boundaries of commerce, potentially had a substantial effect on commerce and were thus subject to congressional oversight. Thus, the substantial effects doctrine was born.

Thomas argued that this typical style of post-New Deal reasoning deeply undermined the original intent of the constitution and expanded the commerce power beyond recognition. In support of his argument, Thomas cited many of the pre-1937 decisions that limited attempts to expand regulation of the national economy through the commerce clause. The substantial effects doctrine was most responsible for the changes with which Justice Thomas was uncomfortable. Substantial effects justifications flourished, he claimed, because of the aggregating power that control over one aspect of a field required. In other words, when Congress was given an inch, it often took a mile. So in *Lopez* the need to ensure that schools produce graduates for the effective continuation of commerce was expanded to include school safety. Thomas vehemently objected to all sorts of little things being pulled under the umbrella of commerce because aggregates of little things potentially have substantial effects on interstate commerce. In his words, "one *always* can draw the circle broadly enough to cover an activity that, when taken in isolation, would not have substantial effects on commerce."[30]

The main dissenting opinion, setting out the pro-commerce position, was that of Justice Breyer. First, to his mind, the court had quite properly refrained from narrowly defining the substantial effects test. For Breyer, the expressions "significant" and "substantial" had been left unclear on purpose. That way the test did not require the court to look for reasons to exclude activities. The court did not demonstrate in either intent or practice that the test was to be severely conducted. Second, he argued that cumulative effects (what Thomas called aggregates) were an entirely appropriate way of considering whether there was a significant effect. Breyer cited *Wickard v. Filburn* (a standing precedent) to this end. Finally, and critically from Congress's viewpoint, Breyer wrote that the court should give substantial leeway to the legislature in determining the significance of the connection between an activity and interstate commerce – both because it was Congress's power and because the legislature was better equipped to make such empirical inquiries.

Breyer did not argue that the court should forgo altogether its responsibility for making an independent judgment. He was, however, prepared to accept congressional findings on the connection between the possession of guns and school performance and some measurable effect on commerce. He did so even though Congress included no evidence of such effects in the initial legislation and provided such justifications only after passing the legislation. Several pages of his dissent were spent documenting this connection with material from congressional findings and academic study. On legal points, he found the majority troubling not so much for refusing to recognize this connection as for being restrictive about investigating such connections when it has been the court's practice to allow Congress considerable leeway in such circumstances. In addition, Breyer was troubled by the majority's attempt to distinguish the activity at hand as non-commercial and thus distinct from the kinds of activities allowed by precedent. He objected to the manner in which the decision unsettled an area of law previously believed to be quite stable. Since the volume of activity and legislation that occurs under the auspices of the commerce clause is substantial, he argued, any tinkering with what is permissible under the clause, especially from a "principle" position, threatens the clarity of a large body of regulation.

Term Limits: Sovereignty Debated

The companion to *Lopez* in 1995 was *U.S. Term Limits, Inc. v. Thornton,* on its face a victory for federal over state power. U.S. Term Limits, Inc., a public interest group, had sought to impose limits on the time that federal politicians serve in office by altering state constitutions to that effect. The group's initial strategy was to work on a state-by-state basis to implement restrictions on the number of terms that congresspersons could serve. Given the difficulty of constitutional amendment at the national level, this seemed to be the most effective route to the imposition of term limits. In addition, the movement took advantage of the availability of the referendum and initiative procedures in many states to exact changes in state constitutions mandating the form of election of members to Congress. Many state campaigns were successful in altering state constitutions, Arkansas among them. The Arkansas amendment was challenged on the ground that the states could not restrict the membership of Congress. The court was left to determine whether or not the states actually had the authority to alter the requirements for congressional membership, whether this was a matter for Congress itself, or if in fact term limits required an amendment of the federal constitution.[31]

The case is important in the current federalism debate as the arguments from both sides solidify the contending theories of federalism and sovereignty that have developed on the court. The federalists (again Rehnquist, Scalia, Thomas, and O'Connor) were on the short side this time, but in their dissent they articulated a theory of federalism with a wholly different concept of where sovereignty lies in the federal system than that propounded by the majority. The majority made reference to the founding and ratification debates and determined that the originators of the constitution intended the qualifications of members of Congress to be fixed and certainly not alterable by Congress itself. In their opinion, a constitutional amendment is the only means to alter the qualifications for membership to Congress. With the limited framework for change at the national level in mind, the majority then addressed the question of whether the states could make changes to the qualifications through the powers reserved to them by the Tenth Amendment. This required, in the majority's opinion, an examination of both the original powers of the states and the nature of the compact entered into through the constitution.

For the majority, it seemed that there was no means by which the states could reserve powers that did not exist prior to the creation of the national government itself. How, they asked, could the states claim that their pre-federation powers included an ability to determine the qualifications for members of a national legislature that did not yet exist? The majority referred to the celebrated nineteenth-century jurist Joseph Story, who wrote that "the states can exercise no powers whatsoever, which exclusively spring out of the existence of the national government, which the constitution does not delegate to them ... No state can say, that it has reserved, what it never possessed."[32] The majority also emphasized the "revolutionary character of the government that the Framers conceived."[33] A national government was created that required national loyalties of its citizens as much as (or more than) it required state loyalties. The national government under the present American constitution, they claimed, unlike its Articles of Confederation predecessor, created a direct relationship between the national government and its citizens. While some elements of national representation were still mediated through the states (the state selection, until the passing of the Seventeenth Amendment, of senators and the state-based electoral college), representation in the House of Representatives was a direct demonstration of popular sovereignty at the national level. The majority ruled that, since members of Congress specifically owed their allegiance to the people and not the states, their conditions of office and qualifications were to be decided by the same constituents rather than by the states. The nature of the federal compact, they claimed, precluded the existence of a state power over qualifications of congresspersons.

The majority further argued that, in order for the states to have such a power, it had to be delegated to them by the constitution. The Elections Clause, in Article 1, section 4, of the constitution was the only possible grant of such power to the states.[34] In the majority's reasoning, there was no legitimate construction of the Elections Clause consistent with the Arkansas term limits amendment. Justice Stevens wrote on this point that "the Framers intended the Elections Clause to grant States authority to create procedural regulations, not to provide States with licence to exclude classes of candidates from federal office."[35] This was consistent with, if not derived from, his theory of sovereignty. The framers, he argued, were acutely conscious of the possibility that jealous or difficult state governments would seek to undermine the national government, especially if they had the ability to determine to any extent the composition of the membership of national institutions. With this fear in mind – Stevens found it in the *Federalist* as well as in convention debates – the framers "adopted provisions intended to minimize the possibility of state interference with federal elections."[36] Allowing the states to impose term limits as a qualification on congressional membership, he found, was clearly not the founders' intent.

The minority opinion was also based on a detailed understanding of sovereignty. Like the majority, the minority did not dispute that sovereignty ultimately lay within the hands of the American people, but they conceived "the people" in a radically different manner. In the most basic sense, the people, for constitutional purposes, are not to be understood as the undifferentiated masses of the nation. Rather, the people are holders of a sovereignty that is mediated through the states. "The ultimate source of the Constitution's authority," Justice Thomas wrote, "is the consent of the people of each individual State, not the consent of the undifferentiated people of the Nation as a whole."[37] This theory was based largely upon the procedures used for the ratification of the original constitution and how those procedures mitigated the expression of popular sovereignty through the states. This theory of sovereignty, in turn, provided a different theory of reserved powers, one that precluded the need for a state power over congressional qualifications. Thomas agreed that the setting of qualifications for members of Congress was not a delegated power; however, he did not agree that it needed to be. Instead, he advanced the claim that setting qualifications was a power inherent to the sovereignty of the people and thus the states. When Thomas spoke of popular sovereignty, he often used the phrase "people of the States" to indicate the mediated character of popular assent. The constitution was of course ratified by state conventions rather than by any single national affirmation. The mediation of sovereignty that this represented was not so much an indication of anti-democratic tendencies for Thomas as a reluctance to surrender authority to the national population. He argued that, when the states entered into the federal compact, they surrendered discrete portions of their authority, but as states they preserved a significant portion of their powers.

The fallacy in the majority's argument, Thomas reasoned, was the suggestion that state governments could not reserve powers that did not exist prior to the creation of the national government. The reserved powers had an altogether different character for Thomas. The powers reserved to the states were those also reserved to the people – the people of the states, to reuse his phrase. It is incoherent, Thomas argued, to claim that the people needed to have exercised their powers prior to the founding in order to claim them afterward. By analogy, he suggested that, "if someone says that the power to use a particular facility is reserved to some group, he is not saying anything about whether that group has previously used the facility. He is merely saying that the people who control the facility have designated that group as the entity with authority to use it. The Tenth Amendment is similar."[38] By conceiving sovereignty differently, Thomas constructed the Tenth Amendment and the powers of the states to restrict those eligible for membership differently. Doctrine was an aid to his decision, but it did not force him to rule in a manner adverse to his structural preference.

Term Limits seems to be a doctrinal wasteland. The majority relied upon *Powell v. McCormack,* a decision of the Warren Court, in its determination of who can set congressional qualifications, but otherwise there is little specific material from previous cases that appeared to guide the two opinions. The constraints that came from previous decisions were much more abstract. The court effectively raised grand theorizing about sovereignty to the status of doctrine. How a judge understood sovereignty became the prime determinant of his or her response to questions regarding federalism. This situation has led one notable commentator to label both approaches "structural default positions."[39] It would seem that, no matter what the issue put before the court, the respective sides can retreat to these structural positions to find the appropriate answer. In contrast to the functionalist approach that had its nadir in *Garcia,* the *Term Limits* opinions demonstrated a growing tendency on both sides of the court to formalize decision making and to use some of the most absolute terms available. The *Term Limits* majority was seeking to protect federal power in much the same way that the *New York* majority sought to protect state power, only this time the swing vote of Justice Kennedy, in a separate concurring opinion, favoured the federal government. His point of view on the sovereignty issue seems to be clear: "In my view ... it is well settled that the whole people of the United States asserted their political identity and unity of purpose when they created the federal system ... Federalism was our Nation's own discovery. The Framers split the atom of sovereignty. It was the genius of their idea that our citizens would have two political capacities, one state and one federal, each protected from incursion by the other."[40]

The last sentence is perhaps most telling of Kennedy's outlook on federalism. His concern for independence within the spheres allotted to both levels of government could be described as classical. This may help to explain his shifting allegiances. One could allege that he is more interested in seeing the clean lines of accountability preserved than proudly trumpeting his understanding of sovereignty. Kennedy was motivated by the doctrine of classical federalism that he articulated in *New York* to find against the states in order to preserve the same value.

The functionalist approach briefly held by the court in *Garcia* need not be inherently centralizing. However, it tended to favour enumerated powers over the less concretely expressed reserved powers. The benefit of the doubt was given to national power. By contrast, a more formalized approach can favour either level of government. Which government it does favour depends upon what reading of the sovereignty question a judge or group of judges favours. Hence the "structural default." The answer to federalism conflicts for the Rehnquist court seemed to lie not in the circumstances of any given conflict but in the judges' understanding of the way that the federation was designed. This approach abandoned some of the specific earlier doctrines of the court, such as those that have slowly grown up around the commerce clause, in favour of more general doctrines about the nature of the constitutional system. Regardless of the source, these structural understandings were clearly embedded in the minds of the judges as they went about deciding specific federalism cases.

Printz: The New Sovereignty Argument Applied

Printz v. United States,[41] decided in 1997, mixed elements of both the *Lopez* and the *New York* decisions in the subject matter that it addressed as well as in its results. The court again found against the extension of federal jurisdiction in gun control and the conscription of state officials in the application of federal law. Congress passed the *Brady Handgun Violence Prevention Act* in 1993, which implemented a system of background checks for prospective handgun buyers, in order to limit the legal possession of such firearms among those with criminal records or histories of violence. The legislation provided for the eventual creation of a national registration infrastructure, but in order to apply the law in the interim the chief law enforcement officials (or CLEOs) of local areas were compelled by the legislation to conduct the background checks and clearances. It was not long before some state officials applied to be absolved from this burden on federalism grounds. Jay Printz, CLEO of a Montana county, and Richard Mack, a colleague from Arizona, applied to be relieved from their obligations under the act. They argued that it was not within Congress's power to compel local officials to carry out federal policy, even on an interim basis.

Justice Scalia's majority opinion agreed wholeheartedly. Scalia admitted that there was no explicit constitutional prohibition on the states being employed in the application of congressional law. However, he found that (1) historical practice, (2) the structure of the constitution, and (3) the jurisprudence of the court suggested that such a prohibition existed.[42] As to the first source, he found no relevant historical instance in which the states had been pressed into the service of the federal executive. Nor did he find any evidence that the founders conceived such a practice. Relying in part on the court's *New York* decision, Scalia claimed that the system of dual sovereignty envisioned by the founders presumed the exact opposite. The constitution was structured to make the two levels of government responsible for their own spheres, not to compel one level to fulfill the edicts of the other.

Scalia argued that the most compelling reason to dismiss the enlistment of CLEOs by Congress was the prior jurisprudence of the court, specifically *New*

York. The government claimed that *New York* was distinguishable from this case in that the "take title" provisions of the act challenged there compelled legislatures to make certain policies, whereas in this case officials, not legislatures, were compelled. The CLEOs were issued a final, non-discretionary directive to help implement the law in the interim. The federal government, claimed this directive, was sufficiently different from the kind of compulsion mandated in *New York*. The federal argument far from satisfied Justice Scalia and the majority. The enlistment of state officials in a non-policy-making role was perhaps distinguishable from the enlistment of state legislatures in a policy-making role, but both offended the principle of state sovereignty affirmed by the majority in *New York*. The fatal flaw in the *Brady Act* was its conscription of state officials, even on a temporary basis.

Justice Stevens wrote for the dissenters in *Printz*. He found the *New York* precedent much less controlling. The enlistment of officials instead of legislatures made all the difference to the minority. They found that the impelling of local officials did not qualify as a matter of impugned state sovereignty. Stevens claimed that no evidence, certainly no written rule, exists to bar Congress from enlisting state officials. In fact, historical practice seems to suggest that in times of emergency the enlistment of state personnel by Congress is common. Why, asked Stevens, was the court willing to substitute its judgment for that of Congress? It should be up to Congress to decide if gun violence is an emergency, and if so the court should not interfere but should defer to Congress's better judgment.

But Stevens did not stop with a simple deference argument. He engaged the *Printz* majority on its own terms, specifically on its interpretation of *New York*. Far from reading *New York* as an indictment of cooperative federalism, Stevens read the case as an endorsement of the practice. Of the three sets of incentives in *New York*, only the take title provisions displeased the majority. Otherwise, the case speaks to exactly how Congress can enlist the states. The take title provisions were thrown out in *New York* because Congress compelled the state legislatures. That was the sole basis for the court's decision. Stevens agreed that compelling a state legislature certainly qualified as an infringement of state sovereignty. Compelling a state official to cooperate in the implementation of federal legislation did not seem to him to be on par as a violation of sovereignty. In fact, he argued, the majority may have done more to upset the federal balance by requiring the federal government to create an entirely new bureaucracy to carry out the routine work that it requested of local officials.[43]

Sovereign Immunity

The Rehnquist court did not limit its influence on federalism strictly to division-of-powers interpretation. Limiting the scope of the commerce power or other powers of Congress is the most obvious means to alter the relative power and activity levels of the federal government. It is by no account the only means. The court's interpretation of the states' sovereign immunity goes hand in hand with its general federalism jurisprudence and places equally severe limits on the ability of congressional legislation to regulate the activities of the states or state agencies and limits the grounds of redress available to citizens. Congress may have wide and recognized jurisdiction in areas such as commerce, but the effect of a robust state sovereign immunity is to limit the applicability of those validly enacted laws to the states themselves.

From 1996 onward, the Rehnquist court developed a set of parallel doctrines to its division of powers jurisprudence promoting state immunity from federal legislation and the use of federal courts. These cases were at the fore of the court's federalism rulings. *Seminole Tribe of Florida v. Florida*[44] first brought the question of state immunity before the Rehnquist court. The case dealt with the validity of the *Indian Gaming Regulatory Act* of 1988, passed by Congress under the auspices of the Indian commerce clause. In order for Indian tribes to undertake gaming activities, they had to enter into compacts with the relevant state government. To ensure that states would not avoid negotiations, the act allowed tribes to sue states in federal court for non-financial relief if the state failed to negotiate in good faith. The Seminole Tribe sued the State of Florida for not negotiating a compact. In turn, the state challenged the tribe's right to sue, citing its sovereign immunity from suits in federal court granted by the Eleventh Amendment.[45]

The court found for the state, with Chief Justice Rehnquist writing for a five-justice majority. The relevant case law to that point had established that Congress could abrogate state sovereign immunity if it did so pursuant to the exercise of an exclusive congressional power under Article 1. In *Pennsylvania v. Union Gas,*[46] a five-to-four court had found that regulations under the commerce clause could be used to justify the abrogation of state sovereign immunity. The *Seminole* majority overruled *Union Gas,* finding it a mistaken departure from prior understandings of the Eleventh Amendment. For Rehnquist, "the background principle of state sovereign immunity embodied in the Eleventh Amendment is not so ephemeral as to dissipate when the subject of the suit is an area ... that is under the exclusive control of the Federal Government."[47] In the majority's reading, the Eleventh Amendment is essentially a trump to federal power, at least as far as limiting suits by private parties against the states in federal courts. States could consent to being subject to such suits, but Congress may not force them to answer to suits in federal courts.

The court sustained the federal court exemption that it first granted in *Seminole Tribe* in *Idaho v. Coeur d'Alene Tribe.*[48] While affirming the immunity idea, the holding argument in the case also upheld an exemption from the general state immunity rule first established in *Ex parte Young*. The so-called

Young doctrine allows relief to be sought in federal court when state officers have violated federal law. If the relevant actor in a dispute is the state, then the *Young* doctrine does not apply. The Coeur d'Alene tribe sought injunctive relief against Idaho state officials to prevent them from regulating or interfering with their claimed possession of submerged lands beneath Lake Coeur d'Alene. Justice O'Connor wrote a plurality opinion in which she tried to minimize the effect of the case. Rather than extending the immunity recognized in *Seminole Tribe* to state officials, she took a more minimalist course and refused to recognize the Coeur d'Alene Tribe's suit as really one against state officials. Properly characterized, this was a suit against the State of Idaho, and *Young*'s exemptions did not apply. O'Connor's opinion essentially kept the *Young* doctrine alive, but she refused to apply it to the case at hand. Since the action was one against the state, the sovereign immunity recognized in *Seminole Tribe* did, however, apply.

In *Alden v. Maine,* the strong version of the state sovereignty argument that first (and briefly) won over the court in *National League of Cities* joined with the emerging immunity doctrine. Unlike the two earlier immunity cases, *Alden* dealt with the applicability of federal labour standards to the working conditions of state government employees. In the case, a group of probation officers alleged violations of the overtime provisions in the federal *Fair Labor Standards Act.* The officers sought financial compensation from the state for these violations in federal court. As the suits were proceeding, the court made its ruling in *Seminole Tribe,* protecting non-consenting states from cases in federal courts. As *Seminole Tribe* made no ruling on the use of state courts to advance federal guarantees, the officers refiled their claim in state court. A majority of the Supreme Court, this time led by Justice Kennedy, extended the sovereign immunity of the states to include a bar on the use of state courts to enforce federal legislation against the state.

Alden v. Maine deals with the same Eleventh Amendment concerns as its predecessors, but the majority cast its findings in much less technical terms. Kennedy contended that the sovereign immunity enjoyed by the states is more than simply a matter of construing the scope of the Eleventh Amendment. The constitution's history and structure, as well as rulings of the court, were invoked as indications that "the States' immunity from suit is a fundamental aspect of the sovereignty which the States enjoyed before the ratification of the Constitution, and which they retain today."[49] The decision continued in this vein, describing the dual sovereignty of the American federation with an emphasis on the preservation of the "dignity" of the states through such structures as sovereign immunity.

Kennedy then proceeded to a long discussion of the founding debates and the apparent intentions of the founders in providing for state sovereign immunity. His historical analysis is put to use to define the broader scope of sovereign immunity created by the ruling. The court's prior jurisprudence had read the Eleventh Amendment as a bar against states being sued in federal courts. In order to extend that immunity, Kennedy looked beyond the Eleventh Amendment. He claimed that there is a structural barrier in the system of federalism that grants the states the necessary immunity from suits in their own courts in addition to the federal court restrictions of the Eleventh Amendment. This structural argument continues the tradition of *Printz* and *Term Limits,* grounding the court's reasoning in strong arguments based on the very origins and an imputed logic of the constitution. Kennedy's language reflects the near absolutism of the position. For Kennedy, it is important to assert that "Congress has vast power but not all power. When Congress legislates in matters affecting the States, it may not treat those sovereign entities as mere prefectures or corporations. Congress must accord States the esteem due to them as joint participants in a federal system, one beginning with the premise of sovereignty in both the central Government and the separate States."[50] The ruling in *Alden v. Maine* does not outlaw entirely the ability of Congress to subject non-consenting states to suits. Under positive grants of congressional authority, the Fourteenth Amendment in particular, Congress may still have leeway. Likewise, state officers are still subject to the *Young* doctrine described above.

Linda Greenhouse, the *New York Times* Supreme Court correspondent, describes the case as "the most powerful indication yet of a narrow majority's determination to reconfigure the balance between state and Federal authority in favour of the states."[51] *Alden v. Maine* certainly upped the rhetorical ante. Justice Souter claimed that the majority's infatuation with state sovereignty, particularly with state immunity from federal law, was on a par with the regressive constitutionalism of the early New Deal court. He wrote, "I expect the Court's late essay into immunity doctrine will prove the equal of its earlier experiment in laissez-faire, the one being as unrealistic as the other, as indefensible, and probably as fleeting."[52]

The last few terms of the Rehnquist court continued to develop and expand this immunity doctrine. In *Kimel v. Florida Board of Regents,*[53] the court considered the scope of congressional power to subject states to suit under the Fourteenth Amendment. The case was brought by university professors alleging violation of federal age discrimination legislation by state-operated universities in Florida. Similarly, in *Alabama v. Garrett,* state employees sought monetary damages for violation by their state employer of the federal *Americans with Disabilities Act.* In both cases, the ability of Congress to abrogate state sovereign immunity was recognized as a possibility but not accepted in the case at hand. In *Kimel,* Justice O'Connor narrowed the possibilities for abrogation of the state immunity rule. Article 1 powers such as commerce, she reasserted, may not be used to abrogate immunity. Other exclusive powers of Congress, mainly the anti-discrimination Fourteenth

Amendment, may be used, but under restrictive circumstances. O'Connor invoked a notion of balance, first articulated in *City of Boerne v. Flores,*[54] to overturn the federal government's reliance on the Fourteenth Amendment in *Kimel.* In *Boerne,* the court held that "there must be a congruence and proportionality between the injury to be prevented or remedied and the means adopted to that end."[55] This balance must be tested by the judicial branch. While age discrimination by a state may be discriminatory, the negative consequences of disrupting federal balance in this case led Justice O'Connor to find that the court could not uphold congressional interference with state immunity. Age discrimination, she argued, was not as pressing as racial or gender discrimination and therefore lowered the acceptability of Congress interfering in state activities. Likewise in *Garrett,* Chief Justice Rehnquist failed to find a sufficient pattern of discrimination against the disabled by state employers to justify the abrogation of state immunity.[56]

State sovereign immunity was used most recently in *Federal Maritime Commission v. South Carolina State Ports Authority*[57] to prevent a quasi-judicial federal administrative agency (the Federal Maritime Commission) from adjudicating a private party's dispute with a state port authority. The logic of *Alden v. Maine* that sovereign immunity was more than an Eleventh Amendment protection was put to good use by Justice Thomas, who found for the majority that the immunity enjoyed by states from federal and state judicial relief also applied to the quasi-judicial findings of federal executive agencies. The structural argument advanced by Kennedy in *Alden* ensures that the expansion of immunity will not be hidebound by the restrictions of the Eleventh Amendment.

Opponents of the state sovereign immunity rulings of the court suggest that the concept of state sovereignty has had too mixed a use by the court to be truly meaningful: "The language of state sovereignty does not embody a coherent, historically accepted concept of the states' role in the federal system."[58] Moreover, the kinds of problems that the court has used state sovereignty arguments to solve, they argue, are not well served by the doctrine since "no such concept has ever secured long term adherence." For its critics, "state sovereignty simply is a diversion from the true task of finding the correct resolution of the particular constitutional or federalism issues that arise."[59]

***Morrison:* Commerce Reconsidered**

The most serious consideration of the commerce clause since *Lopez* is *United States v. Morrison.* With the solidifying state sovereignty doctrinal battle as a backdrop, the court used the case as an opportunity to clarify and, for the majority, amplify its thinking on the most important congressional grant of power. *Morrison* arose out of a sexual assault complaint at Virginia Polytechnic Institute (Virginia Tech). The victim, Christy Brzonkala, brought suit after an unsatisfactory resolution of her complaint by the university's internal procedures. Brzonkala sued Morrison and another attacker as well as Virginia Tech under federal legislation entitling victims of gender-motivated violence to seek civil remedies. The constitutional issue before the court was whether Congress had the authority to enact the sections of the *Violence Against Women Act* that provided for civil remedies of this type. Congress had enacted the legislation under the auspices of the commerce clause and the Fourteenth Amendment to the constitution.

Chief Justice Rehnquist wrote on behalf of the majority of the court. Two dissents were written by Justices Souter and Breyer, who were joined by Justices Stevens and Ginsburg. Justice Thomas added a very short concurrence to the chief justice's majority opinion. The composition of majority and dissent is more than familiar. The chief justice began his analysis in *Morrison* with a review of the relevant branches of the commerce power under which congressional legislation can be justified. As the *Violence Against Women Act* did not deal with the channels or instrumentalities of interstate commerce, in order to be justified as within the commerce power, it must have regulated a topic with a "substantial effect" on interstate commerce.

Rehnquist's analysis then proceeded to reiterate the main points of *Lopez.* This served to emphasize the concern of the court that only activities of an economic nature can be regulated under the commerce clause banner. The regulation of gun possession in school zones, the court found, was non-economic, criminal conduct and not genuinely related to commerce. Likewise for Rehnquist, "gender-motivated crimes of violence are not, in any sense of the phrase, economic activity."[60] Unlike the *Guns Free School Act,* the *Violence Against Women Act* was supported by substantial congressional findings as to the impact of gender-motivated violence on victims and families. Congress in fact argued that gender-motivated violence deterred "potential victims from travelling interstate, from engaging in employment in interstate business and from transacting with business, and in places involved in interstate commerce."[61] For the majority, this amounted to a vast aggregation of effects in order to argue a substantial relation to commerce, a method rejected by the court in *Lopez.* "If accepted," argued Rehnquist, "petitioners' reasoning would allow Congress to regulate any crime as long as the nationwide aggregated impact of that crime has substantial effects on employment, production, transit or consumption."[62] Ultimately, the majority hope to prevent traditional state areas of jurisdiction from being aggregated as national concerns.

Justice Breyer in dissent argued that the economic/non-economic distinction was nearly impossible to apply. He asked, "does the local street corner mugger engage in 'economic' activity or 'noneconomic' activity when he mugs for money?"[63] He objected to breaking apart a nationally recognized problem into bits simply to honour the value of federalism. All of Congress's activities, this logic suggests, could be broken down by a determined court. Most nationwide concerns are still an aggregate of essentially local concerns. Judges, he claims, are in a poor position to patrol this line drawing. For Breyer, Congress is the better judge of state-federal balance. To this end, he cites the structural safeguards argument of *Garcia.*[64] Congress, he argues, respected federalism by seeking out and receiving state support for the *Violence Against Women Act.* The court has simply taken it upon itself to be overly formal and veto the products of cooperative federalism.

The most recent cases of the court confirm two things said here about Rehnquist-era federalism. The first point is that the sovereignty doctrines of both sides remain front and centre to the way that the court decides federalism cases. *Alden v. Maine* in particular demonstrates that those essential positions do not appear to have weakened. Both sides vehemently defended their interpretations of constitutional history. If anything, the rhetoric has increased. In his dissent in the *Federal Maritime Commission* case, Justice Breyer, after noting his consistent objections to the majority's vision of state immunity, emphasized that he and the remainder of the four-justice minority are likely to continue resisting: "These decisions set loose an interpretive principle that restricts far too severely the authority of the Federal Government ... Today's decision reaffirms the need for continued dissent – unless the consequences of the Court's approach prove anodyne, as I hope, rather than randomly destructive as I fear."[65] At the close of the 2002 term, Linda Greenhouse summarized her impressions in a simple phrase: "These days, federalism means war."[66]

The second point is that doctrine does remain a factor that can shape results, even in a manner that seems to be contrary to the stated preferences of the judges. In *Davis,* Justice O'Connor appeared to be quite comfortable defending a federal law that on its surface appears to contradict her greater preference for state solutions and for reining in the federal government. While the exercise of a federal spending power is seen as potentially destructive to states' rights, O'Connor joined a majority that upheld conditions on the receipt of federal funds by state agencies. When one looks at Justice O'Connor's record and reasons for the decision, one is reminded that she has been a longtime proponent of the explicit use of the federal spending power. When incentives have been clear to the states, she has defended Congress's right to impose conditions on the receipt of federal funds. This was exactly the issue disputed in the *Davis* case. Unlike her fellow states' rights colleagues, Justice O'Connor determined that the tests designed to curb abuse of the spending power had been met in the *Davis* case and that federal law could apply to those who received federal funds.

Since state sovereignty is not threatened by a state knowingly accepting conditions, she could not agree with the minority that the "federal balance" had to be considered.

Justice O'Connor's position in the *Davis* case has been suggested by some to be a product of her feminism as opposed to her long-held views on federalism.[67] However, the argument that she makes in the majority opinion does not really contradict her federalism jurisprudence. It shows instead that there are shades of difference between the ideological position that some of the judges have staked on federalism and a position consistent with the court's federalism jurisprudence. For O'Connor, the federal legislation upheld in *Davis* was consistent with conditions that she endorsed in the past, and a beefed-up state sovereignty doctrine could not defeat that understanding. The more recent state sovereign immunity cases suggest that the conservative majority on the court may hold greater sway.

Justice O'Connor's commitment to promoting strict boundaries between federal and state jurisdiction continued into her last full term on the court. *Raich v. Gonzales,*[68] one of the last decisions of the court's 2004 term, upheld the application of the federal *Controlled Substances Act* as a limit on the use of medical marijuana despite legislation from California authorizing limited use of the drug for medical purposes. The majority decision, which accepted the broad interpretation of the commerce power necessary to justify federal intervention, was joined by Justices Kennedy and Scalia, commonly on the side of states' rights in such matters. Many have categorized the case as a true test of the pro-states' majority on the court and their commitment to federalism in the face of ideological outcomes that they do not prefer, in this case the partial legalization of marijuana. Justice O'Connor wrote the court's dissenting opinion, relying on the structural intentions of federalism and sustaining the new vigilance of the court in applying the substantial effects test relied upon to invalidate congressional stretching under commerce in *Lopez* and *Morrison.*

Observers have been tempted to label the Rehnquist court, and particularly its federalism jurisprudence, as revolutionary. Even the regular dissenters have used the language of revolt. In his dissent in *Kimel,* Justice Stevens remarked that "the kind of judicial activism manifested in cases like *Seminole Tribe* ... represents such a radical departure from the proper role of this court that it should be opposed whenever the opportunity arises."[69] While his point is a rhetorical one, certainly at no time since the New Deal has the court been more at the centre of the development of American federalism. The willingness of a majority on the court to challenge congressional exercises of the commerce power is unprecedented in the post-New Deal era. Congressional Democrats in particular have taken the court's interventions as an invitation to be more activist on questions of national policy. Senator Hillary Rodham Clinton, for one, has criticized the court for its "willingness to override common-sense legislation" in a manner "deliberately designed to exclude Congress – and by extension, the American people – from playing a part in defining what the Constitution requires and what it permits."[70] The Supreme Court's intervention in the 2000 election via *Bush v. Gore* suggested to some that it had become an explicit political actor. The extraordinary stability of the court's membership in recent years has allowed it to develop a profile and reputation that turnover usually denies. The justices and their default positions were both familiar and predictable.

Some have cautioned against a strictly political or attitudinal account of why the court's jurisprudence looks like it currently does. Keith Whittington judges the recent federalism offensive on the Supreme Court as the product of both political (external) and legal (internal) forces. In his account, the Rehnquist federalism revolution is not strictly the product of a more conservative ideological cast on the court. Rather, a complete account of the recent turnaround, Whittington suggests, can be explained only if one "takes account of both politics and law. A purely legal explanation would have difficulty accounting for the timing and form of the Court's changing constitutional interpretation. A purely political explanation would neglect the particular institutional features of the Court and its deep concern for the law. The Court must make decisions within a particular social and political environment; it is not immune to the effects of that environment."[71] Whittington's hybrid of politics and law still keeps both forces roughly in their respective spheres. Historical institutionalist accounts of decision making have placed greater explanatory stock in the constraints that come from any decision maker's particular institutional setting. In the case of judges, this means that the constraints of the law work to limit the options open to judicial decision makers.

For Whittington, a "jurisprudential [or internal] explanation of the Court's recent federalism offensive will have to be supplemented with a political [or external] explanation."[72] This account suggests that a federalism revolution can occur if, as at present, the dominant forces on the court have a particular reading of the constitution's provisions and an external environment that is relatively amenable and therefore not interested in challenging their perspective. With the internal and external stars properly aligned, a period of judicial-led constitutional change can occur. For scholars trying to give an accurate descriptive picture, "the real challenge is to bridge the gap between [external and internal explanations] ... to develop accounts that can reconcile the verifiable observations of the externalist explanations with the also significant empirical support for the internalist explanations."[73]

There is something unsatisfying in this account. While it recognizes that constraints of a legal nature count, it still looks on them as constraints on political attitudes held by judges. The agency that matters is still judicial agency and, in this case, a dominant faction on the court that subscribes to the states-first ideology of federalism. According to this thinking, attitudes still drive outcomes; they are just conditioned by the intervening variable of the law. The argument made herein is different. Doctrine has a more independent effect, which, along with other independent variables such as judicial attitudes, determines judicial outcomes and, in a federal system, ultimately shapes the vocabulary and form of the federation.

Others argue that the Rehnquist court has done little to reinvent federalism. Richard Brisbin argues that the court may indeed be interpreting federalism with more favour toward the states than at any time since the New Deal, but that does not constitute a reinvention. To reinvent federalism, the court would have to ask different kinds of questions than these recent cases have. In short, he claims, the Rehnquist court has not challenged the "constitutive" (his term) structures of American federalism in its decisions. Instead, the questions asked by the court "assume that a legally bounded politics, as manifested in the federal Constitution and two centuries of judicial interpretations of the U.S. Constitution[,] should provide rules that divide power between the federal and state governments."[74]

Brisbin might say that the court's current approach is contentedly doctrinal. He believes that, despite the court's current internal differences, the institution as a whole endorses the status quo of American federalism's institutional arrangements. Rather than reconstitute American federalism, as *Garcia* presented an opportunity to do, the court has only revitalized debate about the deployment of government power within the formal legal understanding of federalism. The court has not propounded "a new institutional structure of politics or nonlegal arrangement of political power."[75] I would argue that federalism benefits from such a revival. Consider again the alternative.

Garcia was certainly the most constitutive case of the court in modern memory. And, set alongside *Garcia,* the recent cases do lack constitutive traits. The *Garcia* majority articulated a vision of federalism that did not require the concerted involvement of the court. This so-called functionalist or "political-safeguards" approach claimed that American federalism would operate better without the artificial restraints and false certainties of judicial review.[76] Better, claimed the majority, that the court defer to Congress on matters of federalism than try to impose artificial, if legal, constraints upon the scope of the enumerated powers. The current court takes its inspiration not from *Garcia* but from the approach in *National League of Cities (NLC).*

The *Garcia/NLC* split is a battle between functionalism and formalism as ideal types. Formalism as a method for deciding constitutional cases is currently in the ascendant. Both the states' rights advocates on the court and their opponents have adopted the methodology. What bothers someone like Kathleen Sullivan is that this method seems to structure decisions in rather uncompromising directions. To her mind, this new formalism allows judges to retreat to "structural default rules" rather than spend any time considering the circumstances of a particular case or how the court could help the federal system to function more smoothly. This battle between "duelling sovereignties" is more formal than she believes it needs to be and comes at the cost of removing compromise and concession from the court's federalism adjudication.

But Sullivan presumes too much of the structural positions. The doctrines currently applied by the court are not that rigid. They do not "lock in" positions that compel all future results.[77] The court has not even developed entirely polar doctrinal categories. There is room in the understanding of federalism held by the court generally for considerable manoeuvring by individual judges.[78] The structural positions, like all doctrines, go only part of the way toward determining how a case will fall out. Sullivan's concern suggests that the historical understandings shared by the factions of the court have become all important. They are more important than they were twenty-five years ago, but they are still only one among a host of variables.

The American Supreme Court has abandoned the purely functional position that it articulated in *Garcia*. This is not a small development. Alone, it demonstrates a continuing place for judicial reasoning in the study of federalism. By engaging with federalism as it has, the reasoning of the court has never been more critical to the outcomes of federal-state conflicts. A summary of the recent doctrines and approaches such as that offered in this chapter can also be a summary of recent developments in federalism. These ideas matter to the operation of any federal system. What the court has to say and how it arrives at that outcome are more determinative of the general structure of federalism than has been the case since the New Deal. Divining the preferences of the judges has once again become constitutionalist spectator sport. That there is wiggling room within the positions held by the court makes the reasons for judgment in every case all the more critical. The court has revived the belief that it can decide matters of federalism on the basis of a reasonably defined set of principles and does not need to leave the settlement of division-of-powers disputes to political institutions alone. Doctrine is again an independent variable. The contrast between the federalism of the court in *Garcia* and the present day cannot be overstated. The court has effectively moved from a position that cast doubt upon its own ability and suitability to contribute to the resolution of federalism disputes to a point where federal-state conflicts hang in the balance of evolving and subtle ideas about the interpretation of federalism and the division of powers.

4
The Australian High Court: Legalistic Federalism

Legalism, Literalism, and Doctrine

Australia's High Court has always expressed a preference for formal methods of decision making. Australian constitutionalism has been invariably legalistic. Only recently has the High Court indicated any willingness to question strict legalistic methods. Otherwise, it has expressed continuous endorsement of this "neutral" method ever since its most famous articulation in the *Engineers* case of 1920. The most important consequence of the court's legalist tradition has been that Commonwealth powers in section 51 of the constitution have been read literally or according to the "natural meaning of the text."[1] This literal reading has invariably expanded section 51 powers in preference to the "reserved" and notably unwritten powers assigned to the states.

The *Engineers* revolution cemented an approach to the interpretation of the division of powers that has yet to be anything more than cosmetically altered. With *Engineers,* the early doctrines of the court were abandoned in favour of much stricter analytical techniques. Legalism has its own set of doctrines – even a literalist technique relies upon tools to divine meaning. Legalism does purport to be less dependent on extra-textual aids, but critics of the court have amply demonstrated the reliance of legalism on doctrine to carry out judicial review.[2] That said, some of the same critics have more recently suggested that the court is less interested in using legalism as a justification for its approach to the division of powers. Brian Galligan, for example, argues that legalism was never anything more than a public relations strategy for the court. Legalism reassured the Australian public that undemocratic and unaccountable judges were not just deciding cases on a whim. Legalism, according to this thinking, was never really a philosophy so much as a rhetorical device used to cloak the messier process of balancing interests and preferences that is judicial review. But legalism cannot be written off wholly as an animating philosophy. While there are indications that the court is willing to decide controversies outside the bounds of its traditional lines, literalism and legalism have by no means been wiped off the map. There may be a change in the way that the court makes decisions about federalism, but legalistic methods are still a part of the way that the court forms its results.

Likewise, the court no longer appears as willing to endorse expansion of the central government's power through a generous reading of the Commonwealth headings in the constitution. Going into the 1980s, there was little indication that the court would relent in its favouring of central over state authority. But in order for a revolution to occur, sometimes the extravagance of the existing regime must first be made undeniable. Judges seem to back off a system of reasoning only after it comes to a sort of logical endpoint by forcing obtuse results – the textual equivalent of closets full of Guccis or the palace of Versailles. Once the practice of a court demonstrates an overt degree of circularity or bias, it is much more vulnerable to challenge, particularly if results appear to be perverse. The best example of this phenomenon is the way that the American Supreme Court indulged a radically centralist position in *Garcia* and has since subjected commerce clause regulation to much more rigorous review. A similar change in current Australian developments can be traced to the *Tasmanian Dam* case and the way in which the court pushed the literalist method to an almost absurd but logical endpoint, threatening in the process the very idea of the division of powers.

After writing off federalism in *Tasmanian Dam,* the court appears to have been left with nothing to do but reinvent and revive federalism. This chapter will explore how the court pushed the logic of the division of powers to its brink and has since retreated to a more measured view of the balance between Commonwealth and state powers. The continued role of legalism in this development will be closely noted. This "superdoctrine" has endangered the relevance of the court as a force in federalism, but it is doctrine (albeit of different sorts) that has renewed the role of the court in Commonwealth-state relations.

Koowarta: External Affairs Expanded

It did not take the *Tasmanian Dam* case to alert all observers to the threatened status of federalism. Historian Winston McMinn proclaimed the end of federalism in Australia some years earlier. He credited its apparent demise largely to the liberal interpretation of the powers of the Commonwealth. "There are other definitions of federalism," he noted, "but to accept Wheare's is to accept that Australia has long since ceased to be a federation."[3] The broadly defined Commonwealth powers, in his view, had effectively robbed the states of the independence necessary to live up to Wheare's coordinate definition. That was four years before the *Tasmanian Dam* case.

The trend was not as entirely one-sided or as dramatic as McMinn's evaluation might suggest. The High Court expanded Commonwealth powers only to a point. This is particularly evident when one compares the pace of centralization with the avowedly anti-federal goals of the country's Labor Party. Comparatively, Australia's federal system does seem to be centralized, but the Labor Party's more hostile, anti-federalism agenda was left unfulfilled by the court. The court was not the only, and perhaps not even the most significant, obstacle to centralization. The Labor Party was also stymied by a population unwilling to endorse constitutional change via referendum. Only eight of the forty-four referendums put to the Australian electorate have achieved the double majority necessary for approval, making Australia, in Geoffrey Sawer's words, the "frozen continent."[4] The most intense struggles between Labor and the constitution were confined to the 1940-50 period but continued to mark the tone of judicial review. Thus, the net effect of the High Court's jurisprudence was to centralize power, albeit at a slower rate than the political branches preferred. The fate of the Commonwealth's jurisdiction over external affairs is the best example of this phenomenon.

The Commonwealth was accorded the power to conduct Australia's external relations by section 52(xxix) of the constitution. This power was historically understood to include the making of treaties on behalf of the federation. The treaty power was not limited to those areas in which the Commonwealth government had legislative jurisdiction but was understood as plenary and independent.[5] The implementation of treaties for which the Commonwealth did not have an enumerated power commonly depended upon the goodwill of the states or required the Commonwealth to justify laws as ones made in the name of external affairs. Commonwealth politicians had been advised for some time that a more aggressive use of the external affairs power would provide a legitimate means to increase power at the centre without any likely opposition from the High Court. The stated goal of the national Labor Party for the better part of the twentieth century was the promotion of centralization to better realize the goals of a national welfare state. The great Labor expansionist Gough Whitlam saw the potential of external affairs to provide justification for such centralization without resort to constitutional change. "A Labor Government," he wrote, "should make more use of the external affairs power to extend its legislative competence, in particular by implementing conventions and treaties ... There would seem good ground for believing that the High Court would not be prone to invalidate Commonwealth legislation in such fields."[6] Whitlam's optimism was based on the High Court's decision in *R. v. Burgess; Ex parte Henry,* which upheld the Commonwealth's regulation of aeronautics as a matter "international in character." The majority of the court found that section 51(xxix) encompassed anything reasonably required for living up to a treaty.[7] Robert Menzies too saw the potential of external affairs to expand the scope of Commonwealth power without resort to constitutional amendment.[8] The court necessarily became involved as states challenged the variety of agreements and treaties to which the Commonwealth was a signatory.

The logic of permissible external affairs expansion was simple. The Commonwealth Parliament must have passed legislation to fulfill the obligations made in the course of Australia's external relations. The only apparent limits on Parliament's power were the same ones, such as implied immunity, that applied to all Commonwealth powers. The court also required that the law be a reasonable means of living up to a treaty commitment. Finally, the court argued in *Burgess* that, for matters to qualify as external affairs, the activity in question had to be "international in character." That is, the matter must be perceived to be a subject of legitimate international cooperation and agreement. The court argued that such an activity did not have to take place outside Australia to qualify as a matter of external affairs but had to have an element of legitimate internationalism. What this meant was left largely undefined.

The modern expansion of the external affairs power came with *Koowarta v. Bjelke-Petersen.*[9] The Commonwealth had invoked anti-discrimination legislation to overrule the Queensland State government's decision to refuse pastoral leases to Aboriginal communities. The Commonwealth defended its action as necessary to the fulfillment of a treaty obligation. *Koowarta* presaged much of the *Tasmanian Dam* decision, expanding what was acceptable as an international agreement and thereby the scope of the subject matters in which Commonwealth legislation was permissible. The disposition of lands within the state, the nominal activity in dispute in *Koowarta,* was commonly thought of as a state rather than Commonwealth matter. However, the Commonwealth had passed, some years earlier, the *Racial Discrimination Act* [1975] in conformity with its commitment to the *International Convention on Human Rights.* The Commonwealth was drawn into the dispute as the Queensland government was effectively discriminating against Aboriginals in the exercise of its lands power.

The court was obliged to decide what was permissible under external affairs, the definition left by *Burgess* being relatively unclear. The court's reasoning turned not so much on whether the Commonwealth's agreement to the international convention had an international character as on whether or not it comprised a matter of "international concern." This subtle shift had expansive potential. According to this test, a matter did not need to be international at a functional level. In this example, there was nothing really international about racial discrimination or making laws to prevent its practice. However, by becoming the subject of an international treaty, racial discrimination took on the attribute of an international concern. While the court upheld the *Racial Discrimination Act* as a matter of external affairs, no majority actually agreed upon the reasons why. Three of the four judges accepted the external affairs justification on the ground of the international concern evidenced by the treaty.[10] The fourth justice did not accept such an easy proof of international concern but preferred to consider history and context as necessary to its determination.

The case signalled that the court was willing to permit Commonwealth legislation on wholly domestic matters in traditional state jurisdiction if it arose out of an international obligation. While the court was cautious and divided on just how much proof of international concern was necessary, it was moving away from a definition of external affairs that only included actual relations outside the country. This proved to be a major new policy tool, particularly for a Commonwealth Labor government that faced states unwilling to cooperate with it on Aboriginal and environmental policies.

Tasmanian Dam has been recognized as a landmark in Australian federalism, but *Koowarta* may in fact be the more revolutionary of the two cases.[11] The wide scope that the three judges in the majority gave to the external affairs power differed critically from that accorded the Commonwealth in the still controlling *Burgess* case. After *Koowarta,* matters did not have to possess an international character to qualify under external affairs; they simply had to be matters of international concern. *Koowarta* essentially failed to articulate a single vision of external affairs, or of the race power (section 51[xxvi]), which was also advanced as justification. Much less did it provide an alternative vision that limited the scope of Commonwealth power.

Tasmanian Dam: The Logic of Expansion Confirmed

Australia, like Canada, has no shortage of natural wonders. Also like Canada, it has no shortage of entrepreneurs and corporations eager to draw as much bounty from the earth as possible. Tasmania, the smallest Australian state, is no exception to this pattern. Indeed, given its relative compactness, hardly a single stone has been left unturned in the quest for making the most of what nature has to offer. The state government has traditionally been supportive of this development, the prosperity of its residents being intimately related to the pace of exploitation. The Commonwealth government, not unlike other federal overseers, tends to take a more dispassionate approach to the direct issues at hand, generally seeking "national standards" in preference to promoting development.[12] In the Australian case, these roles are magnified by the already overwhelming size of Commonwealth jurisdiction as compared to the states. The stereotypical roles of reckless developer and overseeing environmental conscience would be fulfilled to the letter in the controversy over the damming of the Gordon River in Tasmania.[13]

The Commonwealth Labor government of Bob Hawke, shortly after its ascension to office in 1983, sought to halt the development of a dam at the junction of the Gordon and Franklin rivers in southwestern Tasmania. This project had been pursued by the Tasmanian Hydro Electric Commission with the cooperation of the state government. The pro-development premier, Robin Gray, found little reason to preserve the natural state of the Franklin. By his description, the river was not among the first rank of Australia's natural gifts; rather, it was "a brown ditch, leech-ridden and unattractive."[14] The area was already protected, at Tasmania's request, in 1981 under the auspices of the United Nations World Heritage list. The state government changed its mind after making the request but failed to convince the Commonwealth to withdraw the region from protection. The Tasmanian Parliament later passed legislation exempting the area from its own conservation legislation, enabling the project to proceed. The Commonwealth government, despite representations from some concerned groups, did nothing to counter this action until the election of the Hawke government, which quickly passed legislation giving effect to the UN protection and stopping Tasmania's attempts to begin the project.

The Commonwealth cited its powers over external affairs as justification for this intervention. Putting a halt to the dam was necessary, it argued, for Australia to meet its treaty obligations as a signatory to the *Convention for the Protection of the World Cultural and Natural Heritage* adopted by the General Conference of UNESCO (the United Nations Education, Scientific, and Cultural Organization). The Commonwealth also argued that it could halt the dam under its power to make laws relevant to race, as some Aboriginal archeological sites would be flooded by the dam's reservoir. If it was constitutional, the Commonwealth legislation would overrule the earlier Tasmanian legislation as the Commonwealth enjoys supremacy (much like the federal paramountcy of Canada's constitution act) through section 109 of the constitution. The court found, by a narrow majority, that the suspension of development was justified under external affairs, keeping the Franklin dam floodgates unbuilt but literally opening the floodgates to substantial exploitation of the external affairs power by the Commonwealth.

The court made it clear in *Tasmanian Dam* that the definition of "external affairs" did not limit the Commonwealth to exercising jurisdiction over areas solely outside the country. The majority upheld the legislation as a necessary adjunct to the international obligation that Australia had undertaken through UNESCO. It ruled that Commonwealth laws, whose purpose is to implement treaty obligations, could be justified as matters of external affairs. What subjects qualified as matters of treaty obligation was a separate issue. Again the international concern test, imported from *Koowarta,* was used, but it was applied very loosely. International concern, according to the majority in this case, was essentially an unenforceable limit. Justice

Mason, as he then was, wrote that, as long as the obligation was incurred by a real international agreement, there was no real limit to the possible subject matters upon which the Commonwealth could enter into agreements. To determine whether there was indeed an "international concern," he believed that it was enough to rely on the executive's discretion: "Whether the subject matter as dealt with by the convention is of international concern, whether it will yield, or is capable of yielding, a benefit to Australia, whether non-observance by Australia is likely to lead to adverse international action or reaction, are not questions on which the Court can readily arrive at an informed opinion. Essentially they are issues involving nice questions of sensitive judgment that should be left to the Executive Government for determination."[15]

The dissenters were more interested in dissecting an international concern test. They found no reason to qualify the damming of a Tasmanian river as a matter of international concern, regardless of a treaty commitment, and thus rejected the need for Commonwealth intervention. Chief Justice Gibbs sought a more definite theory of international concern in the *Koowarta* minority that included matters that "in some way involve a relationship with other countries or persons or things outside Australia."[16] This time, again in dissent, he desperately sought some manner of limiting Commonwealth discretion. He rejected the majority's loose vision of international concern in favour of a more "precise test." "Whether a matter is of international concern," he argued, "depends on the extent to which it is regarded by the nations of the world as a proper subject for international action, and on the extent to which it will affect Australia's relations with other countries."[17] He did not see any of these elements in the specific controversy at hand.

Since the limits of the external affairs power would be defined only by the types of treaties signed by the Commonwealth, the court tried to articulate a minimal standard for these treaties to live up to. At minimum, they argued, international agreements must be entered into *bona fide:* that is, in good faith and not simply for the purpose of accumulating power at the centre. How the court was to ensure that such colourable activities were not undertaken was less clear. A test for *mala fide* agreements was never really contemplated; the court seemed to be prepared to rely on the Commonwealth's good judgment. Considering the genesis of the conflict at hand, that did not seem to be very encouraging for Commonwealth-state relations. For Gibbs, in dissent, the *bona fide* doctrine is at best "a frail shield."[18] Another commentator has referred to the *bona fide* criterion as nothing more than a "purely theoretical limitation"[19] given the genuine difficulty of finding a case in which the Commonwealth could be caught making subversive international agreements. More likely to happen was exactly what happened in this instance – the Commonwealth sought out international agreements to legitimize its intervention when it had an agenda at odds with that of a particular state.

Perhaps a more demanding set of limitations was placed on the Commonwealth by the requirement that even the broad range of feasible international agreements must respect the principle of the *Burgess* case. External affairs were still to "be exercised with regard to the various constitutional limitations expressed or implied in the Constitution, which generally restrain the exercise of Federal power."[20] What were these limitations? Well, they were something short of simply "the federal nature of the constitution" that the *Tasmanian Dam* minority suggested was enough to invalidate the whole scheme. Gibbs forcefully put it for the minority that "no single power should be construed in such a way as to give the Commonwealth parliament a universal power of legislation which would render absurd the assignment of particular, carefully defined powers to parliament."[21] However, the limits of which the majority decision spoke are more modest. Still, they constituted the remnants of federalism in the post-*Tasmanian Dam* era.

Academic criticism has been levelled at the minority judgments in *Tasmanian Dam* and *Koowarta*. Particular issue has been taken with the limits that the minority hoped to derive from the constitution's commitment to federalism. The critics argue that a narrow interpretation of external affairs really seems like a case for reserved powers, a concept unambiguously rejected by the court in *Engineers*. Given the general esteem in which that case is held, both by the legal community and by the bench (it has never been more than cautiously detracted and has never been rejected in principle or result), any effort to revive reserved powers seemed to rest on shaky ground. The minority argument should be taken seriously, however, as it is concerned with federal balance. The legalistic technique that the court has favoured since *Engineers* has precluded it from giving too much stock to the potential outcomes of the court's pronouncements. Unfortunately for the minority, or anyone seeking to achieve federal balance, consequences are important to making such determinations.

But there may be more to the legalistic technique than simply an expansive reading of Commonwealth powers. There was something of a "survivalist" instinct in the way that the minority presented the case for federal balance in both *Koowarta* and *Tasmanian Dam*. For example, Gibbs's plea that no single power ought to be construed so broadly as to make other grants seem absurd is also a plea to make federalism exist in practice as well as in name. Gibbs sounded the most dire notes in *Tasmanian Dam*. With alarm, he wrote, "the division-of-powers between the Commonwealth and the States ... could be rendered quite meaningless if the Federal Government could, by entering into treaties with foreign governments on matters of domestic concern, enlarge the legislative powers of Parliament so that they embraced literally all fields of activity."[22] The only concessions that the *Tasmanian Dam* majority allowed were those from the *State Banking* case; the Commonwealth's power could not be used so as to discriminate against a single state or prevent a state from continuing to exist and function as an independent unit.[23] The federal balance argument, while not determinative, is an important caveat for the court.

Corporations Power

In addition to radically expanding external affairs, the court marginally expanded the federal power over corporations in *Tasmanian Dam*. Section 51(xx) of the constitution provides the Commonwealth with a power over "foreign corporations, and trading or financial corporations formed within the limits of the Commonwealth." At issue in this part of the case was whether the Tasmanian Hydro Electric Commission qualified as a trading corporation and, if so, whether or not its activities in relation to the dam were then subject to Commonwealth regulation. The court took the *Concrete Pipes* case as its starting point in this regard. That case, we may recall, prevented the reserved power of the states to regulate the internal state activities of trading corporations from barring Commonwealth regulation. *Concrete Pipes* essentially introduced *Engineers*-style thinking to the corporations power and set aside the presumed reserve powers of the states. This made the Commonwealth power over trading corporations plenary and independent. In addition, *Concrete Pipes* made it clear that the Commonwealth's power was not limited to the trading activities of corporations but designed to deal with corporations themselves. However, the High Court did not leave the power completely open ended. Legislation justified under the power was required to have a substantial connection to the topic of corporations rather than to simply apply to them. For example, the corporations power did not open the door to environmental legislation simply because it applied to trading corporations. Rather, the legislation had to be about the kinds of specific activities undertaken by trading corporations. Trade practices, such as monopolies and trusts, were considered relevant enough, and most expansions of the Commonwealth power after *Concrete Pipes* were made in such areas.

The *World Heritage Act* related not to trade practices but to the activities involved in the building of a dam: namely, cutting down trees and building roads. If the corporations power was extended to include these "non-trading" activities of trading corporations, it would represent a substantial increase for the Commonwealth as to the kinds of activities that it could control under the auspice of the corporations power. The court demonstrated some restraint and took the narrowest view available. It found the Hydro Electric Commission to indeed be a trading corporation and thus subject to corporations legislation. The court also allowed Commonwealth jurisdiction to apply to those activities that were strictly "for the purposes of trading," even though the acts themselves were non-trading. The court formed no conclusive majority behind a wider interpretation that would include all activities undertaken by trading corporations. As it stood, the court's definition was wide enough. The court found that the building of a dam was an activity related to the trade in which the corporation was engaged and thus could be halted by the Commonwealth legislation.

The crux of the corporations power analysis was defining which activities relate to trade. This definition becomes critical in the aftermath of the *Tasmanian Dam* decision. With a wider scope of activities covered by the corporations power, those subject to Commonwealth corporations regulation were potentially in for more. Thus, there was an automatic incentive for corporations to avoid falling within the definition of a trading corporation. According to the court, manufacturing corporations, if they intended to sell their wares, automatically fell within the ambit of the power. The test used by the court was whether or not trading makes up a "substantial" part of the corporation's activities. The test not only included manufacturing interests but also other enterprises such as football clubs and leagues. Previous distinctions had been built into the test to exclude mining and municipal corporations, but the court found the maintenance of such distinctions problematic.[24] *Tasmanian Dam* essentially standardized the accepted definition of trading corporations up to that point. It left open one crucial exception. States could not be characterized as trading corporations; their activities were considered to fall under the rubric of public service. In *Tasmanian Dam,* the state was exempt, but the Hydro Electric Commission, having been created as an autonomous organization by the state, was not.[25]

The exception of states from the corporations power is reminiscent of the implied immunity doctrine. The states do engage in trade and trading activities, so by a perfectly literalist reading they should be considered subject to the Commonwealth's power. But federalism imports the implied immunity of the states regardless. The implied immunity doctrine has not been rejected by the court, as has the doctrine of reserved powers. Unfortunately for the Tasmanian government, the Hydro Electric Commission was too far removed from the state to qualify for immunity. However, the doctrine's survival remains an important potential limit for the central government to heed.

Like *Garcia* in the United States, *Tasmanian Dam* left the protection of the states to the political rather than the legal realm. Michael Coper, for one, refused to take the High Court's obvious centralism too seriously. "It should not be forgotten," he argued, "that the High Court has determined and can determine only that certain powers exist, not whether or how those powers should be exercised. There is still room for political constraints and for political negotiation."[26]

External Affairs after *Tasmanian Dam*

The High Court has restrained its expansion of Commonwealth powers since the *Tasmanian Dam* case. Occasionally, the states have claimed small victories. However, literalism has endured as a technique, despite showing some signs of wear. Literalism, true to the test of doctrine, has proven to be flexible. Despite presumptions to the contrary, it will likely outlast some of the challenges made to its legitimacy by a "states' rights faction" (albeit a small one) that has always claimed it was due for such an evaluation.

Justice Daryl Dawson, who throughout his career strongly dissented from the court's centralizing decisions, cautioned that not only was the external affairs power open-ended and infinitely expandable as a result of *Tasmanian Dam* but also, "even with existing treaties to which Australia is party, the Commonwealth presently has the capacity to cut a swathe through the areas hitherto thought to be within the residual powers of the States."[27] Thus, even if the Commonwealth did not consciously seek to grow its jurisdiction at the expense of the states, the external affairs power would increase it almost by default. Such a situation has not come to pass. Brian Galligan sees some gains in the national government's power over the environment in the wake of *Tasmanian Dam* but recognizes that "in practice ... the potential expansion of Commonwealth powers under external affairs has been limited by the countervailing political power of the States."[28] In fact, in the post-*Tasmanian Dam* world, external affairs have yet to become the plenary power that doomsayers such as Dawson believed they would.

The High Court held back from further expanding external affairs in the two major decisions on that power since *Tasmanian Dam*. In *Richardson v. Forestry Commission* (1988),[29] the court did little more than affirm the basic principles of *Tasmanian Dam*. This time a larger majority of the court accepted a broad interpretation of external affairs. The judges really had little choice. The circumstances in the case were similar to those in *Tasmanian Dam*, and thus the latter served as a clear precedent. Dawson wrote what could at best be considered a qualified endorsement of *Tasmanian Dam*. In *dicta*, he rejected the general approach to external affairs taken by the *Tasmanian Dam* majority, but he agreed that the *Tasmanian Dam* precedent was binding regardless of whether he believed it to be right or wrong.

In *Queensland v. Commonwealth* [*Tropical Rainforests* case],[30] the court continued its pattern of deferring to the Commonwealth on what actually qualified as a matter of international concern. In fact, the court's deference extended one degree further. The State of Queensland contested the protection of a portion of its tropical rainforest by the Commonwealth. The Commonwealth protected the area at the urging of the World Heritage Committee. The committee, not the Commonwealth, determined that the affected area required protection under the auspices of the World Heritage List. Queensland objected to such a determination on the ground that the

Commonwealth could not pass its decision-making authority off to an international body. The court disagreed. In this case, the international community had been empowered to make a determination on behalf of the Commonwealth government, and protecting those areas was part of the Commonwealth's treaty obligation.

Again Dawson dissented from the majority. States, in his opinion, were better able to determine which areas of their natural heritage were in need of protection. But again he deferred to the majority and the controlling status of *Tasmanian Dam*. His reasoning in the *Richardson* case helps to explain why: "Precedent must, however, have a part to play, even in the interpretation of a constitution. Considerations of practicality make it necessary that the law should as far as possible, take a consistent course. The constant re-examination of concluded questions is incompatible with that aim."[31] For the record, Dawson was willing to articulate his objection but deferred to precedent.

The most recent considerations of the external affairs power have not involved domestic activity undertaken by the Commonwealth under the guise of external affairs. The court has instead been asked what kinds of activities fit within the definition of external affairs. In 1991, the *War Crimes Act* case decided if crimes committed outside Australia were within the scope of external affairs. The Commonwealth had amended its war crimes legislation to permit the prosecution of Australian residents who had committed war crimes abroad during the Second World War. The court found that the act was within the purview of external affairs by virtue of its extra-territorial application. This extended the Commonwealth's power under external affairs beyond the scope already afforded to it by the broad reading of treaty powers. The willingness to defer to the discretion of Parliament was again affirmed. Mason argued that "it is not necessary that the court should be satisfied that Australia has an interest or concern in the subject-matter of the legislation in order that its validity be sustained. It is enough that Parliament's judgment is that Australia has an interest or concern. It is inconceivable that the Court could overrule Parliament's decision on that question."[32]

Similarly, in *Horta v. Commonwealth*,[33] the court found that the extraterritoriality of Commonwealth action was sufficient to bring it under the external affairs power. The case itself was politically controversial. The litigation sought to void a treaty between Australia and Indonesia over the Timor Gap. Both governments laid claim to the oil and gas reserves in the gap, which is outside both of their territorial waters. They were unable to settle the sovereignty dispute but reached a working agreement in the form of a cooperation zone treaty in 1989. Complicating matters was the legitimacy of Indonesia's claim to sovereignty in East Timor; while cautiously accepted by the international community, it is contested by many non-state actors. East Timor remains something of a cause célèbre among international activists, and a source of infamy for the Indonesian government, which occupied the area with considerable force in 1975. The Australian activist community was a flag bearer of international dissent as it included many former East Timorese who had been forced to flee the occupied province. In an effort to embarrass the Australian government for bargaining with Indonesia over the spoils of its occupation, activists applied to the court to invalidate the treaty. They argued that cooperating with Indonesia violated Australia's international obligations under the *Universal Declaration of Human Rights* and other UN commitments. If the agreement was contrary to international law, a question that the activists hoped the High Court itself would examine, the Commonwealth could not justify its treaty with Indonesia under the external affairs power. The court found it unnecessary to examine this question. Rather, writing as one, its members found that the matter was unquestionably extra-territorial and therefore *prima facie* within the scope of external affairs. Even if the Commonwealth was contravening the international law to which it was already a party, the agreement itself was still justified as an exercise in external affairs on the ground that it was concerned with extra-territorial matters.

The High Court has stuck by its broad interpretation of external affairs. Fortunately, it has not been met with a rash of litigation from disgruntled states bullied into compromises by an overbearing Commonwealth. However, the effect of the power has been noticeable, serving as something of a chill on ambitious state-led development projects.[34] The Commonwealth has even found itself subject to the environmental protections that it agreed to in international treaties. The current Commonwealth government, led by a Liberal Party coalition, has been stymied by the international community in what has been referred to by one newspaper as the biggest "environmental stoush since Franklin Dam." Activists sought to halt the development of the Jabiluka uranium mine in Kakadu National Park. UNESCO inspectors were invited to the site to determine if it should receive the protection of the convention's provisions. The proposed mine is in the Northern Territory, an area administered by the national government. Unfortunately for the protesters and Aboriginal groups seeking the halt, the Commonwealth appears to be less sympathetic to their aims than it was in 1983. The UN, however, has argued that the area requires protection. The Commonwealth has vowed to ignore the UN's wishes, and development is proceeding.

The court seems to have collectively (and somewhat subconsciously) seen an abyss in *Tasmanian Dam* and turned back lest it fall into the bottomless pit of emasculated federalism. This response has not diminished the external affairs power. To be fair, the court has not had to settle a tough case on external affairs since *Tasmanian Dam*. It has not been required since to test for the *bona fides* of an international agreement. Nor has it been required to expand the power to cover further types of domestic regulation under the auspices of external affairs. *Richardson* and the *Tropical Rainforests* case were both on their facts essentially similar (albeit on a smaller scale) to the dispute in Tasmania.

More recent decisions have dealt with entirely non-domestic applications of external affairs and have not pressed the international concern logic of *Tasmanian Dam.* Every indication is that, if the Commonwealth is so inclined, it could continue to expand its jurisdiction over the environment through the external affairs power. One observer has noted that commitments made by the Commonwealth at the Rio Summit on the environment in 1992 could potentially expand that power considerably.[35] This remains more a matter of potential than reality given the present Commonwealth government's lack of inclination and even hostility to initiatives such as the Kyoto Accord.[36] External affairs has not grown by leaps and bounds, nor has it obliterated the logic of the division of powers. The potential for expansion remains, though, as the modest upholding of *Tasmanian Dam* in *Victoria v. Commonwealth* demonstrates.[37]

Corporations Power Revisited

Important developments have continued in other division of powers matters. These cases have largely relied on the continuing guidance of literalism as a technique. While centralists had reason to be optimistic about the corporations power in the wake of the *Tasmanian Dam* decision, there was a degree of qualification therein that made the future of the power more uncertain than that over external affairs. Expansion of the corporations power was halted when the Commonwealth tried to develop a general law of incorporation that regulated how trading companies were structured and registered. A major package of corporations legislation was put together by the Commonwealth government in an attempt to exact new control over corporations and securities law with a national regime of incorporation. The court rejected this attempt in *New South Wales v. Commonwealth* [*Incorporation* case], limiting the scope of the section 51(xx) power significantly.

The court was nearly unanimous in this decision. It did not rely upon federalism to limit the corporations power. Rather, the old technique of literalism did the trick. For centralists, literalism giveth, but literalism may also taketh away. The court used what has historically been a centralizing technique to exclude the registration of corporations from the definition of the corporations power. Crucial to the decision in the *Incorporation* case was the generosity with which the court read the power to make laws with respect to corporations. At issue was whether or not the process of incorporation could be included in the general corporations power. Section 51(xx) gives the Commonwealth power over "foreign corporations, and trading or financial corporations formed within the limits of the Commonwealth."

For the literalists on the court, the presence of the word *formed* was critical. By having a power to regulate "formed" corporations, was the Commonwealth left to wait for corporations to be formed before they could come under the corporations power? Rather than simply provide a wide reading, the majority dwelt on their belief that use of the word *formed* excluded the regulation of incorporation and envisaged the regulation only of existing corporations by the Commonwealth. To support this contention, the majority looked to federation-era evidence of the founders' intent when including corporations in the Commonwealth's list of powers. Based on a perusal of the federation-era debates and successive drafts of the constitutional bill, the majority concluded that "the history of section 51 (xx) confirms that the language of the paragraph was not directed towards the subject of incorporation."[38]

Much has been made of the fact that the court relied upon the federation debates to seek the intentions of the founders. Some wonder if this amounts to a rejection of literalism in favour of "intentionalism." Greg Craven has been an unremitting critic of the literalist approach and has made some effort to articulate intentionalism as an alternative. The *Incorporation* case seems to him to support such an approach.[39] Intentionalism works from a different "objective" standard than literalism. If the literalist technique places great stock in the common meaning of phrases in the constitution, the intentionalist method seeks to make more of those phrases than simple semantics. Much like the "original intent" school in the United States, intentionalism seeks to interpret the constitutional text on the basis of the stated aims of the founders. The method presumes that the founders had cause for assigning particular powers to the Commonwealth. For an intentionalist court, it is a matter of consulting the detailed records of the debates and conventions that produced the federation compromise to sift out intent. Given the decentralized leanings of the founders (so plainly exemplified by the first-generation High Court), relying upon these sources will likely produce a less centralized jurisprudence.

Craven advocates intentionalism because he believes that the literalist method has been nothing more than a beard for the centralist leanings of High Court appointees. He recognizes that intentionalism is unsuited to new and unforeseen subject matters and may give the impression that the country is being ruled by the "dead hand of the past."[40] Craven has altered the concept somewhat in response and instead of specific intent looks to the guidance of "fundamental constitutional values." This approach still has its roots in an intentionalist reading of the constitutional document. In addition, the fundamental values approach compensates for intentionalism's weakness in dealing with new matters by dictating that new subjects be approached through the lens of intent, seeking to reproduce with contemporary subjects the balance originally struck by the founders. Again this method favours the states, which have consistently lost power since the federation's inception.

Other commentators have approached the *Incorporation* case differently. Geoffrey Lindell, for example, emphasizes the fact that the case was the first major decision in some time in which the Commonwealth had lost a claim to jurisdiction. In contrast to Craven, who is struck by the historical intent approach of the court, Lindell stresses the role that literalism played in the decision and the relative novelty of literalism working to the benefit of state power. For him, the case is a testament to the flexibility of literalism. Lindell actually contends that the case may have been wrongly decided as the court failed to live by its own practice of reading an indeterminate power liberally rather than narrowly. This technique of liberal interpretation, while not necessarily literalist, has been something of a handmaiden to literal expansion of the Commonwealth headings. That the court departed from this routine, and summoned the federation debates as evidence, signals a potential shift away from favouring the Commonwealth. From this observer's view, it seems to signal little difference in the manner of judicial reasoning – either way the court is simply refining the practice of its literalist superdoctrine.

The Commonwealth was further restricted under the corporations power in 1995 in Dingjan's Case.[41] For the first time since *Tasmanian Dam,* the court was asked to determine the extent to which the activities of "constitutional corporations" (those within the definition of section 52[xx]) were subject to Commonwealth law. Dingjan and his wife operated as subcontractors to a wood-chipping operation in Tasmania. The Dingjans supplied timber to a contractor who subsequently sold it to a pulp and paper mill. When the contractors sought to change the terms of their arrangement with the Dingjans, the latter objected and applied through the labour union to which they belonged for relief under the Commonwealth's *Industrial Relations Act.*

At issue in the case was whether the subcontracts were subject to Commonwealth law since they were some degree removed from the trading and financial activities of the pulp mill corporation. The act provided, in section 127C(1), a review by the Australian Industrial Relations Commission for contracts entered into by constitutional corporations that were suspected of being harsh or unfair. The court found in a close four-to-three decision that the scope of the corporations power could not be extended so far as to include just any contract related to the business activities of a constitutional corporation. Justifiable Commonwealth laws, it argued, had to be laws "with respect to" constitutional corporations. Chief Justice Mason, in the minority, strongly protested that the scope of the Commonwealth power was never intended to be limited solely to the financial and trading activities of constitutional corporations. Rather, he argued, the regulation of the everyday business activities of these corporations seemed to be contemplated by the power. He found that contracts and subcontracts are part of how some constitutional corporations do business and thus should be part of the regulated activity of these corporations. Despite the indirect relationship that the subcontractor had with the constitutional corporation, what "the subcontractor does in performing the subcontract is ultimately done for the purposes of the corporation and constitutes a relevant part of its business operations."[42] The majority were not persuaded to this view.

Dingjan's Case did not really alter the overall scope of the corporations power; the court could only rule that contractors were exempt from it. According to the majority, a Commonwealth law regulating the activities of the people with whom corporations do business was not a law for corporations. The case did not answer the question of whether the Commonwealth can make rules controlling all the activities of corporations. The *dicta* – which seemed to contemplate a wide scope of application – may prove critical to future discussions of the corporations power and eventually turn the tide in the Commonwealth's favour.

In response to these limitations from the High Court and in the words of a state solicitor general, "a general acceptance by all governments of all political persuasions that uniform corporate regulation was not only desirable, but necessary,"[43] greater efforts at state-Commonwealth cooperation have been attempted. Their initial form came in a non-justiciable cooperative agreement known as the "Corporations Agreement," which established a ministerial council and a cooperative legislative scheme that coordinated the objectives and practices of state and federal law and provided for Commonwealth investigation and prosecution of offences under the scheme. This arrangement was challenged in a pair of High Court cases that sent the states and the Commonwealth back to the drawing board.

In *Re Wakim; Ex Parte McNally*[44] and *R. v. Hughes,*[45] elements of the cooperative corporations scheme were put into question by the High Court. In *Wakim,* the court rejected the Corporations Agreement's practice of vesting state "functions" in federal courts for the purpose of advancing uniformity of application. The "cross-vesting" of state jurisdiction into the federal courts is the kind of practice typical of cooperative schemes. The High Court found, however, that other constitutional guarantees may not be ignored even if they are advancing cooperative purposes. In this case, Chapter 3 of the constitution, which speaks to the nature of the judiciary, was invoked as a limit on such practices. While Chapter 3 contemplates the vesting of federal jurisdiction in state courts, it does not explicitly provide for the reverse. A state's obligations or limitations under the constitution operate as affirmative limits on what might be handed over, even willingly, to the Commonwealth.

The effects of *Wakim* were not terribly drastic; the bulk of prosecutions for corporations law offences as a matter of practical reality were handled by the New South Wales Supreme Court, and that court was willing and able to continue that work. State attorneys general agreed that a constitutional amendment might be necessary to legitimate the scheme as previously put but that the need was not sufficiently pressing to require immediate action.[46]

Concerns about cross-vesting were advanced further in *Hughes,* in which a defendant accused under the Western Australia *Corporations Law* challenged the whole scheme as an unconstitutional abdication of state power. Members of the High Court entertained concerns about accountability in cooperative federalism, but the majority did not base their decision on that question. The central issue in the case was whether or not the Commonwealth Department of Public Prosecutions could validly prosecute state law as the cooperative scheme required. Western Australia had certainly conferred such a power in its legislation, but the constitutional validity of that exercise was still unclear. While the court accepted that the Commonwealth department could in fact undertake prosecutions of state corporations law, it could do so only because of the Commonwealth Parliament's power over corporations in section 51(xx) and the finding that the relevant corporation in the prosecution fit under that power.[47] Only provisions of the scheme that fit under the corporations power or other headings of section 51 that delegated explicit power to the Commonwealth would be legitimate. According to one observer, *Hughes* "suggests that the powers conferred by State legislation ... may have been invalid in relation to those areas where the Commonwealth lacks constitutional authority to legislate."[48] *Hughes* was a close call for the corporations scheme and effectively frightened governments at the state and Commonwealth levels into reconsidering the basis for their joint enterprise. Neither *Wakim* nor *Hughes* overturned the core of the corporations scheme, but the willingness of the court to interpret relevant clauses of the constitution legalistically put a fire under governments to solidify the constitutional mechanisms of their scheme.

The practical result has been to send governments back to the negotiating table to create a more constitutionally certain corporations power. The states have invoked the little-used practice of "referring" relevant powers to the Commonwealth to realize a uniform national corporations law. Under section 51(xxxvii) of the constitution, the Commonwealth Parliament can make laws regarding matters referred to it by a state parliament. Effectively, the states can delegate their powers to the federal Parliament through this procedure. "A Commonwealth law pursuant to a reference," writes Cheryl Saunders, "has all the usual qualities of a Commonwealth law. While it lasts, a referred 'matter' becomes a [Commonwealth] head of power."[49] On 15 July 2001, a uniform corporations law, with references to the Commonwealth from all the states, came into effect. The references last for five years and can be renewed by proclamation. Saunders calls the present corporations reference notable as "the most extensive use yet made of the reference power." In addition, she argues that the use of the reference procedure has ensured that the "new scheme overcomes the constitutional problems that threatened the core of the previous arrangements."[50]

Taxation and Excise

The tax regime in Australia seems to be entirely unsuited to a federal nation. The development of a uniform income tax system during the Second World War, approved by the High Court, grants a *de facto* monopoly on income taxes to the Commonwealth. This has left the states with a dearth of revenue sources, certainly nothing commensurable with their jurisdictional responsibilities. Commonwealth revenues before intergovernmental transfers were 69.1 percent of total government revenues in 1996. Comparatively, federal revenues in the United States are roughly the same. The Canadian federal government's revenues are generally just below 50 percent of total government revenues.[51] The Commonwealth grants scheme, which actually predates the income tax monopoly, involves substantial transfers to the states to ensure that they are able to meet their responsibilities. However, the dependency on the Commonwealth that it creates robs the states of flexibility in fiscal matters. The Commonwealth's predominance is further enhanced by section 90 of the constitution, which provides it with exclusive power over excise. In the quest for alternative revenue sources, the states are limited to those fields in which the Commonwealth does not hold exclusive power.

In a broad historical account of federal finance, Russell Mathews and Robert Jay laid blame squarely on the shoulders of the High Court for much of the "vertical fiscal imbalance" that characterized Australian fiscal federalism.[52] To help remedy the fiscal imbalance, the states have traditionally collected excise-like revenue from business franchise licences for retailers of products such as tobacco, alcohol, and petrol. The Commonwealth had turned a wilfully blind eye to these fees in an effort to provide the states with some discretionary revenue and to lighten its own fiscal burden. The states effectively taxed consumption by including a surcharge, equivalent to a percentage of sales, in the fee for a business licence.

These so-called franchise fees proved too ingenious to hold up to judicial scrutiny. In order to give the appearance that the fee was not a tax on the direct consumption of goods, the fee was "back dated" and calculated on the basis of past sales. In a typical case, a percentage of product sales from two months prior to the issuing of a licence was added to a base licence fee. The states were actually forced into this cumbersome means of collection by the High Court. The so-called *Dennis Hotels*[53] formula of collecting on the basis of past rather than current sales was legitimized by an extremely close decision in 1960. Although the fee was obviously anticipatory of further sales and was necessarily passed on by retailers to their customers (characteristics of excise), the court was originally willing to look the other way.

The court was unwilling to entertain challenges to the authority of the *Dennis Hotels* formula for some years. Indeed, it approved of it again in *Dickenson's Arcade,*[54] allowing the system of business licences to continue. The court's patience did not preclude continual challenges to the various state provisions by the retailers and manufacturers of the affected products. One such challenge occurred in 1989 in *Phillip Morris.*[55] Although divided, the court maintained the system of business licences as it then existed. It excluded the licence fees from the definition of excise and thus kept them out of exclusive Commonwealth jurisdiction. At the same time, the case, like many of the other challenges to licence statutes, revealed some of the inconsistencies and oddities in the court's definition of excise. The field remained ripe for reconsideration.

When the tobacco licence fee in New South Wales was again challenged in *Ha v. New South Wales,*[56] state governments hoped that the court would take the opportunity to settle the doubt that always hung over the fees and clean up the "dog's breakfast"[57] that jurisprudence in this area had become. The reasonably positive result in *Philip Morris* gave the states some reason for optimism. Given the opportunity to reconsider, the court certainly simplified the field but did so by finding that all charges on commodities were excise and that the state franchise fees were constitutionally insupportable.

The reasoning of the court was quite simple, and the decision was short given its drastic consequences for the states. As in the *Incorporation* case, the court betrayed a reliance on literalism. For the court, excise was only to be defined in the simplest terms. The majority believed that previous attempts to fashion a form of excise that allowed the coexistence of franchise fees lacked definitional clarity. Thus, the court amply cited former Chief Justice Dixon's dissent in the *Dennis Hotels* case. Dixon refused to characterize the liquor taxes challenged in that case as anything other than excise. The judicial history of this field showed that many attempts, Dixon's among them, were made to read excise literally. Several close judgments had allowed the excise-like franchise fees to continue. This time the court refused to consider the fees generously. In fact, state dependence on these revenues was so great and the fees themselves had increased so dramatically over the years that they could no longer reasonably be characterized as licence fees. The court found that "the *Dennis Hotels* formula cannot support what is, on any realistic view of form and of 'substantial result' a revenue-raising inland tax on goods. The States and Territories have far overreached their entitlement to exact what might properly be characterized as fees for licenses to carry on businesses. The imposts which the Act purports to levy are manifestly duties of excise on the tobacco sold during the relevant periods. The challenged provisions of the Act are beyond power."[58]

With the franchise fee on tobacco outlawed, the states were immediately left in the lurch and out of pocket for fees not only on tobacco but on petroleum products and liquor too, imposts that had been conceived according to similar constitutional reasoning. The shortfall immediately amounted to close to five billion dollars a year, nearly one-sixth of the revenue collected by the states.[59] The Commonwealth intervened with an emergency measure to collect the fees and remit the proceeds directly to the states. The John Howard government introduced comprehensive tax changes in 1999 that eliminated the Commonwealth's wholesale tax and nine of the indirect state taxes, all of which were replaced by a Commonwealth-collected Goods and Services Tax (GST). All the revenue collected from the GST is distributed to the states on an equalized basis through the Commonwealth grants scheme.[60] The revenues from the GST have been greater than projected, which has been good news for state budgets.

Through successive decisions, the High Court expanded the definition of excise. Whenever it expanded excise, it subsequently contracted the independent revenue-generating power of the states. When the states were finally forced out of excise-like fields, the imbalance of fiscal capacities was further exacerbated. The uniform tax scheme and the judicial expansion of excise were the main contributors to federal fiscal imbalance. The court had a great deal of influence in this field, and literalism was central to the way it exerted that influence.

Implied Immunity

Implied immunity is a pre-*Engineers* doctrine that had its strongest support in the court of the founders' era. However, unlike the doctrine of reserved powers, so unambiguously rejected by the *Engineers* case, immunity managed to live on. The idea of implied immunity has already been described in detail above. Essentially, the doctrine has drawn the implication from the mere existence of a federal system of government that the individual levels of government need immunity from the application of each other's laws in order to operate independently within their jurisdictional spheres. The doctrine has worked in both directions – protecting the states from Commonwealth law and vice versa. The *Cigamatic* case in 1962[61] left the Commonwealth with a somewhat enhanced scope of immunity based upon the Crown's prerogative. In the post-*Tasmanian Dam* era, the immunity doctrine has found continued expression.

The Commonwealth tested the limits of its ability to compel the states in 1985. The court's decision in *Queensland Electricity Commission*[62] nullified Commonwealth legislation intended to fast-track an industrial dispute involving the Queensland state utility. Again, as in *Koowarta,* a Commonwealth Labor government clashed with the Queensland Liberal government. The court found that the Commonwealth legislation violated the protection that states enjoy from "discriminatory" national legislation. At a minimum, it ruled that immunity still existed in the form established by the *State Banking* case, which had affirmed that the Commonwealth was stopped from forcing states or their instruments into doing their financial business with the Commonwealth's choice of bank. In *Queensland Electricity Commission,* the court extended this principle of non-discrimination to include discrimination against states vis-à-vis other states: a state could not be singled out from other states for discrimination. The fast-track arbitration attempted by the Commonwealth was specifically designed to circumvent the regular procedures of the labour arbitration system in order to resolve a single Queensland dispute. The court ruled that such discrimination could not occur in a federal system.

While *Queensland Electricity Commission* protected the states from discriminatory Commonwealth legislation, the Commonwealth has tended to enjoy equal or greater immunity from state legislation. In *Cigamatic,* a broad scope of Commonwealth immunity was created that has since irked many state officials. The court recently undertook the task of reexamining the *Cigamatic* principle of Commonwealth immunity from state law. In the 1997 decision *Re: Residential Tenancies Tribunal (NSW),*[63] the court once again endorsed the twofold protection enjoyed by the states: first, that Commonwealth legislation could not seek to single out states; second, and more radically, that Commonwealth legislation could not alter the status of states as entities. The latter was recognized as a baseline protection that actually prevented more than just the dissolving of states.

The court also attempted to articulate the extent of the reciprocal immunity enjoyed by the Commonwealth. On the basis of *Cigamatic,* the Commonwealth enjoyed a wider grant of immunity from the application of state law. This was particularly evident when contrasted with state immunity. The court reconsidered the immunity granted by the 1962 decision. The Commonwealth sought to have its agency, the Defence Housing Authority, exempted from the New South Wales landlord-tenant act on grounds of Crown immunity. The court found against the Commonwealth by a sizable majority.

The majority went to great lengths to distinguish the general perception of Commonwealth immunity as nearly unlimited from a more qualified version. The popular legal perception going into the case was that, under the protection of section 61 of the constitution, Crown immunity (bolstered by the finding in *Cigamatic*) gave the Commonwealth a special (and broad) exemption from the laws of the states. The court found this not to be the case at all. In fact, it affirmed that, in the matter of laws of general application, the Commonwealth enjoys no special immunity whatsoever. Therefore, in the case at hand, the Commonwealth Crown had to enter into contractual relationships on the same grounds as its subjects and should be subject to the same state laws. Chief Justice Brennan, in concurring reasons, pointed to the need for a distinction between "capacities and functions of the Crown" and the transactions into which the Crown may choose to enter. It is undoubted, he argued, that the Crown in the "capacities and functions" sense has an immunity from state law. No state, for example, could seek to alter the character of the Crown through its laws. Yet, he argued, the Crown does not enjoy anything resembling total immunity from state laws. The court did leave the Commonwealth an escape hatch. If the Commonwealth Crown wished to be exempt, it must have a similar law to take precedence over the state law, legislate an exemption for itself under its "protective power," or prove that the state law is not one of general application. Otherwise, the Commonwealth, when entering into a transaction or engaging in an activity covered by state law, must be prepared to be bound by it.

These immunity cases do not represent a great shift either way in terms of centralization or decentralization. The Commonwealth may be more cautious in conforming its behaviours to certain state laws, but the court has clearly signalled the more appropriate means by which the Commonwealth can circumvent the application of state restrictions if it so chooses. The Commonwealth Parliament will simply have to be more candid about not wanting to obey state regulations. More importantly, these cases are relevant to the discussion because the court has relied on the doctrine of immunity as a guide.

Greg Craven suggests in a series of articles that the High Court's literalism may be a victim of its own success.[64] The centralization that it enabled has been realized in spades. Literalism has been so successful at concentrating power in the Commonwealth government that he claims "the federal balance of power is largely a dead (or comatose) issue."[65] Craven is unhappy with the duplicitous politics that he believes the formal methods of the court cover up. "To the extent that literalism is underpinned by centralism," he argues, "one is faced with the spectacle of a constitutional methodology whose avowed essence is an inadvertence to political issues, but whose intellectual genesis lies in precisely such considerations."[66] Seeking to fight fire with fire, Craven advocates his own method – intentionalism. If the court looks to the intent of the founders, he argues, it will be able to overcome its present subjectivity. The American court has shown how contrasting understandings of the federation period can be used to bolster contrasting interpretations of the founders' intentions.

Brian Galligan continues to be one of the court's most watchful observers. He also criticizes the court for being essentially dishonest about its politics. He believes that the court has had undeniable effects upon the balance of federalism and the form of politics in Australia, despite its claims to being apolitical. The court, he argues, has retreated behind a cloak of legalism because it is fundamentally uncomfortable with admitting to its political role and thereby risk criticism for its lack of democratic pedigree or accountability.

In his most recent appraisal of the High Court's politics, Galligan has written that, by "abandoning legalism and taking a more active role as shaper and developer of the Constitution, the current High Court has indeed put itself at the eye of the political storm. The court will need to develop a defensible methodology and give a better public presentation of itself if it is to retain the support of the people in continuing to carry out its constitutional function of judicial review."[67] Like Craven, Galligan believes that the legitimacy of legalism appears to be waning, both on and off the bench. "In particular," he adds, "the court needs to jettison the legalistic methodology of *Engineers,* which is antithetical to Australia's federal Constitution. It is quite inappropriate to interpret the Commonwealth's enumerated heads of power in a literal way irrespective of the broader federal architecture of the constitution and regardless of the centralizing effect that such a method produces." He closes, "the High Court needs to develop an interpretive method appropriate for a federal constitution for the next century of federation. That ... should be its primary constitutional agenda for the centenary decade."[68] In Galligan's opinion, a dismissal of the general legalist approach and the specific literalist technique is central to the proper reorientation of the court's energies. Whether the evidence from the cases indicates this to be true has, in retrospect, been the task of this chapter. It seems that legalism – which can be loosely affiliated with formalism of the American sort – may be the best means to ensure that the court remains relevant in the coming years.

Federalism in Australia may very well have died somewhere in the muddy waters of Tasmania's Gordon River, but if it did its passing was brief. *Tasmanian Dam,* much like the US Supreme Court's ruling in *Garcia,* provided the court with all that it needed to abdicate its role in containing the national government's power. The subsequent interpretation of external affairs has not brought such a reality to pass. Such developments demonstrate that idle judicial hands, while not necessarily the devil's playthings, do seek to make themselves relevant. Redressing the federal imbalance, particularly as states continue to demonstrate their relevance to the political life of Australians, has become the new challenge for the court. As part of that revival, *Engineers*-style literalism, some believe, is under threat. The court's overt role in centralizing power in Australia, demonstrated so fully by *Tasmanian Dam,* may have given it second thoughts. Craven believes that "the present High Court has clearly had occasion to look somewhat askance at the Commonwealth juggernaut that it has helped to create."[69] As part of that re-evaluation, he believes, it has started to experiment with new techniques.

But do the developments surveyed above really resemble a different approach to constitutional adjudication? I do not think they do. The rejection of literalism, much less legalism, does not seem at all complete or even really begun. They may be out of favour as ways of publicly justifying the court's role in federal politics, but as techniques both seem quite alive and well. The court has not taken the *Tasmanian Dam* case as an opportunity to ask "constitutive" questions; rather, it seems to have seen the danger of going that route. The moderate approach to judicial review is to remain legalistic but to develop new lines of argument that favour both levels of government. Craven's option would be to replace one potentially biased technique with another. The American evidence shows that this is clearly not necessary to enliven debate about federalism. Indeed, a formal approach to the division of powers might prove more invigorating than any attempt to divine guiding "intentionalist" principles. Legalism can be abandoned as public rhetoric, but the doctrinal discipline inspired by legalism remains in the court's best interest.

-decision-making done by the JPPC - not Supreme Court.

B ever, the decisions that have had the most impact on Canadian federalism came from the Judicial Committee of the Privy Council (JCPC)

↓

and elsewhere - the impact is debatable

5
The Canadian Supreme Court: Balanced Federalism

Low-Impact Judicial Review?

The Canadian Supreme Court has the shortest history as a court of final resort among the three surveyed here. While the court has practised the task of judicial review for more than 100 years, 2005 marks only the fifty-sixth year that the court had the final word in matters of Canadian law.[1] As a result, the court has had less of an opportunity than its counterparts to put its defining mark on the way that federalism is understood and practised. In addition, the Supreme Court has made no decisions that have dramatically demonstrated the capacity of judicial review to change a federal system. There has not been a wholly Canadian equivalent to the *Engineers* case or an *NLRB v. Jones*. The decisions with the most measurable impact on Canadian federalism have come from the Judicial Committee of the Privy Council (JCPC), and even there the relative importance of judicial interpretation has been disputed. There has been no period when the Supreme Court's vision of federalism has been in serious conflict with the vision of the political branches of the Canadian federal system.

During its tenure as Canada's final court, the JCPC generally favoured the provinces and had a profound effect on the balance of Canadian federalism as a result. However, in the period since, the work of the Canadian court has had far less apparent or overt impact on the powers of either level of government. Nevertheless, political scientists want to know what effect the court has on the balance of powers between the federal and provincial governments. The conventional belief is that the court, over the long term, has been relatively even-handed.[2] Even those who contend that recent jurisprudence has tilted somewhat to the favour of the federal government acknowledge that the court has been measured in its style. John Saywell, for example, writes that, "during the last two decades of the [twentieth] century, the Supreme Court had continued on its course of rebalancing the structure of the federation by expanding the field of activity of the federal government without narrowing the traditional enclaves of provincial power."[3] Not only is the net effect of the Supreme Court's intervention in Canadian federalism balanced, but also most decisions seem to be balanced within themselves. Rarely are members of the court identifiable as enthusiastic supporters of a "states' rights" style of provincialism or an excessively centralist position. The Supreme Court's decision in the *Reference Re: Secession of Quebec,* while

had all the potential for political
read as a
e impor-
preted all
ommerce
ce, order,
n to the
r offered
terpreted

. The Su-
ncements
ences for
he court's
ctrine, not

wers juris-
. As in the
o evaluate
important
eace, order,
commerce
provincial
categories,
udicial doc-
ie to shape
ine has also
cooperative
leralism oc-
ourt has not
been called
agreements
ctrine in this

Reference Re: Anti-Inflation Act

The *Anti-Inflation* reference of 1976 is not chosen as the starting point for the clarity of its vision of federalism. Unlike the *Tasmanian Dam* case in

is the net effect of the Supreme Court's intervention in Canadian federalism balanced, but also most decisions seem to be balanced within themselves. Rarely are members of the court identifiable as enthusiastic supporters of a "states' rights" style of provincialism or an excessively centralist position. The Supreme Court's decision in the *Reference Re: Secession of Quebec*, while not about the division of powers per se, had all the potential for political disaster. The reasoning of the court was sufficiently balanced to be read as a victory by both Quebec sovereigntists and federalists. Perhaps more importantly, no portion of Canada's federal constitution has been interpreted all out of recognition, as one could legitimately contend the US commerce clause or the Australian external affairs power have. Even the peace, order, and good government clause of section 91, which in comparison to the aforementioned is probably the most potentially expansive power offered to any level of government in the three federations, has been interpreted with continued caution.

The devil is in the details of Canadian federalism jurisprudence. The Supreme Court's decisions on federalism are not dramatic pronouncements on the nature of the federation, imbued with ideological preferences for centralized or decentralized political control. What animates the court's decisions and divisions are much finer points of distinction in doctrine, not global theories of federalism.

This chapter surveys developments in Canadian division-of-powers jurisprudence, from the *Anti-Inflation* reference of 1976 to the present. As in the previous two chapters, doctrine is the primary variable used to evaluate trends in the jurisprudence of the court. Doctrine has been most important in the interpretation of the federal power to make laws for the peace, order, and good government (POGG) of the nation and the trade and commerce power. In addition, it has been critical in balancing the parallel provincial category of property and civil rights. These three jurisdictional categories, primarily due to their generality, have been the source of most judicial doctrine on federalism, and decisions about these powers continue to shape the kind of federalism that Canadians experience. Judicial doctrine has also been developed in recent years to clarify the legal position of cooperative federalism. Much of the day-to-day operation of Canadian federalism occurs regardless of the niceties of the division of powers. The court has not refrained from supervising this activity, largely because it has been called upon to patrol the terms of some of the extra-constitutional agreements hammered out between governments. The chapter reviews doctrine in this area as well.

Reference Re: Anti-Inflation Act

The *Anti-Inflation* reference of 1976 is not chosen as the starting point for the clarity of its vision of federalism. Unlike the *Tasmanian Dam* case in

5
The Canadian Supreme Court: Balanced Federalism

Low-Impact Judicial Review?

The Canadian Supreme Court has the shortest history as a court of final resort among the three surveyed here. While the court has practised the task of judicial review for more than 100 years, 2005 marks only the fifty-sixth year that the court had the final word in matters of Canadian law.[1] As a result, the court has had less of an opportunity than its counterparts to put its defining mark on the way that federalism is understood and practised. In addition, the Supreme Court has made no decisions that have dramatically demonstrated the capacity of judicial review to change a federal system. There has not been a wholly Canadian equivalent to the *Engineers* case or an *NLRB v. Jones*. The decisions with the most measurable impact on Canadian federalism have come from the Judicial Committee of the Privy Council (JCPC), and even there the relative importance of judicial interpretation has been disputed. There has been no period when the Supreme Court's vision of federalism has been in serious conflict with the vision of the political branches of the Canadian federal system.

During its tenure as Canada's final court, the JCPC generally favoured the provinces and had a profound effect on the balance of Canadian federalism as a result. However, in the period since, the work of the Canadian court has had far less apparent or overt impact on the powers of either level of government. Nevertheless, political scientists want to know what effect the court has on the balance of powers between the federal and provincial governments. The conventional belief is that the court, over the long term, has been relatively even-handed.[2] Even those who contend that recent jurisprudence has tilted somewhat to the favour of the federal government acknowledge that the court has been measured in its style. John Saywell, for example, writes that, "during the last two decades of the [twentieth] century, the Supreme Court had continued on its course of rebalancing the structure of the federation by expanding the field of activity of the federal government without narrowing the traditional enclaves of provincial power."[3] Not only

Australia, or the *Garcia* decision in the United States, the contemporary era in Canada begins with a less than bold statement on the division of powers and the place of the court in its adjudication. Not that the court lacked the opportunity for such a statement. With the *Anti-Inflation* case, the court had to deal with some of the most political circumstances that it had faced since 1949 and with the most ambivalently decided clause in the constitution, the federal government's power over POGG. The court's inability to live up to expectations suggests that the case might be better labelled the "anti-climax" reference. Only in that sense does it serve as a landmark for the present era. The internal balance on the court and the subtle distinctions between the contending views of POGG among its members did not make for compelling jurisprudence. Nevertheless, the style of the judgment has been replicated many times over in the nearly thirty years that have passed since it was handed down.

The *Anti-Inflation Act,* passed by the federal Parliament in 1976, provided for the control of prices and wages in some sectors of the economy in response to the oil crisis and escalating inflation. With a number of interest groups in business and labour clamouring to challenge the legislation, the Liberal government led by Prime Minister Pierre Trudeau decided to refer the act to the Supreme Court to test its constitutionality.

In its submissions to the court, the federal government argued that jurisdiction for such an exercise of federal authority existed under POGG because inflation was a matter of national concern and had attained the status of a crisis or emergency. The members of the court responded in a decidedly mixed manner. However, out of the welter of opinions, Chief Justice Laskin managed to cobble together a majority to uphold the act. The victory was by no means complete. Laskin wrote an opinion for himself and three others allowing both the national concern and emergency arguments of the federal government. The Laskin-led four were joined by three who approved the act's constitutionality, but only on the basis of the emergency justification. The final pair, led by Justice Beetz, dissented, accepting neither justification for the act.[4] By a margin of seven to two, the court accepted federal jurisdiction, but by five to four it rejected the most centralist route, favoured by the chief justice, that treated inflation as a matter of national concern.

Part of the reluctance of the court to ever accept a national concern argument in support of POGG jurisdiction had always been the potential limitlessness of such reasoning. If matters were to be routinely promoted to the status of national concern, there would seem to be bountiful incentives for an expansionist central government to define whatever fields it wanted to involve itself in as fitting that description. The emergency doctrine was always a more risk-averse strategy for the judicial umpires of federalism to take. While the kinds of circumstances that constituted an emergency certainly waxed and waned, the scope of POGG was always confined by some logic of emergency. By contrast, any effort to narrow the scope of national concern seemed to require much more explicit limits. In that sense, national concern is a highly doctrinally dependent construct. The limits must be articulated by the courts for them to become real and effective. Various attempts have been made in the constitutional literature to provide a sound basis for the use of the national concern branch. The task has been particularly favoured by those enamoured of POGG's possibilities but not willing to expand it as generously as someone like Laskin might have.

W.R. Lederman, in his article "Unity and Diversity in Canadian Federalism," argued that the structure of the *BNA Act* effectively put the enumerated powers in competition with one another. Unlike the American and Australian constitutions, the two-list system used in the Canadian constitution created an immediate tension between the lists. With some exceptions, for every federal grant of power, there is a provincial grant that might be characterized in such a way as to justify provincial control over a roughly similar matter. This logic is especially true of the general powers left to both levels of government. In Lederman's view, POGG was neither a mere appendage nor the source of all federal power, with the twenty-nine subject matters of section 91 being mere illustrations. The federal general power, he argued, had to be seen as on par with the provincial general power. The main difference between the two was simply that the provincial general power was for matters of a local nature, and the federal general power was for matters of a national nature. He asserted that, in order for excursions of federal power to be justified under the national general power, they had to be demonstrated, as a matter of evidence, to be (1) "something that necessarily requires country-wide regulation at the national level" and to have (2) "an identity and unity that is quite limited and particular in its extent."[5]

Looking for examples, Lederman suggested that aviation was an ideal candidate for inclusion under the national power. The Fathers of Confederation obviously did not conceive of aviation as a potential field of government regulation, and as such it should fall to one of the two residual categories. But rather than hand aviation to the federal government by dint of its newness or because all residual subject matters should fall to the federal government, as the most expansive interpretations of POGG would suggest, the assignment can be made on a more qualified basis. Lederman argued that, as a subject, aviation belonged to the federal category as it appeared to require country-wide regulation and was sufficiently different from other modes of transportation to have the necessary unity of purpose and demonstrable limitations on its scope required to keep expansion under POGG discrete.

Lederman actually represented one of the unions challenging the wage controls in the *Anti-Inflation Act.* As counsel, he presented this narrow view of national dimensions to the court. He argued that, absent emergencies, the POGG clause supports federal legislation only in discrete, narrowly defined subject matters that clearly fall outside provincial jurisdiction.[6] The Laskin faction did not accept such limits on national concern. However, Justice Beetz was writing for a majority of the court on the question of national concern.

Beetz, long known to harbour strong views on the issue, took this case as an opportunity to state definitively his theory of federalism. He presented the national concern and emergency branches as the respective "normal" and "abnormal" branches of the POGG power. Under the normal, national concern branch, he wrote, the dominating factor to consider has to be the newness and indivisible distinctiveness of the subject matter. Otherwise, he argued, the door is open to unlimited expansion of federal jurisdiction under such ubiquitous headings as inflation or the environment.[7] In order to limit the reach of national concern, Beetz sought to delegitimize the use under POGG of broad categories that tend to engulf provincial powers. His means to this end was to require unity and coherence in subject matters. These traits appeared to be difficult to acquire and would hopefully be uncommon.

In a detailed analysis of the *Anti-Inflation* case, Peter Russell suggests that Laskin and Beetz were not so far apart in their interpretations of POGG as might first appear. Where they did differ was a matter of some import, though. The chief justice tried to rule out an interpretation of POGG that required either the extreme of national emergency or national concern. In Russell's phrase, Laskin "tries to weave a single piece of cloth out of all the strands to be found in previous decisions."[8] By recognizing both a national concern and an emergency branch for POGG, Beetz was similarly unwilling to build doctrine entirely anew. However, he favoured a more limited form of national concern than the version preferred by Laskin. Ultimately, what divided them was what qualified as a matter of national concern. Laskin took a relaxed and consequently expansive view. Beetz was more demanding, particularly if provincial jurisdiction appeared to be threatened. In the end, the *Anti-Inflation* case left a constrained view of what qualified under the national concern branch, despite the fact that it favoured the federal government's intervention to control inflation.

It is plain that the court did not satisfy centralist hopefuls, although Laskin did try. What the court did do was begin a new tradition of essentially ambivalent federalism jurisprudence. The anti-climax of the *Anti-Inflation* decision was enough to convince Russell that judicial review had limited importance to the politics of Canadian federalism. By taking the middle ground, the court had done nothing more than endorse the model of Canadian federalism already at work. Rather than direct the shape of Canadian federalism as the Privy Council's law lords had attempted, judicial review now seemed to mirror the federalism status quo. The decision, Russell argued, reflected the balance of political power in the federation fairly accurately. His implicit criticism was that although the court acted in an essentially political manner by reflecting this balance, the end product, the judicial decision, was still legalistic and framed in the formal language of federalism. According to Russell, this contrived formalism contributed to the waning relevance of the court. While intergovernmental relations would continue partly to play itself out through the law, the provinces and the federal government had already changed the real rules of the game.[9] This was to be the era of cooperative federalism. Negotiation was to have pride of place over legal wrangling.[10] In the nearly thirty years since the case, the preference for cooperative over litigated federalism has prevailed.

In contrast to the increasingly dynamic field of intergovernmental relations, the court after *Anti-Inflation* looked as though it could contribute only an uncreative and confined legalism to the dialogue of Canadian federalism. Perhaps this was the only contribution that fit its lack of electoral legitimacy and accountability. In order to give clearer policy reasons for their decision, Russell argued, the court's majority would have needed to be much more explicitly in favour of the federal government. The only policy-based reasoning he saw was that of Justice Beetz, who favoured the provinces. Russell noted with some irony that, "for policy reasons, a jurisprudential style which would make policy reasons more transparent is rejected. As a result, Canadians cannot expect judicial reasoning to add very much to the country's stock of constitutional wisdom."[11] By its unwillingness to make bold constitutional pronouncements (or refrain from dispensing constitutional wisdom), the court signalled that the tenor of Canadian federalism would have to be set by someone else.

Has the court's approach changed since then? Or have the judges continued to mask judicial power and thus constrain their influence in the development of Canadian federalism? Developments in POGG jurisprudence suggest that the court has continued to avoid broad pronouncements about federal power but in the search for such avoidance may have created an entirely different monster. To demonstrate, the chapter turns to more recent developments in federalism jurisprudence.

Provincial Inability and POGG

Anti-Inflation seemed to indicate judicial ambivalence about the interpretation of POGG. Unlike older decisions that betrayed more overt preferences for either the centralist or the provincialist interpretation of POGG, *Anti-Inflation* could equally be read as an endorsement of POGG as a general power or as a restricted power. Since *Anti-Inflation,* the court has continued to seek limits on the national concern branch of the power. Emergency, however, has almost disappeared from the vocabulary of POGG decisions. The most relevant doctrinal stream today is the concept of provincial inability.[12]

Provincial inability is the product of a generation of JCPC naysayers such as Lederman who hoped to place national concern on a more solid footing in order that the post-1949 system of judicial review would look more favourably upon POGG as a justification for federal power. To make national concern a more palatable concept, a limited and prudent version had to be available to the court. If national concern could be found to exist in discrete categories, the court would be more likely to endorse it as a justification. Limits would also help national concern to avoid descending the slippery slope of a general power interpretation of POGG. Centralist thinkers came to realize that, in order to achieve centralization through POGG, it was critical to define limits on the scope of the power, or it might never be used to justify federal government activity. Otherwise, POGG always risked being a victim of its own potential. While Lederman was busy putting such an argument before the Supreme Court in *Anti-Inflation,* Dale Gibson formulated a complementary theory of national concern with similar limits on the scope of federal power to ensure its palatability. In an article entitled "Measuring National Dimensions,"[13] Gibson proposed a test of provincial inability as a principled way to concede jurisdiction to the federal government without establishing a broad or open-ended grant of power. The test basically ensured that jurisdiction could be claimed under the national concern doctrine only after all provincial capabilities had first been exhausted. He argued that this would give a limited, residual scope to POGG.

For Gibson, *"a matter has a national dimension to the extent only that it is beyond the power of the provinces to deal with it."*[14] "Power" appears to be understood ambiguously as a measure both of jurisdiction and of actual capacity. Provincial inability is first determined by reference to the enumerated powers of the provinces. If the provinces were not accorded jurisdiction by the constitution, then provincial inability exists.[15] This is something of a tautology; the provinces cannot do what they cannot do. But making the point confirmed Gibson's characterization of POGG as a residual power, even in those instances where a national dimension exists. In the secondary and more important sense, the dimensions of the problem at hand are to be considered. The question becomes whether a province is actually able to control all the necessary elements of a problem or has the capacity to regulate it effectively.

As an example of the phenomena that he was concerned with, Gibson considered the capacity of a province to deal with a pestilence. Airborne diseases do not respect provincial boundaries, so they cannot legitimately be expected to be contained by just one province, and a national need or concern is created. Less catastrophic examples can also be imagined, the important characteristic being that some trait prevents a single province from coping effectively with the problem on its own terms. National concern ensures that the potential harm to all provinces, which may ensue when one province does not act, or is unable to cope with the scale of a threat, is avoided. In order to maintain a narrow view of POGG, Gibson argued that the federal jurisdiction that exists as a result of this provincial inability must be limited solely to those matters that are beyond provincial competence. Inability, he argued, is not an invitation to plenary federal jurisdiction. Rather, it is an attempt to take advantage of federal competence to deal with issues that overlap provincial boundaries and to "fill the gap in provincial powers."[16]

Anti-Inflation actually provided fertile soil for germinating this concept and allowed provincial inability to emerge quickly as the prevailing orthodoxy on national dimensions. A year after the reference, in the first edition of his now standard text on Canadian constitutional law, Peter Hogg approvingly cited Gibson on the point.[17] Hogg's formulation of provincial inability, however, omitted reference to jurisdiction and focused exclusively on the lack of capacity of a province, or even a few provinces, to accomplish some ends or cope with threats. Hogg wrote that, when uniformity of policy or standards is necessary, and not simply just desirable, federal jurisdiction should be granted. In a passage that came to play a clear role in subsequent judicial reasoning, Hogg described national concern: "The most important element of national dimension or national concern is a need for one national law which cannot realistically be satisfied by cooperative provincial action because the failure of one province to co-operate would carry with it grave consequences for the residents of other provinces. A subject-matter of legislation which has this characteristic has the necessary national dimension of concern to justify invocation of the p.o.g.g. power."[18]

The Supreme Court endorsed Hogg's interpretation shortly thereafter. In three decisions following the *Anti-Inflation* reference, the court legitimated the concept of provincial inability as a standard for measuring national dimensions or concern. In the first of these cases, *Labatt Breweries of Canada v. A.-G. Canada,*[19] the court considered the constitutionality of federal legislation regulating the production and labelling of malt liquors and beer. Labatt Breweries, in a whimsical attempt at marketing semantics, produced and bottled a beer with 4 percent alcohol and labelled it "special lite." However, the federal *Food and Drug Act* only permitted beer with 2.5 percent alcohol or less to be labelled "light." Altering the spelling to do an end-run around the regulation was looked upon unfavourably by federal authorities. Equally unhappy with being hauled to court for replacing two consonants with a vowel, Labatt challenged the legislation regulating alcohol levels as *ultra vires* the federal Parliament. Justice Estey, writing for the majority, found in Labatt's favour and rejected the idea that federal regulation of the brewing and labelling of light beer was a matter of national concern, as such regulation did not appear to transcend the legislative abilities of the provinces.[20]

His finding was based in part on Hogg's reasoning and conformed to Gibson's narrow vision of POGG, which maintains provincial jurisdiction where it is clear that the provinces have the capacity to be effective.

Three years later, in *Schneider v. The Queen,* the court again had an opportunity to consider provincial inability as a test of national concern.[21] At issue in this case was whether British Columbia's *Heroin Treatment Act,* which provided for a mandatory six-month treatment program for heroin abusers, was *intra vires* the legislature of the province. Schneider, wishing to avoid the mandated treatment, challenged the legislation, arguing that the control of narcotic drugs and their users was the responsibility of the federal government.[22] While agreeing that traffic in drugs was a national matter, the court failed to find a national dimension to the problem of heroin dependency. Instead, it found the treatment of abusers to be an aspect manageable under the health jurisdiction of each province. The case was a critical step in the development of the provincial inability doctrine. In *Schneider,* the court showed that it was willing to look at older cases through the lens of provincial inability. Gibson admitted in 1976 that his formulation of provincial inability could not be found explicitly in the case law. However, he did believe that the concept conformed to much of the court's jurisprudence.[23] *Schneider* confirmed this belief. In applying the test, the court basically reinterpreted several important national concern cases, such as *Re: Regulation and Control of Aeronautics* (1932), *Canada Temperance Federation* (1946), *Johannesson* (1952), and *Munro* (1966). While none of these decisions contained any explicit reference to the term or concept of provincial inability, the court in Schneider implied that they conformed to such a model of thinking about national dimensions.

The final case of the trio was *R. v. Wetmore.* Again at issue was the *Food and Drug Act.* The federal government initiated a prosecution against pharmacist Steven Kripps for violations of the act related to selling contaminated or adulterated drugs. Kripps countered that the sections of the act in question were criminal law, and thus the provinces were responsible for the prosecution of offences under them. County Court Judge Wetmore agreed, and his decision was appealed by the federal government. The Supreme Court reversed the initial finding and allowed the federal prosecution of Kripps to proceed. However, in dissent, Justice Dickson rejected federal involvement as there appeared to be nothing in the offence at hand that necessitated it. He failed to see anything that went "beyond local or provincial interest and must from its intrinsic nature be the concern of the dominion as a whole."[24] For Dickson, there was in effect no provincial inability, and thus federal involvement appeared to be unnecessary. In this case, like the two before it, the provincial inability test clearly stood as an impediment to central government expansion under POGG. Further refinements of the test, however, served to diminish this potential.[25]

The real tests of provincial inability as a doctrine have only come in the past twenty years. The most important initial case was *Crown Zellerbach* in 1988. There the court took the opportunity to define provincial inability in a much more precise manner than it had in the three previous cases, which admittedly made much more oblique reference to the concept. While the decisions above legitimated the spirit of provincial inability, the court never endorsed the term specifically. It referred only to conceptual elements of the test as propounded by Gibson or Hogg, despite the clarity that it seemed to bring to thinking about national concern. Such ambiguity disappeared in *Crown Zellerbach*.

The case provided ideal circumstances for a nuanced application of the test. Crown Zellerbach, a major lumber producer with logging and milling operations in British Columbia, had been charged with dumping wood waste into the sea without a permit, in violation of the provisions of the federal *Ocean Dumping Control Act*. The company challenged the legislation as *ultra vires* the federal Parliament, arguing specifically that waste not shown to have a pollutant effect on extra-provincial waters could not be regulated by the federal government.[26] In response, the court deemed that Parliament's power over fisheries and the sea coast did not give it jurisdiction in these circumstances. However, the majority did find that the legislation, as a measure to control marine pollution, could still be justified on the basis of POGG as a matter of national concern. In doing so, the majority attempted to provide a clear and systematic test of what qualifies as an object of national concern.

Justice Le Dain's majority opinion explicitly referred to provincial inability for the first time in judicial text. Le Dain sought to develop a consistent set of criteria for the evaluation of claims made under the national concern branch of POGG. Drawing from jurisprudence that he believed to be "firmly established," he articulated a four-step test of federal jurisdiction, the last step of which entailed a determination of provincial inability. In short, the test required (1) that matters of national concern be divorced from matters of national emergency, the latter being distinguishable chiefly by their temporary nature; (2) that they be new or, if old, be matters of a local or private nature that have become ones of national concern; (3) that they have a singleness, distinctiveness, and indivisibility, a requirement necessary to avoid national matters being created out of aggregates of provincial powers, and does not upset the basic balance inherent in the distribution of legislative powers; and (4) that singleness and distinctiveness be tested by an examination of provincial inability or the "effect on extraprovincial interests of a provincial failure to deal effectively with the control or regulation of the intraprovincial aspects of the matter."[27] In construing the test the way he did, Le Dain effected nothing less than a complete alteration of provincial inability from its original character as a limit on national concern.

Le Dain's formulation used provincial inability to determine singleness and indivisibility. Since this differed from the approach of the court in earlier decisions, Le Dain offered reasons for his modification. He made direct reference to Dale Gibson's argument that a subject matter attains national dimensions under POGG only in the parts that the provinces cannot address. Le Dain believed that this "appears to contemplate a concurrent or overlapping federal jurisdiction,"[28] as opposed to the "classical federal" notion of single ownership of fields.[29] He was unwilling to venture into the overlapping jurisdictions that flow from such a test, so he rejected Gibson's positioning of it and put provincial inability to the task of testing singleness and indivisibility, thereby helping to keep federal divisions clear. Le Dain drew on Hogg to affirm this change. The provincial inability test in Hogg's formulation, he wrote, "is adopted simply as a reason for finding that a particular matter is one of national concern falling within the peace, order and good government power."[30] This fit more readily with Le Dain's desire to test for singleness. The provincial inability test's utility, he wrote, is not in "providing a rationale for the general notion, hitherto rejected in the cases, that there must be a plenary jurisdiction in one order of government." Rather, it is the ability of the concept to aid in the determination of "whether a matter has the requisite singleness or indivisibility from a functional as well as a conceptual point of view."[31] Le Dain held up the spectre of a plenary federal power, the long-feared tool of rampant centralization, as a realistic possibility in order to justify removing provincial inability as a precondition of national concern. His preoccupation with singleness revealed a preference for a different, more classical form of national concern.

Understanding Le Dain's repositioning of provincial inability is crucial to appreciating the potential effect of an evolving doctrine of national concern. In its academic, pre-Supreme Court formulation, provincial inability was proffered as a means to determine national concern without unduly infringing upon the jurisdiction and autonomy of the provinces. Indeed, in the first few cases in which the court loosely applied the idea, that is how it was used. In *Labatt, Schneider,* and *Wetmore,* when the court failed to see a need for federal involvement or could not find the existence of any genuine inability on the part of the provinces, national concern was excluded as a justification. However, if provincial inability is used at a later stage in the analysis, as it is by Le Dain, it loses some of its limiting effect. In Le Dain's version, provincial inability is a last chance to deny the existence of national concern rather than a means of proving the possibility of a national concern. Whether the new and improved provincial inability would still serve as a check on national expansion in this role is revealed in the application of the test.

Armed with his revised concept of national concern and provincial inability, Le Dain went to work on the matters at hand in *Crown Zellerbach.*

With provincial inability no longer a question of capacity and more a test of singleness, the initial determination of "national concern" became a less restrictive process. National concern could be claimed on grounds such as "extraprovincial" effects or the existence of an international dimension, both of which Le Dain advanced as reasons for national concern in *Crown Zellerbach.*[32] The scope of federal power seemed likely to increase under such reasoning. Justice La Forest, writing in dissent, recognized this possibility. "As I see it, the potential breadth of federal power to control pollution by use of its general power is so great that ... the constitutional challenge in the end may be the development of judicial strategies to confine its ambit."[33] In *Crown Zellerbach,* little effort was devoted to examining the existence of national concern – it was almost assumed to exist without debate given the extra-provincial or international elements involved. The difficult question, as Le Dain saw it, was not the *prima facie* existence of national concern but whether pollution in marine waters, including provincial marine waters, could be considered a single, indivisible matter. He wrote that, given the evidence before the court, the difficulty of finding the terminus of provincial marine waters and the beginning of federal marine waters "creates an unacceptable degree of uncertainty for the application of regulatory and penal provisions."[34] Thus, provincial inability existed, and federal jurisdiction under POGG was justified.

In dissent, Justice La Forest dismissed this kind of broad reasoning by taking a more detailed approach to the facts of the case. Crown Zellerbach was charged with dumping wood waste, not chemicals or by-products, an activity that La Forest believed could not strictly be defined as pollution. If the material was toxic or dangerous, the matter would be resolved as extra-provincial marine pollution, which was already the domain of the federal government. La Forest used provincial inability in the "effect on extra-provincial interests" form. Since he could not perceive an effect in the dumping of benign material, he found no need for national concern, despite the extra-provincial or international elements that might have been involved.

Provincial inability did not enter La Forest's test of singleness and distinctiveness. La Forest, like Le Dain, shared Beetz's *Anti-Inflation* concern that "one can effectively invent new heads of federal power under the national dimensions doctrine, thereby incidentally removing them from provincial jurisdiction."[35] He found that Le Dain's formulation of provincial inability did not offer a clear enough approach to avoid this problem. Instead, it actually offered the opportunity to take a number of areas of jurisdiction and consider them collectively as single and indivisible without first asking if such an exercise was at all necessary. La Forest situated this matter in the historical struggle over POGG much better than Le Dain by noting that the attempts to accumulate jurisdiction through broad general headings are "fighting on another plane the war that was lost on the economic plane in the Canadian new deal cases."[36] Just as Bennett was denied broad power to deal with the crisis of the Depression, new crises do not necessarily justify the granting of broad powers. By applying provincial inability the way he did, Le Dain weakened its initial, necessity-based, narrowing effect and opened doors for national concern.

Provincial Inability Post-*Crown Zellerbach*

Although the POGG clause is infrequently considered by the court, concepts that emerge from POGG cases can have an influence on other federalism decisions. The doctrinal effect of provincial inability is a good example of this phenomenon. The concepts of national concern and provincial inability did not arise again in the Supreme Court until four years after *Crown Zellerbach,* in *Friends of the Oldman River Society v. Canada.*[37]

The society sought to halt the development of a dam on the Oldman River in southern Alberta. It challenged the Alberta government's authority to build the dam without first subjecting the project to a federal environmental review as per the federal *Environmental Assessment and Review Process Guidelines Order* since some areas of federal jurisdiction such as Indian lands and fisheries were potentially affected. While the case was largely occupied with issues other than POGG, the court did allude to the provincial inability test in its reasoning. The Alberta government, wishing not to incur further delays, challenged the validity of the federal legislation conferring authority for the review. Part of that challenge was to suggest that federal review would upset the balance of federal/provincial jurisdiction over the environment. The court affirmed the federal government's legitimate place in environmental assessment. It agreed with the society, but it did not compel the federal government to undertake an actual assessment in this instance.

Justice La Forest wrote the majority decision for the court. He had argued in the dissent in *Crown Zellerbach* that "pollution" and "the marine environment" did not have the requisite distinctiveness to qualify as subject matters of national concern. Here he had the opportunity to readdress his views on the environment as a subject matter of federalism. In large part, La Forest picked up where he left off in *Crown Zellerbach,* pursuing a version of provincial inability that would be more to Dale Gibson's liking than to Justice Le Dain's. Given that jurisdiction over the environment is not a power specifically assigned to either level of government, La Forest affirmed that both levels of government had to accept a degree of responsibility for ensuring that environmental concerns are taken into account in the exercise of their respective jurisdictional activities.[38] In La Forest's mind, the federal government must be responsible for reviewing projects that fall under or affect federal jurisdiction and the provinces likewise. He denied a plenary jurisdiction over the environment to either level of government, preferring that both levels intervene on the basis of their capacity or incapacity.

At the same time, La Forest recognized that environmental assessments, if they are to be at all useful, must be comprehensive and not be restricted by the affected heads of federal or provincial jurisdiction. Where jurisdiction permits an assessment, it must be as comprehensive as possible. While alert to the possibility of a Trojan Horse in this line of reasoning, La Forest was confident that such a threat would prove negligible. Environmental impact assessments, he suggested, are just that, assessments, and they are strictly decision-making adjuncts. Since whatever policy might result from a review was still made by the government that had jurisdiction, any "unbalancing" effect would be diminished.[39]

Ontario Hydro v. Ontario,[40] a decision handed down by the Supreme Court in the fall of 1993, is the first post-*Zellerbach* test of national concern and provincial inability. The appeal dealt with the applicability of federal labour regulation to employees in Ontario Hydro's nuclear power plants. Labour relations as a general category, like the environment, are not assigned to the federal or provincial governments. However, most labour matters have fallen under the provincial heading of property and civil rights, the exception being labour relations in federal agencies and in industries of enumerated federal jurisdiction, such as fisheries or shipping and navigation.[41] Also important to the appeal was the accepted understanding that works and undertakings for the production of atomic energy are considered to be for the general advantage of Canada and therefore fall under the declaratory power of the federal Parliament.[42] Atomic energy has also been specifically confirmed as one of the few subject matters that falls under the national concern branch of POGG.[43]

Whether federal jurisdiction over atomic energy also included labour relations at an atomic energy plant was the question before the court. A prospective union for the employees of Ontario Hydro who worked in nuclear plants sought certification under provincial law from the Ontario Labour Relations Board. The board denied certification, and the union challenged the board's decision. Much of the court's ruling hinged on issues surrounding the declaratory power of Parliament. However, for good measure, the court tested POGG jurisdiction as well. The POGG argument was presented by the attorney general of Canada as a fall back in the event that the court did not extend the declaratory power to include labour relations. The majority of the court, led again by La Forest, agreed that Parliament was responsible for atomic energy on the grounds of the declaratory and POGG powers and that this responsibility required jurisdiction over all labour relations at the atomic energy plant. Chief Justice Lamer concurred but limited federal jurisdiction to those workers specifically concerned with the production of nuclear or atomic energy and excluded those workers responsible for the transformation or transmission of the energy as electricity. In dissent, Justice Iacobucci argued that control over labour was not essential to the federal government exercising its rightful role over atomic energy and that federal and provincial regulation could coexist.

The court was forced to consider directly the expanded national concern criteria enunciated by Le Dain in *Crown Zellerbach*. All three opinions noted the "onerous threshold" that the court had created for a matter to qualify as one of national concern. However, the real effects of the test can be seen in the way that the judges responded to this purportedly difficult set of criteria. Of particular interest is how they determined national concern at the outset and where and how provincial inability entered their analysis.

In the determination of national concern, the opinions did not differ greatly. La Forest's majority followed Le Dain's example in *Crown Zellerbach* by advancing little evidence to demonstrate that the matter was *prima facie* of national concern. The fact that atomic energy has international and extra-provincial characteristics was deemed reason enough to justify the existence of a national concern. Extra-provincial or international characteristics had effectively replaced provincial inability as the means to determine that a potential national concern exists. The Iacobucci dissent did not stray far on this point. In fact, Iacobucci noted that the existence of a general POGG jurisdiction in the field of atomic energy was an undisputed point – the issue was simply whether the extension of that jurisdiction to include labour relations could be justified. Thus, Iacobucci actually advanced no argument to justify national concern and limited his discussion to the scope of Parliament's jurisdiction.

Provincial inability entered the analysis only as a determinant of the singleness and distinctiveness required by *Crown Zellerbach*. La Forest simply stated that power over labour relations was necessary for the proper regulation of the subject matter. He remarked that he was "at a loss to see how one can have exclusive power to regulate, operate and manage a work without having exclusive power to regulate the labour relations between management and the employees engaged in that enterprise."[44] La Forest offered further evidence of this necessity through an expanded concept of security, noting that "safety and security are as much in jeopardy from the manner in which employees do their work as in the manner in which a facility is constructed."[45] In his concurring opinion, Chief Justice Lamer agreed and amplified the need for labour regulation as part of the general authority over atomic energy. However, Lamer struck a note of reserve by separating the workers specifically engaged in the production of atomic energy from those responsible for other functions in the nuclear plant. With this distinction, he narrowed the subject matter through the distinctiveness criterion. The workers engaged directly in energy production were seen as sufficiently distinct to justify their exclusion from provincial labour legislation. La Forest, like Le Dain in *Crown Zellerbach,* did not see a clear enough distinction and, like Le Dain, gave the benefit of the doubt, as well as the expanded jurisdiction, to the federal government. Whether it was truly necessary for labour relations to be included in the regulation of atomic energy became the provincial inability issue.

This latter point was well demonstrated by the dissent. Iacobucci did not deny jurisdiction over atomic energy to the federal government, but he did deny that control over labour relations was part of that jurisdiction. Using the singleness test of *Crown Zellerbach,* he was unable to find that labour relations were part of the single, distinctive problem of atomic energy and therefore subject to Parliament's control. For Iacobucci, "to allow Parliament to control labour relations at these facilities where such regulation is not integral ... [to the regulation of atomic energy] would not be reconcilable with the distribution of legislative powers."[46] The doctrine did act as a limit in this sense, at least as far as it limited the scope of federal power. When it determined national concern, the court never considered what the province was unable to do jurisdictionally or practically or the potential harm that could come from provincial inaction on this issue. Why would the province of Ontario be unable to deal with the local aspects of atomic energy generation? For Iacobucci, it was not clear that it could not, so he proposed that the federal government be excluded from intervening.

In the manner in which it was used by Iacobucci, provincial inability lived up to the limiting role that Gibson first proposed for it and ensured that federal jurisdiction extends only to those matters that are proven cases of inability. However, even if Iacobucci had written for the majority, he was defending provincial authority on the margins. The court was not using provincial inability to determine if a subject matter qualified as one of national concern; instead, it was using the test to determine which provincial powers the existence of a national concern allowed Parliament to plunder. Conceding greater power to the federal government up front through national concern and then scaling it back through the singleness test substantially weakens the capacity of provincial inability to control central government expansion.

It is perhaps for this reason that, in the aftermath of *Ontario Hydro,* the Supreme Court has seemingly turned away from POGG justifications for federal jurisdiction. In the most recent attempts to maintain federal regulatory power under POGG, the court has preferred to accept the federal government's power over the criminal law as an alternative justification. Little has changed in the way that the court approaches the provincial inability test, but, by ignoring POGG justifications entirely, the court has implicitly expressed some reservation about working under the national concern heading – provincial inability or not.

In *RJR-MacDonald v. Canada (A.G.)*,[47] a major multinational tobacco company challenged strict federal regulations that almost entirely prohibited the advertising of tobacco products. RJR-MacDonald argued first that the legislation was *ultra vires* the federal Parliament and second that, even if it was within federal jurisdiction, the legislation offended section 2(b) of the Charter, the right to freedom of expression. The court agreed with the challenge and repealed the tobacco advertising regulations. Popular and academic attention has thus far focused on the expansive scope that the court gave to the freedom of expression and the section 1 "reasonable limits" analysis in Justice McLachlin's ruling.[48] The federalism issues raised by the case are generally overlooked. And they are easy to overlook. The court dispensed with a POGG analysis almost entirely by subsuming the issue under the much less controversial federal criminal law power.

The Quebec Court of Appeal, whose decision was disputed, demonstrated the difficulties that Le Dain's concept of provincial inability poses for POGG analysis. Despite undertaking an extensive overview of the provincial inability test's history, the Quebec court failed to implement the test in a manner true to the Le Dain doctrine. By looking at the history of the concept in greater detail, the court imported elements of Gibson's provincial inability into Le Dain's test. The result was chaotic rather than refining. However, the evident confusion of the court demonstrated some of the subtle but important alterations that the test has undergone.

Writing the decision for the lower court, Justice Le Bel (who has since been appointed to the Supreme Court) suggested that tobacco advertising was a matter of national concern based on "the nature of the activity aimed at."[49] Specifically, Le Bel found "this problem has so developed that ... the inaction of one province and its practical inability to regulate certain forms of interprovincial or especially international advertising may seriously impede, if not render impossible the realization of the objective sought."[50] The problem was one of national concern not because of extra-provincial aspects specifically but because the provinces appeared to be unable to grapple with the reach of the issue.

Thus, Le Bel determined national concern on the basis of provincial inability. He also used the test to determine whether the matter had the requisite singleness or indivisibility as required by Le Dain.[51] In this instance, tobacco advertising was considered a sufficiently distinct problem. In so doing, the Quebec court put provincial inability to two uses, thereby implying that a dual function is consistent with the interpretation of the concept. Given the court's careful attention to Gibson's approach, such a result is not surprising. It is not a result, however, that seems to be commanded by Le Dain's presentation of provincial inability. As the *Ontario Hydro* decision showed, the Supreme Court appears to use provincial inability only to test for singleness and distinctiveness. The

Supreme Court's silence on the matter in consideration of *RJR-MacDonald* left POGG unchanged.

The evasive manoeuvring on national concern begun in *RJR-MacDonald* continued in *R. v. Hydro-Québec*. There the court turned away from POGG even more resolutely than it had in *RJR*. The circumstances in *Hydro-Québec* (unlike *RJR*) closely resembled those in *Crown Zellerbach*, yet the court noticeably refrained from dealing with matters under the national concern branch of POGG.

Hydro-Québec was charged with violations under the *Canadian Environmental Protection Act* because it had dumped PCBs in contravention of the legislation. A narrow majority of the court dismissed the company's challenge that the applicable portions of the act were outside the federal government's competence. The court preserved the federal government's guidelines under the rubric of the federal power to write the criminal law. It did so in preference to the argument before the court that the regulation of toxic substances was a matter of national concern. Thus, the court again forestalled the centralist logic of provincial inability in favour of a more discrete grant of federal power.

Writing for the majority of the court, Justice La Forest recognized the power of the post-*Zellerbach* national concern doctrine: "Determining that a particular subject matter is a matter of national concern involves the consequence that the matter falls within the exclusive and paramount power of Parliament and has obvious impact on the balance of Canadian federalism."[52] This was not his preferred approach to environmental law. Citing *Oldman River,* La Forest reiterated that neither level of government is assigned exclusive control over the environment by the constitution. Accordingly, the environment must be dealt with on a case-by-case basis – the provinces and the federal government can minimize environmental impacts or impose environmental standards in the course of exercising their traditionally assigned functions.[53] The source of legitimacy is always the originally occupied field of the government in question. If a provision cannot be adequately related to an original grant, then it is likely to be insupportable.

The arguments made to the court by counsel paid considerable attention to national concern. As a result, La Forest argued, the stakes for federal balance raised by the case may have been exaggerated. He noted that national concern "inevitably raises profound issues respecting the federal structure of our Constitution which do not rise with anything like the same intensity in relation to the criminal law power."[54] Essentially, he posited that environmental matters such as those involved here were reasonably dealt with under the criminal law without opening the floodgates of national concern. A criminal law justification permitted "discrete prohibitions to prevent evils falling within a broad purpose such as, for example, the protection of health."[55]

The immediate result of this line of thinking was a tempering of provincial inability and the national concern test. The seeming menace of the national concern doctrine for cautious observers was defused by La Forest in a conscious effort to avoid the potential excesses that he recognized in previous applications of the current criteria. He noted, for example, that in *Crown Zellerbach* "this court held that marine pollution met those criteria and so fell within the exclusive legislative power of Parliament under the peace, order and good government clause. While the constitutional necessity of characterizing certain activities as beyond the scope of provincial legislation and falling within the national domain was accepted by all members of the court, the danger of too readily adopting this course was not lost on the minority."[56]

It is too early to tell whether or not the criminal law power has become a proxy for national concern. Presumably, there is a more restricted scope available under the criminal law power than there would be under an increasingly expanding national concern doctrine.

In the *Reference Re: Firearms Act,* decided in the summer of 2000, the Supreme Court again upheld federal jurisdiction over national problems by giving room to the criminal law. At issue in the case was controversial federal gun control legislation, which provided for the registration and licensing of all types of firearms and their owners. The government of Alberta, one of the constituencies most hostile to gun control, referred the federal law to its Court of Appeal for a ruling on its constitutionality. In particular, the government wondered if the registration of guns was not more properly a matter for property and civil rights and thereby provincial jurisdiction. The provinces (Alberta was joined by intervenors Saskatchewan, Ontario, Nova Scotia, and New Brunswick in its objections to the law) argued that some classes of firearms, in particular long guns, are simple property and that possession of them should not be a matter of criminal law. The Alberta Court of Appeal upheld the constitutionality of the federal legislation but not without a strongly worded dissent.[57] Writing in dissent, Justice Conrad argued that the proper question before the court was to what degree the federal criminal law power can be used to invade provincial jurisdiction. The majority upheld federal jurisdiction as a matter of "double aspect"[58] and on the basis of the broad definitions of criminal law found in *Hydro Québec* and *RJR-MacDonald.* Justice Conrad argued that "federal balance" should be a consideration for the court.

Prior jurisprudence on the criminal law power, including *Hydro-Québec,* suggests that if the behaviour or subject regulated poses a threat to public safety it has a criminal law purpose. Furthermore, if it is regulated by prohibitions that are backed by penalties, the sanction is likely to be a valid exercise of the criminal law. This seems to leave a lot of potential for federal activism under the auspices of the criminal law power. The Alberta brief to the court noted as much: "If the act is valid criminal law, it is difficult to conceive the bounds that could be placed on a federal desire to regulate in traditionally provincial areas."[59] A unanimous Supreme Court found that gun control legislation, despite having some regulatory attributes, is a valid purpose of the criminal law.[60] Given that the court found the dumping of toxins to be well within the rubric of the criminal law in *Hydro-Québec,* the regulation of guns – on its surface a more logical part of criminal law – was easy to place within the same confines. In response to Alberta's fears of a rampant criminal law power, the court has suggested that only when effects on provincial jurisdiction remain incidental (as they were in the case of firearms) will the federal power prevail. If the effects of legislation are more than incidental, the law is in pith and substance something other than criminal law and thereby will be ruled *ultra vires.* The court ruled that federal balance would be considered but only when it is so upset as to suggest an altogether different purpose for a law. The court has left it for itself to draw those distinctions in the future.

When the court has been faced with the opportunity to choose between criminal law and the POGG power, it has increasingly opted for the former. This trend was confirmed in the latter part of 2003 when the court was asked to rule on the constitutionality of the federal *Narcotics Control Act* in *R. v. Malmo-Levine.*[61] Criminal provisions related to marijuana possession were challenged in the case. While the more controversial constitutional issue was whether or not imprisonment for simple possession of marijuana was a violation of the Charter's section 7 right to "security of the person," there were also questions raised as to the appropriateness of federal jurisdiction. To the chagrin of decriminalization activists, the majority of the court rejected the Charter argument, suggesting that such questions were ones of policy best decided by Parliament. Three justices penned individual dissents on the Charter question, but all justices of the court agreed that the control of marijuana was a matter within the scope of Parliament's powers. In the late 1970s, the court had accepted a POGG argument as justification for federal control of narcotics.[62] In *Malmo-Levine,* the majority again backed away from the POGG justification and opted for the umbrella of the criminal law. The majority explicitly left consideration of a POGG justification under the *Zellerbach* test to another day given the comfortable fit that it found in the criminal law power.[63] Thus, the pattern of avoiding POGG arguments when a criminal law justification is available continues.

Other Federal Powers

Similar trends have emerged in cases that do not bear on the POGG power and the doctrines that support it. Under the trade and commerce and property and civil rights powers, most of the court's activity has been concerned with testing the legitimacy of federal competition policy. The tendency of the court has been to justify such regulation under the general branch of the trade and commerce power with reasoning similar to that expressed in regard to the national concern branch of POGG. In addition, the Supreme Court has been obliged to rule on the status of intergovernmental agreements, a major feature of federalism since the 1960s that has largely escaped judicial supervision.

In trade and commerce, doctrine has closely mirrored the developments in POGG jurisprudence. Like POGG, the power in section 91(2) for the federal government to "regulate trade and commerce" is potentially very expansive. One need only look at the scope of the commerce power in the United States to see how a general power over commerce can be interpreted widely to include most matters of modern government and regulation. The JCPC ensured that such a power never emerged while it presided as Canada's final court. Trade and commerce were always narrowly interpreted, with preference given to the provincial power over property and civil rights instead. The power was effectively divided by judicial review into two branches: (1) a power over international and interprovincial trade, and (2) a power over general trade and commerce affecting Canada as a whole. A number of landmark cases from the JCPC era confirmed the preference held by the law lords for the provincial heading of property and civil rights. The committee narrowly defined the scope of the first branch of trade and commerce.[64] The second branch was effectively ignored altogether – as Chief Justice Dickson wrote for the court in 1989, it was *terra incognita.* In the post-1949 era, the Supreme Court continued to take a narrow view of the power over trade and commerce, particularly the second branch, allowing Dickson to quote the claim that, "at least until relatively recently, the history of interpretation of the trade and commerce power has almost uniformly reinforced the federal paralysis which resulted from a series of Privy Council decisions."[65]

In the trade and commerce cases of the past three decades, a five-part test for a matter to be included under the power has emerged. Three elements of the current test were drawn from Bora Laskin's decision in *MacDonald v. Vapour Canada Ltd.*[66] In that case, the court refused to endorse a portion of the federal *Trade Marks Act*[67] prohibiting business practices "contrary to honest industrial or commercial usage,"[68] under the trade and commerce power. In his reasons, Laskin pointed to the three criteria that he considered essential for a legislative scheme to be justifiable as an exercise of the general trade and commerce power: first, the governmental activity supported must be in the form of a regulation or a general regulatory scheme; second, the scheme must be enforced by a regulatory agency, not left to "the chance of private redress"[69]; and third, it must regulate trade and commerce as a whole rather than be concerned with a specific industry. In the *Vapour* case, Laskin found nothing in the disputed section of the *Trade Marks*

Act that was regulatory or enforced by such an agency, and thus he could not sustain the impugned sections under the trade and commerce power.

Dickson added to those three criteria two of his own in the *Canadian National Transportation* decision.[70] The case was concerned with whether federal prosecutors were constitutionally able to apply the federal *Combines Investigation Act* or if the prosecutions would have to be pursued, like most criminal matters, by provincial attorneys general. The companies involved in the case had been charged with anti-competitive behaviour in the interprovincial shipping industry. They sought to preclude charges being brought by the federal attorney general on the grounds that the act depended for its validity upon the criminal law heading of section 91(27) of the constitution, which is enforced by the provinces.[71] The Alberta Court of Appeal agreed and did not allow prosecution by the federal attorney general to proceed. The Supreme Court allowed the appeal, ruling that the federal Parliament could have certain cases pursued by federal prosecutors under the auspices of section 2 of the *Criminal Code.* In *obiter,* Dickson agreed with the section 2 justification but also gave a justification for the *Combines Investigation Act* under the general branch of trade and commerce.

The requirement that regulation under the second branch of trade and commerce be general obligated the court to determine some way of distinguishing what is general from what is specific. The requirement of generality was the federalism consideration of the analysis. Apart from that test, the validity of trade and commerce regulation depends very little on any clear federalism requirements. No test for the need of such regulation in a federal system is made. The only federalism exemption was a prohibition on targeting a specific industry or trade. Such regulation risked being too local in its effects. Unresolved was the distinction between two categories of regulation that could not be considered specific: those that are genuine attempts at national control of trade but have local effects, and those that are amalgams of local matters centralized simply for the assertion of national control. To distinguish between these two, Dickson argued for the inclusion of a much more explicit federal test in addition to the Laskin criteria. Dickson's innovation was a spin on provincial inability, operationalized in the form of two requirements: first, "that the provinces jointly or severally would be constitutionally incapable of passing such an enactment"; and second, "that failure to include one or more provinces ... would jeopardize successful operation in other parts of the country."[72] In the case at hand, national anti-combines legislation could be justified, Dickson argued, as "an example of the genre of legislation that could not practically or constitutionally be enacted by a provincial government." Specifically, he cited the fact that "Canada is, for economic purposes, a single huge market-place. If competition is to be regulated at all it must be regulated federally."[73]

Dickson continued this line of reasoning in *General Motors of Canada v. City National Leasing*. City National leased car fleets to other companies across the country. It bought General Motors cars, among others, from franchised dealers and subsequently leased the cars to its customers. City National brought suit against General Motors, claiming that the manufacturer offered "preferential interest rate" incentives to some of the national fleet-leasing companies that bought cars from it but not to City National. This practice threatened City National's competitive position with its market rivals. City National was able to bring the matter to court under the *Combines Investigation Act*.[74] This federal legislation, created under the trade and commerce power, was designed to curb anti-competitive and monopolistic practices. General Motors contested the constitutional legitimacy of section 31(1) of the act and consequently the act as a whole. GM claimed that the legislation was *ultra vires* the federal Parliament since it created a cause for civil action, a matter more properly within the scope of the provincial power over property and civil rights. The court disagreed and affirmed that the legislation was in fact *intra vires* the federal Parliament under the second branch of trade and commerce.

Dickson built upon his position in *Canadian National Transportation*. Again he emphasized the nature of the Canadian free market as a justification for national competition policy. Quoting from Professors Peter Hogg and Warren Grover, Dickson wrote that "goods and services, and the cash or credit which purchases them, flow freely from one part of the country to another without regard for provincial boundaries."[75] This substantiated his belief that the provinces alone could not cope with the scale of the national economy. Unlike the trademark provisions at issue in the *Vapour* case, the initial three criteria were abundantly satisfied by the *Combines Investigation Act*. How the final two criteria were met is of some interest, especially given the court's track record of offering slim justifications for provincial inability in POGG cases. For Dickson, the national character of the economy was sufficient to preclude the provinces from being able to cooperate at enforcing competition policy. Quoting again from Hogg and Grover, he argued that "the market for goods and services is competitive on a national basis," proof enough that "provincial legislation cannot be an effective regulator."[76] To support his claim, Dickson cited a further study prepared for the federal government in 1974 suggesting that the toleration of a monopoly by any one province could lead to a need for tariffs or subsidies to support the monopoly and end up frustrating the national free market. Dickson concluded that the consequences of one province's reluctance to regulate competition, especially in a product or service with a national market, could have negative effects for all provinces.

What Dickson did with trade and commerce jurisprudence was to reintroduce some degree of federalism analysis. His reason for doing so was fairly clear. Like many of the generation reared on disdain for the JCPC's provincialism, Dickson believed that the trade and commerce power was unwisely restrained. However, he also looked for appropriate criteria to apply to trade and commerce claims, thereby preventing the power from becoming overinclusive. Laskin imported no federalism analysis into his test in *Vapour.* In retrospect, this may have been intentional. While he was ruling against federal power in that instance, his sympathies with a centralist position were clear, and by default he might have made it easier for general schemes at national regulation to squeak by as long as they lived up to the structural needs that he identified. Dickson softened that possibility by testing for inability or the risk of adverse effects from a provincial failure to regulate some types of activities in trade and commerce. This put the second branch of trade and commerce on a bit more solid ground. It has not been tested since *City National.*

Cooperative Federalism

One of the dominant themes put forward in this book is that a doctrinally-centred judicial review helps to support a more formally legal federalism. In turn, such legalism keeps the wolves at bay for those in a federation who would suffer were raw power to be the only means of determining outcomes. A federalism based on less concrete commitments to constitutional guarantees can hurt even the presumed powerhouses of a federation when they are up against the federal government, a lesson that the "have provinces" discovered in 1990.

In that year, the federal government, in a concerted effort to control its expenditures, took aim at one of the largest liabilities on its books, transfers to the provinces. Before the changes made by the Liberal government in 1995, most transfers to the provinces flowed through three programs: (1) Established Programs Financing (EPF), which funded the bulk of "established programs" for health and higher education; (2) the Canada Assistance Plan (CAP), which provided 50 percent of the cost to the provinces for programs in social assistance and welfare; and (3) equalization, which provided block funding to those provinces that fell below a complexly calculated national average of revenue-raising capacity. In what by later standards would seem to be a modest cut (the Liberal government post-1993 would make much deeper cuts in transfers that affected almost all provinces),[77] the Conservative federal government in 1990 sought to place a limit on the amount that payments under CAP could grow for those provinces that did not receive equalization. Rather than allow the transfers to the "have" provinces to continue growing at a rate consistent with provincial spending on social assistance, as the CAP had operated in the past, the federal government sought to limit growth for those three provinces (Alberta, British Columbia, and Ontario) to 5 percent per annum. When enacted, this "cap on CAP" would make the federal contribution in those provinces less than 50 percent of the cost of delivery if expenditures grew at any rate higher than 5 percent.[78]

The British Columbia government referred the legislation, *The Government Expenditures Restraint Act,* to the BC Court of Appeal inquiring as to whether Parliament had the authority to limit its obligations under the CAP without the consent of the provinces affected by the cuts. CAP, along with EPF, covered a whole generation of programs begun in the late 1960s under the auspices of cooperative federalism. Both were statutory programs rather than a constitutionally enforced system of fiscal federalism and redistribution of federal dollars. The BC Court of Appeal agreed with the provincial government that changes in CAP could not be made without the consent of the provinces affected. The Supreme Court overruled the BC decision, largely on the basis that to do otherwise would have compromised the sovereignty of Parliament. By affirming the legal (if not political) flexibility of the commitments made by the federal government through cooperative federalism, the court affirmed the superiority of the federal government in setting governmental priorities through its spending power.

A generation of scholars from the 1950s, Pierre Trudeau among them, objected to the use of the federal spending power because it would have a distorting effect on Canadian federalism.[79] Federal spending, they argued, should not be used as a lever to control the policies of the provinces in the jurisdictions assigned to them by the constitution. The worry of these classical federalists (particularly those concerned with the democratic theory of federalism) had been that governments should only raise the money that they needed to fund the responsibilities accorded to them by the constitution. This, they argued, was the only true method of assuring democratic accountability.

A prototype of this problem was the federal government's effort to provide direct financial aid to Canadian universities in the 1950s. Section 93 of the *Constitution Act, 1867,* assigns the provinces authority for education in and for the provinces. To many provinces, particularly Quebec, this has been read as an exclusive power, albeit one routinely circumvented by the federal spending power.[80] Not yet a Liberal politician, Pierre Trudeau even went so far as to agree with his nationalist foe Maurice Duplessis, who, as premier, objected to the receipt of such funds and actually turned down the money for a number of years. Trudeau argued that the program was the "direct negation of federalism."[81] While unitary states could pass out money with little doubt for the taxpayer as to where it came from, it was much easier to blur the lines of accountability in a federation. Trudeau conceded that there may be instances when funding from the federal government for subjects outside its jurisdiction is justified, especially in the promotion of equalization among the provinces. But he did not think that the university grants were among them since the federal government was providing grants to all of the universities regardless of the fiscal health of their home provinces. In the end and for years to come, however, the federal "power of the purse" has prevailed.

CAP, originally unveiled in 1966, was hailed by many as an example of how the federal and provincial governments could cooperate to better serve the needs of Canadians. The era of cooperative federalism continued for some time, with major initiatives jointly undertaken by the provinces and federal government. All were initiated by a fiscally flush and dominant central government. As long as there were half-price dollars available to the provinces for social spending, the system was sustainable. The funding was predictable, and the money was all administered (as long as certain conditions were met) by the provinces on their own. Indeed, one observer heralded CAP as "the ultimate in co-operative federalism."[82] The issue of accountability was buried until the era of fiscal restraint.

But what of the court's doctrine? How did the court justify its position on this important issue in Canadian federalism? The central points settled by the case were the degree to which the federal Parliament is bound by prior commitments to the provinces and whether a legitimate provincial expectation of federal funding can compel the federal legislature to keep funding in place. In a unanimous judgment, the court ruled decisively that the federal cabinet, through the cooperative measures of executive federalism, could not bind the federal Parliament should it wish to alter the provisions of a statutory device such as CAP. Similarly, the court argued that the legitimate expectation of funds could not override parliamentary sovereignty by obliging transfers regardless of the wishes of Parliament. The court asserted that the hands of the federal Parliament cannot be bound by anyone, including the federal executive. It is Parliament that will decide what Parliament will disburse to the provinces. Agreements made by the federal executive with the provinces could only serve as a guide; they could not compel Parliament's assent. With those arguments rejected, the last hope for the provinces was a claim that federal cutbacks amounted to an invasion of provincial jurisdiction.

The Manitoba government, as an intervenor in the case, tried to frame the federal government's contributions under CAP as effective regulation of provincial programs that were all matters of exclusive provincial jurisdiction. Manitoba argued that the federal government, by altering the terms of CAP funding, was invalidly regulating provincial matters. Initiating a program such as CAP was well within the rubric of the federal spending power, but making alterations to the terms of those plans, after creating a legitimate expectation of funds, amounted to setting policy in those provincial fields. What for the federal government was a simple austerity measure amounted to an atom bomb for the provinces. In the more reserved words of the attorney general for Manitoba, the federal law "impacts upon a constitutional interest" outside the jurisdiction of Parliament.[83] The court did not accept this argument. It found instead that "the simple withholding of federal money which had previously been granted to fund a matter of provincial jurisdiction does not amount to the regulation of that matter."[84] In sum, the court affirmed that the federal spending power is unrestrained, in good times and in bad. It ruled that the federal Parliament can alter the terms of its contributions to the provinces at will and without consultation from them. The court claimed that it could not supervise the exercise of the federal spending power even if the stability of intergovernmental compromise was at stake.

Trudeau's concern in the 1950s was dramatically demonstrated in the 1990s. The federalism that Trudeau, as much as anyone, promoted through the use of the federal spending power turned out to be built on a very shaky foundation.[85] Cooperative federalism, which in practice meant ever-growing commitments to social welfare programs bankrolled by fifty-cent dollars from Ottawa, became by the 1990s one of the largest liabilities on the federal government's books. Fortunately for the cost-conscious federal government, it could end this decades-long practice by its own initiative. The "cap on CAP" was only the first step in the fiscal downsizing to come. The so-called off-loading of the federal deficit through massive cuts to transfers continued in the 1990s. The Liberals introduced the Canada Health and Social Transfer (CHST) in 1995; it combined and at the same time decreased in total terms transfers to the provinces. Fortunately for Ottawa, the commitments made to provincial programs over the years have not been set in stone. The fact that these agreements were reached extra-constitutionally, yet lie at the heart of any given province's ability to acquit its responsibilities, has rightly put fiscal federalism at the fore of intergovernmental relations. The Social Union Framework Agreement (SUFA) reached between the federal government and the provinces in the spring of 1999 was a rational response to the uncertainty that emerged in the post-CAP era. Initial evaluations of the agreement suggest that it failed to realize all of its potential, largely due to a lack of commitment on the part of its signatory governments.[86] Yet the constitutional phobia that has plagued federal and provincial politicians in the post-Charlottetown Accord age will likely keep formal amendment off the table.[87]

If we think of federal judicial review as simply a mechanism of resolving intergovernmental disputes, the main candidates to replace it are still the numerous other forms of intergovernmental cooperation and dispute settlement found among the ranks of executive and cooperative federalism. These methods usually find their expression in the accords, frameworks, and communiqués that are the main product of intergovernmental consultation and bargaining. The CAP case only confirmed what was long suspected about the weak degree of legal enforceability that these agreements have. As Katherine Swinton notes, "the method for resolving disputes about obligations between governments tends to lie in the political, rather than the legal, arena. Indeed, some intergovernmental agreements are designed not to be enforceable in any other forum."[88] This claim is only bolstered by the unwillingness of the Supreme Court to interfere.

Thus, the CAP case is a warning to the provinces about the risks that they take by dealing with the federal government in the strictly non-constitutional realm.[89] But the CAP reference only touches on what might be called the external dimension of enforceability. Since the Canada Assistance Plan never took a constitutionalized form, altering Parliament's obligations was as simple as passing new legislation, and the provinces had little grounds on which to appeal. However, when agreements go unaltered but remain unimplemented by one party or another, there is an internal dimension of enforceability. On the basis of a pair of cases from Manitoba, Swinton is more hopeful about the possibility of courts being able to enforce those obligations.[90] The cases demonstrate to her that "intergovernmental agreements are not the preserve of the signatory governments ... [as] the Court gives the citizen status to patrol the intergovernmental relations process and to enforce obligations between governments."[91] She qualifies her claim, though, by stating that "there will be different degrees of judicial oversight depending upon the nature and detail of any particular agreement."[92]

The CAP reference confirmed doubts about the external enforceability of cooperative federalism. Now Swinton's optimism that cooperative agreements have some internal enforceability seems to be headed for the same fate. One of the successes of the flexible federalism of the 1990s, the Agreement on Internal Trade (AIT), provides some idea of where things may be headed. The AIT also embodies the wishes of those like Patrick Monahan and Paul Weiler who have sought to replace the Supreme Court as the arbiter of intergovernmental conflict. A prominent feature of the AIT is the inclusion of an internal mechanism for dispute resolution.

The AIT was signed in July 1994.[93] Its primary goal is the elimination of trade barriers and barriers to economic mobility between the provinces. Like the Social Union Framework Agreement to which it is a precursor, it is a decidedly non-constitutional form of federalism renewal. The agreement commits its signatories to the removal of economic barriers generally but also under a number of sectoral chapters on issues such as government procurement or environmental protection. In the event that either a government or a person wishes to challenge the policies of any provincial government as being in conflict with the commitments of the agreement, the document provides for institutions of dispute settlement.

The dispute settlement mechanisms are contained in Chapter 17 of the AIT. From the start, the provisions signal that cooperation is the overriding principle. The chapter provides for the general mechanism of dispute resolution but refers all conflicts initially to chapter-specific methods of dispute avoidance. Before a government or person can engage the general mechanism, the relevant governments must first exhaust the negotiation, consultation, and alternative dispute resolution mechanisms dictated by the sector-specific chapters. These processes provide the government or governments involved with the opportunity to adjust policies or legislation to keep in tune with the commitments of the AIT. In this initial stage, a premium is placed on working out differences quietly and with a minimum of conflict and publicity. To that end, the sector chapters include fairly rigid deadlines meant to progress claims through the process reasonably quickly. If disputes remain unresolved after the chapter-specific processes, only then may they proceed to Chapter 17 resolution.

Disputes under the AIT are administered by the Internal Trade Secretariat, with the actual resolution being undertaken first by the Committee on Internal Trade (made up of ministers from the provinces and federal government) and then with appointed panels drawn from a roster maintained by the governments. Person-to-government disputes have an additional initial hurdle in the form of a pre-panel screening conducted by a roster-appointed screener who determines whether claims are simply vexatious or harassing. This provision was meant to "root out frivolous charges or cases."[94] If the dispute cannot be worked out by confidential consultation and a panel is struck, it follows procedures fairly analogous to those of a court, hearing briefs from either side and releasing a written decision. The enforcement of panel rulings depends upon the goodwill of the signatory governments and the bad publicity associated with breaking the agreement's commitments. In the case of government-to-government conflicts, permissible retaliatory action is also contemplated for cases of non-compliance.

The relatively weak enforcement mechanisms and the ad hoc nature of the panel process were necessitated by provincial suspicion of a more permanent institution for dispute settlement. Provincial governments in particular objected to the idea of an independent "third tier" institution or even to the courts settling disputes under the AIT. G. Bruce Doern and Mark MacDonald associate this objection with the provincial belief that the "provinces were sovereign entities within a system of federalism and that no enforcement mechanism should be ceded."[95] The models looked to for solutions were the Canada-US Free Trade Agreement and the North American Free Trade Agreement. The specific virtue of the dispute resolution mechanisms in those agreements was that they were structured to be "clearly government driven and controlled rather than private-sector-access driven."[96] That goal has clearly been met. Of the 43 complaints initiated since 1995, only 10 have proceeded to a formal panel. Only 2 of th[illegible]se 10 were person-to-government complaints.[97] The record co[illegible] Patrick Monahan's concern that "the most serious sh[illegible]ea of dispute resolution involves the numer[illegible] the way of private persons."[98] Anec[illegible]he dispute resolution m[illegible]ime consuming" and [illegible]

Ac[illegible]nents opted for decide[illegible]T are obvious. Given t[illegible] and conciliation of [illegible] to initially perform [illegible]is likely to involve tra[illegible]ernments and unduly [illegible] trust the courts to ma[illegible]nts "remain reluctai[illegible] unaccountable bod[illegible]ution mechanisms wi[illegible] its signatories to abide by thei[illegible]ental agreements, the AIT and the decis[illegible] justiciable.[101] From the standpoint of smaller g[illegible]ing their larger partners in Confederation, or businesspeo[illegible]ing to get around protectionist provincial policies, the will of governments is the barrier that they were hoping to overcome in the first place.

Federalism litigation, we should not forget, is routinely commenced by individuals or societal actors who believe that the enacting government does not possess the constitutional authority to proceed as it has. Opportunities to avail oneself of guarantees against governments are all but smothered in the AIT. It puts numerous hurdles in the way of individuals who wish to seek redress. The evidence suggests that individuals find the process stacked against them, and the numbers suggest that the agreement works efficiently to stop disputes before they happen. The bulk of the consultation and the alteration that take place stays confidential. How are interested publics to stay aware of what those negotiations sacrificed or committed? Dispute resolution in the AIT has simply exaggerated the already negative tendencies of cooperative federalism.

Evaluating Balanced Federalism

David Beatty, for one, is not happy with the recent federalism decisions of the Supreme Court. In particular, he is irked by what has happened to the provincial inability test. On its face, there is much that would seem to impress Beatty in such a doctrine. Indeed, he writes that the provincial inabil-

goal has clearly been met. Of the 43 complaints initiated since 1995, only 10 have proceeded to a formal panel. Only 2 of those 10 were person-to-government complaints.[97] The record conforms with Patrick Monahan's concern that "the most serious shortcoming in the area of dispute resolution involves the numerous hurdles that are placed in the way of private persons."[98] Anecdotally, the business press has labelled the dispute resolution mechanisms "complex, inaccessible, expensive [and] time consuming" and "frighteningly vulnerable to bureaucratic inertia."[99]

According to Katherine Swinton, the reasons why governments opted for decidedly non-judicial forms of dispute resolution in the AIT are obvious. Given that the initial onus in the agreement is on negotiation and conciliation of disputes, courts are probably not the best institution to initially perform such oversight. Since interpretation of the agreement is likely to involve trade-offs between permitted "legitimate objectives" of governments and unduly restrictive barriers, governments are also unwilling to trust the courts to make those trade-offs. According to Swinton, governments "remain reluctant to surrender their sovereignty to such a politically unaccountable body."[100] The effectiveness of the AIT and its dispute resolution mechanisms will always be dependent on the willingness of its signatories to abide by their promises. Like other intergovernmental agreements, the AIT and the decisions of AIT panels are not justiciable.[101] From the standpoint of smaller governments battling their larger partners in Confederation, or businesspeople trying to get around protectionist provincial policies, the will of governments is the barrier that they were hoping to overcome in the first place.

Federalism litigation, we should not forget, is routinely commenced by individuals or societal actors who believe that the enacting government does not possess the constitutional authority to proceed as it has. Opportunities to avail oneself of guarantees against governments are all but smothered in the AIT. It puts numerous hurdles in the way of individuals who wish to seek redress. The evidence suggests that individuals find the process stacked against them, and the numbers suggest that the agreement works efficiently to stop disputes before they happen. The bulk of the consultation and the alteration that take place stays confidential. How are interested publics to stay aware of what those negotiations sacrificed or committed? Dispute resolution in the AIT has simply exaggerated the already negative tendencies of cooperative federalism.

Evaluating Balanced Federalism

David Beatty, for one, is not happy with the recent federalism decisions of the Supreme Court. In particular, he is irked by what has happened to the provincial inability test. On its face, there is much that would seem to impress Beatty in such a doctrine. Indeed, he writes that the provincial inabil-

The dispute settlement mechanisms are contained in Chapter 17 of the AIT. From the start, the provisions signal that cooperation is the overriding principle. The chapter provides for the general mechanism of dispute resolution but refers all conflicts initially to chapter-specific methods of dispute avoidance. Before a government or person can engage the general mechanism, the relevant governments must first exhaust the negotiation, consultation, and alternative dispute resolution mechanisms dictated by the sector-specific chapters. These processes provide the government or governments involved with the opportunity to adjust policies or legislation to keep in tune with the commitments of the AIT. In this initial stage, a premium is placed on working out differences quietly and with a minimum of conflict and publicity. To that end, the sector chapters include fairly rigid deadlines meant to progress claims through the process reasonably quickly. If disputes remain unresolved after the chapter-specific processes, only then may they proceed to Chapter 17 resolution.

Disputes under the AIT are administered by the Internal Trade Secretariat, with the actual resolution being undertaken first by the Committee on Internal Trade (made up of ministers from the provinces and federal government) and then with appointed panels drawn from a roster maintained by the governments. Person-to-government disputes have an additional initial hurdle in the form of a pre-panel screening conducted by a roster-appointed screener who determines whether claims are simply vexatious or harassing. This provision was meant to "root out frivolous charges or cases."[94] If the dispute cannot be worked out by confidential consultation and a panel is struck, it follows procedures fairly analogous to those of a court, hearing briefs from either side and releasing a written decision. The enforcement of panel rulings depends upon the goodwill of the signatory governments and the bad publicity associated with breaking the agreement's commitments. In the case of government-to-government conflicts, permissible retaliatory action is also contemplated for cases of non-compliance.

The relatively weak enforcement mechanisms and the ad hoc nature of the panel process were necessitated by provincial suspicion of a more permanent institution for dispute settlement. Provincial governments in particular objected to the idea of an independent "third tier" institution or even to the courts settling disputes under the AIT. G. Bruce Doern and Mark MacDonald associate this objection with the provincial belief that the "provinces were sovereign entities within a system of federalism and that no enforcement mechanism should be ceded."[95] The models looked to for solutions were the Canada-US Free Trade Agreement and the North American Free Trade Agreement. The specific virtue of the dispute resolution mechanisms in those agreements was that they were structured to be "clearly government driven and controlled rather than private-sector-access driven."[96] That

ity test "establishes an objective and normatively attractive standard for co-ordinating federal and provincial initiatives on this or indeed any other matter of common concern."[102] "Objective" is the nicest thing that a positivist can say about a constitutional concept. But, according to Beatty, something has gone wrong with the test's application, particularly in *R. v. Hydro-Québec*. While supportive of the ultimate result in the case, Beatty believes that the "reasoning that supports it turns out to be shockingly inadequate."[103] The test has not lived up to his expectations largely because the court has failed to use it properly. Beatty's disappointment demonstrates acutely why a different understanding of doctrine and its role in judicial reasoning needs to be advocated.

Beatty accuses the court of endorsing a subjective theory of constitutional law by choosing the criminal law over provincial inability in *Hydro-Québec*. Although the majority had an objective and tested standard available, they opted to "rewrite the rules of constitutional law" and decide the case according to the judges', and specifically Justice La Forest's, personal views. This practice goes against all that Beatty claims about the potential of constitutional law. The provincial inability test, if the judges of the court were faithful to it, should have compelled a much different result. If they had followed a principled approach, the court would have had little trouble finding in favour of the federal government without resort to the criminal law. The result in *Hydro-Québec,* he argues, is the equivalent of a toxic spill polluting the law. The metaphor is telling – Beatty believes that a careless or even belligerent court has tainted the pure and objective standards of the law.

But should one expect so much of doctrine? Doctrine is not capable of the objectivity and certainty of result that positivists demand of it. By making such demands, Beatty and others demonstrate one of the real dangers of studying and understanding a court's approach to constitutional questions: namely, rooting for the answers and approaches that one prefers. Provincial inability might show better than any other test surveyed here the risk of taking doctrine too seriously as a variable. The court modified the test from its original form and has since been less willing to use the revised doctrine. This is a disappointment for someone who liked the effect that the doctrine had on the interpretation of federal power. But to be disappointed misses the essence of what doctrine is truly capable of. Recall that from the outset the claim made here has been that doctrine is an independent variable that influences judicial outcomes. For Beatty, it clearly should do more than just influence outcomes; it should also compel them. Provincial inability certainly influenced the result in *Hydro-Québec.* La Forest admits in his decision a preference for dealing with the matter under the criminal law heading because it is less likely to raise issues that threaten the federal balance. The provincial inability test may be a dream come true to centralists, but the court is likely to back off from applying it too generously for just that reason.

It is difficult to divine exactly what Beatty would prefer from the court. He claims that "generations of constitutional law teachers have taught that artificial categories and rigid rules lead to arbitrary distinctions and inconsistent decisions."[104] Yet he waxes nostalgic for the brief period during Brian Dickson's tenure as chief justice when "an effort was made to find common principles and tests in the large grants of power to the federal government in p.o.g.g. and section 91(2) (trade and commerce)."[105] The "generation" of constitutional law teachers that he calls to his aid includes Monahan and Weiler. They would be the first to make the claim that the developments of the Dickson era are no more objective or praiseworthy than prior efforts at constitutional interpretation before Dickson came to the court's helm. Indeed, Monahan suggests that the decade prior to 1987 (three years of which were presided over by Dickson) provides some of the best evidence of the "essentially political nature of the Court's decision-making in the federalism arena."[106] Does Beatty consider provincial inability natural and flexible (as distinct from artificial and rigid)? It appears that his vision of doctrine is equally as rigid as the rules that he decries. With *Hydro-Québec,* the court demonstrates flexibility, not rigidity. And that is exactly what upsets Beatty. It is far better to be realistic about the limitations of doctrine and just be alert to the potential that various interpretive schemes hold.

An endorsement of this flexible, doctrinal approach is not just a post hoc apology for the court's ultimate politics and inconsistency. I agree with Beatty that there is a place for formal law in federalism. But I disagree with his idea of how that law has to be put into effect. "Principled" doctrines should not be expected from the court, but some kind of doctrines should. That does not mean that judges should just follow their gut feelings or ideological preferences. The doctrines that the Supreme Court of Canada has developed to aid the interpretation of federalism are useful guides to determining outcomes. So, to use the same example, provincial inability provides a useful frame for consideration of the federal general power, but it need not preclude all options. What is clear is that, in having to reckon with the doctrine, the court has come up with a different result than a clean slate or a purely political process would allow it. Most of all, the use of doctrine, however variable it may be, contributes to the maintenance of a federal legalism. There are tasks best done by the courts in a federation. Doctrine helps them to be done without a slide into politics.

POGG jurisprudence right up to *Reference Re: Firearms* affirms the contention of Hogg and Russell that the court is balanced in its federalism jurisprudence. Other areas of division-of-powers jurisprudence may not be as internally balanced, but they too demonstrate that "uncanny" ability for balance in the long run. Doctrine is a significant tool in helping to achieve

"contrived formations",
provincial inability +
POGG

- Anti Inflation decisions
signalled an ambivalent
view of interpretation of POGG
- energy rationale disappeared +
- provincial inability
is most prevalent
↓
if national concern could
be limited by the creation
of sub categories, this
~~too~~ justification may be
accepted

that balance. It is inherently flexible, and when a court pushes too much in one direction it clearly helps it to have the doctrinal alternatives that maintain the core of a balanced approach. All the while, the legal structure of federalism provides guarantees and securities that cooperative federalism cannot. The court's contributions may still be veiled in the language of law, but that might be the best thing that the court has to contribute to the federal system. Peter Russell was to be disappointed by the clumsy legalism and lack of constitutional wisdom in the *Anti-Inflation* case. Achieving federal balance through clumsy but still non-political means might just amount to constitutional wisdom after all.

- reinforcing the
status quo sought
to avoid controversy

& not good

(4) seen to be a political
decision

---

yet
→ other cases →
(4) political realism not
~~taken~~
taken.

Conclusion

Does Doctrine Matter?

There is empirical proof that doctrine plays a role in the decision making of federal high courts. From the evidence presented in the previous chapters, it is abundantly clear that doctrine is a formative force in the way that judges settle division-of-powers disputes. Even if one were to wholly accept the attitudinal or instrumentalist contention that judges simply use decisions to put their preferences into force, one could not deny the way that doctrine conditions the expression of those preferences. But doctrine is more than cover for naked preference. In all three of the federations examined here, doctrines have been developed to help courts cope with the challenge of adjudicating federalism disputes. To be sure, they are not the only variable that judges use to come to a decision. However, as Chapters 2 through 5 have shown, isolating doctrine as a variable helps to explain how a federal system evolves and how intergovernmental disputes can be reconciled when competing aims or agendas come to a head.

The American experience is perhaps the most challenging to explain on these terms. Ideological differences between the judges are certainly identifiable, and the court commonly finds itself at the epicentre of some of the country's most divisive issues. But the robustness of doctrine in the federalism cases of the now-passed Rehnquist era is apparent to all who observe it. This is in keeping with historical practice. Tests such as the "stream of commerce" doctrine have been relied upon by the American court since its earliest days. Today the extent of state sovereignty, and tests for how that sovereignty might be offended by congressional legislation, are critical to determining the scope of Congress's legislative jurisdiction.

The course of federal-state relations and the scope of congressional activity literally hang on the developing doctrinal logic of the court. Probably the most important doctrinal dispute currently engaging the court is the degree to which federal legislation can compel states or state instrumentalities. Disputes over state sovereignty frame almost all of the most recent federalism cases. Congress's attempts to regulate state employees or to provide mechanisms of relief against the states for private citizens are compromised every time a "state sovereignty" exemption is granted by the court.

But even as a narrow and alternating majority pursue a preference for protecting the states, they do so by relying on well-articulated and reasonably consistent doctrines that support their interpretation of those constitutional guarantees. When individual members of the court invoke ambiguous values such as a need for "federal balance" or the need to minimize "federalism costs," they are regularly less successful in convincing a majority to join them. For example, the more extreme position on state sovereignty advocated by Justice Thomas rarely, if ever, finds favour with concurring judges, much less a majority of the court. In fact, one of the strengths of the current state sovereignty position is that it derives from a strong doctrinal strand of the court's jurisprudence and can be upheld with a reasonable reading of the history of the constitution. That the contending minority holds its position with the same fervour does not diminish the place of doctrine; it just further proves its importance. That both sides are remarkably confident of the truth of their positions further proves the futility of seeking a principle-based approach to doctrine. Those principles are ultimately normative and not objective; they will always be what their creators make of them. That does not make them irrelevant.

The Australian High Court continues to stand by its rather traditional approach to federalism adjudication. In practical terms, the main technique of the court has been to take literal readings of the enumerated powers given to the Commonwealth. This practice has generally benefited the central government when it has sought to gain jurisdiction, in particular helping it to achieve fiscal dominance over the states. A literalist philosophy alone has not been enough to realize this course of interpretation. Specific doctrines have been developed along the way to clarify the scope of Commonwealth powers, such as external affairs or the corporations power. The court's decision in the *Tasmanian Dam* case appeared to relax the application of doctrine to the point where specific tests almost seemed to be irrelevant. The court has since retreated from that loose application and has been more measured in its recent rulings.

One doctrine in particular seems to offer hope to the states in jurisdictional struggles with the Commonwealth. The doctrine of implied immunity offers them some breathing room in cases where federal law is applied to them as agents. The development of doctrine in this field has also worked to keep the Commonwealth honest by denying it blanket immunity from state legislation. The doctrines used by the court have not generally been to the advantage of the states, but there is some small evidence that the court is more amenable to balancing Australian federalism than it has been in the past.

Doctrines are also critical to the Canadian Supreme Court's approach to federalism. The POGG power has always been shaped by doctrine. Over the past two decades, the court has slowly adjusted the scope of the POGG power through a provincial inability test for national concern. Provincial inability embodies just how a doctrine can be slowly altered and selectively applied. Provincial inability proves the contention made at the outset that doctrine has a degree of agency but cannot be wholly determinative of outcomes. The court will make what it will of the tests and measures attached to the concept, but it must work within the confines of the idea itself, for better or for worse. An advocate of certainty such as David Beatty would prefer to see provincial inability restrain judges, and any time that it plays a less than determinative role he blames misapplication of the test rather than the test itself.

There is an even more important lesson to draw from the Canadian experience. The court's intervention in areas such as the environment suggests that judicial review is of continuing importance for Canadian federalism. The approach of the court to unspecified fields, especially as they gain in importance, is central to jurisdictions such as environmental protection. *Friends of the Oldman River, Ontario Hydro,* and *Hydro-Québec* all dealt with environmental issues where the division of federal and provincial jurisdiction is far from clear. When there are political obstacles to cooperation and compromise in such a field, the legal structure of federalism provides a baseline that political manoeuvring cannot waylay.

While different doctrines have emerged to deal with different constitutional problems in all three countries, there is something similar in the way that these tests come about. They are always a response to distinct interpretational problems, some specific and discrete, others more encompassing. The comparative evidence does not indicate that there is a core of universal federalism values or principles that motivates courts. This is of little surprise given the approach to doctrine that this study has taken. The only truly universal lesson to be drawn from the practices of the courts investigated here is that the technique of developing tests and modifying definitions is widespread and frequent in the practice of judicial review.

The zeal with which doctrines are applied and the degree to which they operationalize deep divisions of opinion on a court may vary. Currently, the deepest divisions of interpretation are probably to be found on the American court. The Canadian court is least likely to come out with polar positions, and disputes among the members of the court are probably the least predictable as they do not seem to turn on fundamental sets of beliefs. The Australian court seems to be in the middle, with only occasional strong-minded dissents coming from judges such as the now-retired Daryl Dawson. While the American example shows that doctrine can often have the effect of entrenching polar positions, American experience also shows the capacity for compromise that doctrine can offer. In short, the divisions of the Rehnquist court may have been overstated. Despite the fact that such vitally held positions on federalism are found on the American court, many cases are still unpredictable from the seeming ideologies of the court's membership. Routinely more important are the enduring doctrines of the court's cumulative work.

Should Doctrine Matter?

Legal scholars and theorists would generally agree that doctrine is a necessity in most areas of jurisprudence. Rules and tests, developed over time, are the analytical tools with which judges work to come to resolutions. Doctrine appears to be much more readily accepted in fields such as contracts or torts. In these areas, the practices of the common law are much more apparent and accepted. Indeed, an important part of the "law" governing these kinds of topics in common-law jurisdictions is completely judge-made and unlegislated. Tests of fairness in contracts or of the "reasonable person" in torts all come from precedent and traditional practice rather than directly from statutes. Such tests are by no means inherently perfect or rational and have developed alongside changing societal attitudes and practices. If doctrine is so readily accepted as a legitimate method in these fields, why is it so much more contested in constitutional law? Perhaps it is because the stakes are so much greater. Constitutional judicial review is about the task of interpreting a nation's blueprint, and it is easy to believe that this is best done on the basis of motivating constitutional principles.

The debate between positivists and realists or attitudinalists chronicled earlier in this book demonstrates the place of normative constitutional principles in thinking about doctrine. Positivists advocate the law as something universal in its truths. The simple task for courts, in this view, is to stick to the principled application of the law. When it comes to specific areas of the law, such as federalism, a positivist such as David Beatty identifies two primary values or principles that have to be upheld – mutual modification and concurrency. Through these tools, the law of federalism is perfectible and holds within it the potential for the neutral and fair settlement of disputes. It is up to the judges to ensure that the law lives up to this potential by staying disciplined and loyal to inherent constitutional principles.

Realists and attitudinalists see much less determinacy in constitutional law. For every principle articulated by a judge or court, they claim that almost anyone could locate and defend an equally compelling counter-principle. For political scientists, this means that judicial review cannot be understood as anything but political, and any other approach to the role of courts in politics is both naïve and ill considered.

A different approach has been taken here, one less interested in canonizing or demonizing doctrine or courts. Rather, following the norms of the new institutionalism, an effort has been made to be neutral about the content of doctrine and to study it for its own sake. What this means is that legal controversies in a federal system can be understood independent of a debate over the objective possibilities of law. Doctrine is still used by the courts whether observers believe that it is perfectible or deeply flawed. The evidence of Chapters 2 through 5 indicates that the courts are functioning in their federalism jurisprudence with a set of tools drawn largely from prior jurisprudence. Those developments have clear ramifications for federalism. Constitutional law serves a task in the maintenance of federalism that is not reliant upon the law's internal purity or lack thereof.

Some critics claim that a rarefied conception of the law is responsible for misconceiving the political role played by high courts. Using rules, doctrines, and so-called objective tests, they argue, is the constitutional equivalent of the noble lie. High courts in particular play politics, but under the guise of doing otherwise. The methodology employed by the courts leads to certain kinds of outcomes that a formalist interpretation suggests are inevitable or dictated by principles inherent in the law. Critics of judicial power have claimed that this is by no means the case and that decisions that have been made under the guise of objectivity are no more than political decisions cloaked in idealistic legal cover. Moreover, the political role of a court is actually hampered by these artificial constraints. The result is a poorly informed jurisprudence that, if not directly detrimental to the health of a federal system, at the least is illegitimate and undemocratically arrived at.

Defending Doctrine

A more modest case needs to be made for doctrine. By lowering our expectations for doctrine, we might actually derive more value from it. Doctrine is a reminder of the legal attributes of federalism, which, as A.V. Dicey knew, is uncommonly bound to the law. A critical understanding of the law of federalism has distanced political science and constitutional study from considering judicial review's contribution to federal development. Federal theory should recognize that, despite the frailties of law, the legal order is the cornerstone of how a federal system operates. The legal forum is available to mediate conflicts and is unique in the way that it serves this function.

Cass Sunstein commends legal reasoning as a tool for reaching what he calls "incompletely theorized agreements." Legal reasoning, Sunstein argues, plays a critical role in the mediation of political conflicts by not obliging parties to fully accept each other's principles but still resolving their disputes.[1] The federal legal order provides a baseline set of rules and protections from which the rest of the intergovernmental system takes important cues. While it may not be the most critical element of a federal system, judicial review is the most important determinant of how that baseline order will be understood.[2]

Patrick Monahan discounts the influence of federal judicial review on the overall federal system by positing what he considers a fundamental maxim of Canadian federalism: "It is *always* possible to do indirectly what you cannot do directly."[3] Executive federalism remains the defining feature of Canadian federalism and makes the constitutional division of powers potentially less relevant to questions of how public policy gets made. When premiers and the prime minister agree on new initiatives or approaches, the Canadian federal order can be remarkably flexible. If the courts tell governments that they are limited in the areas that they may properly legislate, that does not preclude them from ironing out cooperative agreements to do what they would prefer. The relevance of judicial sanctions, Monahan can thus argue, is undermined by the ability of the parties in federalism conflicts to resolve their differences some other way or for governments to collectively achieve their policy goals with alternative strategies. Add to that the impression that there is nothing apparently neutral or objective about judicial decision making and the disfavour in which judicial review has been held is all the more understandable. But this attitude underestimates the importance of judicial review. Canadian federalism may create incentives for governments to collaborate and cooperate, but that does not mean they always will.

In contentious policy fields such as the environment, international treaty making, or the regulation of financial and securities markets, judicial review matters a great deal. Governments cannot always be counted on to agree. And if they agree too much, sometimes the public interest is not foremost in their calculations. The backbone of federalism has always been its legal character, both in providing autonomy for governments to make choices in the spheres defined for them by the constitution and in being accountable for those choices to their respective publics. Executive federalism suffers from the temptation to put pragmatism first. Working with a different kind of reasoning, the calculus of courts is never wholly political – judges must deal with constraints alien to political decision makers. Those constraints, doctrine among them, matter. All the more important then that one understands the way that courts reach decisions.

The conception of doctrine and judicial reasoning as something rarefied or derived from self-evident and self-enforcing truths has been challenged for several decades now. Good riddance to the notion. But in the process, doctrine has become the proverbial baby thrown out with the bath water. That high courts engage in judgment through doctrine is a trait that has been overlooked by those who legitimately seek to remove the veil from judicial power. In their zeal to unmask judges as politicians, the critics support an equally distorted view of the role of the law in a federal system.

The mistake is an easy one to make. Judges usually present their task as finding law and principle. Controversy over judicial activism on rights has tempted members of the Canadian court in particular to defend their work as the application of "principles" alone and not politics. The present chief justice, Beverly McLachlin, has made efforts to defend the court from the charge of judicial activism: "Long before charters of rights were dreamed of, the English spoke ominously of 'palm tree' justice, evoking the image of a colonial magistrate, seated under his judicial palm tree, meting out whatever decisions happened to seem right to him in the particular case at hand. The opposite of palm tree justice ... is justice *rooted in legal principle* and appropriate respect for the constitutional role of Parliament and the legislatures. The law has developed rules and ways of proceeding to assist judges in avoiding the evils of unprincipled, inappropriately interventionist judging" (emphasis added).[4]

The chief justice conflates the use of doctrine with a principled approach. She thereby implies that the legitimacy of the legal method comes from principles rather than something more modest such as routine and the buildup of precedent. Mistaking doctrine for principle throws one unnecessarily into the debate over politics and law and away from an understanding of doctrine in its own right. The temptation to include principle, however, is understandable. On what other grounds can one defend doctrine? Is a doctrine justified because it has been around a while? Because it is reasonably logical and consistent? Principle is a nice way of suggesting that something nobler than caprice is at work. Principle is a counter to caprice, but neither needs to be invoked to defend doctrine. The public face of judging will likely continue to claim objectivity and ideal neutrality. The severest critics will continue to cry "politics!"

McLachlin's account, sans principle, is fairly congruent with the characterization of doctrine that has been offered here. Doctrine is an empirical fact of judicial reasoning. The tests and definitions used by courts are reasonably consistent and offer judges alternatives when faced with complex choices. Doctrine provides judges with the analytical tools to approach federalism problems in a legal manner. Doctrine narrows the compass of political or policy decision. Thus, doctrine should be important to political scientists not for the particular principles that it enacts, or the particular philosophy of federalism that it envisions, but for the account of federalism that it can help to create. To discount doctrine because it is unprincipled or obfuscates real decision making misses the point. The effort expended on judicial reasoning is real. Doctrines and consistency matter to those who fill high courts, and they matter to the results. To ignore them is to construct an impoverished account of federalism.

What does this study add to our understanding of federalism? Simply put, if one pays heed to the doctrine of the courts, a fuller account of what is happening in a federal system can be constructed. The disfavour into which the study of judicial review has fallen has bred an ignorance of judicial developments. This ignorance is an ironic counterweight to the overreliance once placed on judicial review as an all-encompassing explanatory variable in the study of federalism. Judicial review does not explain everything that one needs to know in order to understand a federal system. By the same count, it is not irrelevant. Doctrine is clearly a variable in the way that courts grapple with federalism problems, and it is clearly a useful tool for ensuring that the baseline guarantees of a federal legal structure are maintained.

This does not mean that one should expect policy wisdom from the courts. Neither should the courts "stand up" for abstract and ultimately contentious principles. The tendency of high courts to try to do the latter may be what convinced governments to avoid judicial review whenever possible. But formal institutions, the courts among them, are not as easily avoided as cooperative federalists might once have thought. The "political safeguards of federalism," so enthusiastically endorsed in *Garcia,* are unreliable and even counter to the spirit of federation. In federations, the division of powers will continue to be adjudicated by the courts. If, in the process of doing so, judges insist upon advocating an interpretation of federalism, let them use doctrine. Doctrines can be amended much easier than constitutions and much easier than dramatically stated principles. All federations must deal with the disparity between rules and needs or between existing structures and societal changes. Given the proven difficulty of constitutional amendment in all three of the countries surveyed here, other mechanisms to solve the problem of adjustment are certainly needed. Judicial review can serve that purpose, and it need not do so in a deceptively political way. The continued use of doctrine in federal high courts is a healthy sign for federalism as a system of governance.

The judicial review of federalism is a difficult practice to defend. Judicial reasoning is not always as consistent or as objective as its practitioners profess. Attitudinalists and realists have demonstrated that the ideological preferences of judges certainly go some of the way toward explaining outcomes. While the practice of federal judicial review in Canada has a more muted political character than is generally true of other federal high courts,[5] the Supreme Court is still routinely accused of a centralist bias.[6] Structurally, the Supreme Court's power in the federation runs up against the incrementalist, pragmatic style favoured by the intergovernmental relations protocol. As John Saywell describes it, judicial power is "a frightening third estate in a federal system." Particularly troublesome to him is the "awful finality" of decisions, immune as they are to legislative override and constitutional amendment. "Occasionally," he notes, "the decisions of the judicial law-makers have encouraged the political actors to seek compromise solutions."[7] However, to his thinking and to that of many others, judicial power is often the last say. Given the centralization that Saywell and others see as endemic in the Canadian court's jurisprudence over the past twenty years and the still vigorous influence that courts exercise over the shape of constitutional law, it comes as little surprise that governments have opted out of judicial settlement of disputes over federalism practice. But the creeping informalism of Canadian federalism may not always be to the advantage of governments or democracy.[8]

The comparative inquiry conducted here reminds us of federalism's origins in written constitutionalism. Federations differ in their societal structures and cultural diversities, but their constitutional differences can explain as much about their differing experience of federal government as those organic differences. Federations have both political and legal dimensions that find expression through different institutions and help to establish an equilibrium in the inherent tension between unity and diversity that all federations share. The judicial function in federalism is the reinforcement of the legal order in the face of political innovation. Judges keep the tilting train of political evolution on the constitutional track. The incrementalism of courts and the malleability of legal doctrines over time suggest that the courts are much less dangerous than they are sometimes made out to be. In fact, experience suggests that high courts exhibit some unique competencies in addressing federalism disputes. Legal reasoning asks different questions and provides different answers than political processes would. A good dose of formalism through reinvigorated judicial umpiring may just be essential to a properly functioning federation.

Notes

Introduction

1 François Rocher and Miriam Smith, eds., *New Trends in Canadian Federalism* (Peterborough: Broadview, 1995), 20. See the specific chapters by Rhada Jhappan, "The Federal-Provincial Power-Grid and Aboriginal Self-Government," and Kathryn Harrison, "Federalism, Environmental Protection, and Blame Avoidance." Also see the latter's book-length study. Kathryn Harrison, *Passing the Buck: Federalism and Canadian Environmental Policy* (Vancouver: UBC Press, 1996), especially Chapter 3, "The Constitutional Framework: Constraints and Opportunities."

2 A. Wayne MacKay, "The Supreme Court of Canada and Federalism: Does/Should Anyone Care Anymore?" *Canadian Bar Review* 80 (2001): 241-81, is an exception whose title portrays the problem well.

3 Alan Cairns, "The Judicial Committee and Its Critics," *Canadian Journal of Political Science* 4, 3 (1971): 319.

4 F.R. Scott, "The Consequences of the Privy Council Decisions," *Canadian Bar Review* 15, 6 (1937): 485.

5 John T. Saywell, *The Lawmakers: Judicial Power and the Shaping of Canadian Federalism* (Toronto: University of Toronto Press, 2002).

6 Peter H. Russell, "Overcoming Legal Formalism: The Treatment of the Constitution, the Courts, and Judicial Behaviour in Canadian Political Science," *Canadian Journal of Law and Society* 1 (1986): 21.

7 J.R. Mallory, *Social Credit and the Federal Power in Canada* (Toronto: University of Toronto Press, 1954).

8 Russell, "Overcoming Legal Formalism," 10.

9 Mallory, *Social Credit,* 56.

10 C. Herman Pritchett, *The Roosevelt Court* (New York: Macmillan, 1948); Glendon Schubert, *The Judicial Mind: The Attitudes and Ideologies of Supreme Court Justices, 1946-63* (Evanston, IL: Northwestern University Press, 1965).

11 Russell, "Overcoming Legal Formalism," 11.

12 Martin Shapiro, "Public Law and Judicial Politics," in A. Finifter, ed., *Political Science: The State of the Discipline II* (Washington, DC: American Political Science Association, 1993), 365-81, quoted in Howard Gillman, "Martin Shapiro and the Movement from 'Old' to 'New' Institutionalist Studies in Public Law Scholarship," *Annual Review of Political Science* 7, 1 (2004): 7, 374.

13 Jeffrey A. Segal and Harold J. Spaeth, *The Supreme Court and the Attitudinal Model* (New York: Cambridge University Press, 1993).

Chapter 1: Judicial Doctrine as an Independent Variable in Federalism

1 A.V. Dicey, *Introduction to the Study of the Law of the Constitution*, 10th ed., ed. E.C.S. Wade (London: Macmillan, 1959), 179.

2 Michael Burgess, *The British Tradition of Federalism* (London: Leicester University Press, 1995), 17.
3 Dicey, *Law of the Constitution,* 165.
4 E.S. Corwin, "The Progress of Constitutional Theory between the Declaration of Independence and the Meeting of the Philadelphia Convention," *American Historical Review* 30 (1925): 511-36.
5 Martha Fletcher, "Judicial Review and the Division of Powers in Canada," in J. Peter Meekison, ed., *Canadian Federalism: Myth or Reality* (Toronto: Methuen, 1977), 100.
6 William Livingston, *Federalism and Constitutional Change* (Oxford: Clarendon, 1956), 1-13.
7 Dicey, *Law of the Constitution,* 149.
8 David Beatty, *Constitutional Law in Theory and in Practice* (Toronto: University of Toronto Press, 1995), 21.
9 Charles Fried, "Constitutional Doctrine," *Harvard Law Review* 107 (1993-94): 1140.
10 Andrew Heard, *Canadian Constitutional Conventions: The Marriage of Law and Politics* (Toronto: Oxford University Press, 1991), 3.
11 Charles Fried, *Saying What the Law Is: The Constitution in the Supreme Court* (Cambridge, MA: Harvard University Press, 2004), 12.
12 Peter Hogg, *Constitutional Law of Canada*, 4th ed. (Scarborough: Carswell, 1996), 216-17.
13 Literalists include Geoffrey Sawer, *Australian Federalism in the Courts* (Carlton, Victoria: Melbourne University Press, 1967), and Leslie Zines, *The High Court and the Constitution* (Melbourne: Butterworths, 1991). Realists are well represented by Brian Galligan, *The Politics of the High Court* (St. Lucia: University of Queensland Press, 1987), and Greg Craven, "The Crisis of Constitutional Literalism in Australia," in H.P. Lee and George Winterton, eds., *Australian Constitutional Perspectives* (Sydney: Law Book Company, 1992), 1-28.
14 Beatty, *Constitutional Law in Theory and in Practice,* xi.
15 Ibid., 18.
16 David M. Beatty, "Polluting the Law to Protect the Environment," *Constitutional Forum* 9, 2 (1998): 55-58.
17 Beatty's "constitutional values" do not go unnoticed by judicial authorities, including the Supreme Court of Canada. Its decision in *Reference Re: The Secession of Quebec* (1998), 161 D.L.R. (4th) 385, recognizes these two values as well as a commitment to the rule of law as fundamental tenets of the Canadian state.
18 In the Canadian case, the courts must decide between the two lists of powers contained largely in sections 91 and 92 of the *Constitution Act, 1867,* assigning powers to the federal and provincial governments respectively. The only exception would be powers recognized in the constitution as concurrent, of which three provisions speak. They enumerate agriculture and immigration, the export of natural resources, and old-age pensions as concurrent powers shared by both the federal and the provincial governments. In the Australian and American constitutions, there is only one list of governmental powers, and they are assigned to the national level. The residue is left to the states. Various commentators approach this division of powers as having a much more concurrent nature. The residual nature of state power characterizes federal power differently. Except for a few powers explicitly listed as exclusive, most powers held by the federal government are concurrent with the states. The federal government has supremacy (or paramountcy in the Australian lexicon) when a conflict arises, but unless one does both the states and the federal government are presumed to operate within the majority of the enumerated powers. The judicial task is twofold, then. The court must decide if indeed a matter is one for the federal legislature and, if it is, whether there is a substantive conflict of action, in which case the supremacy of the federal government must be invoked. Hogg, *Constitutional Law of Canada*, 363-64.
19 Ronald Watts, *Comparing Federal Systems*, 2nd ed. (Montreal and Kingston: McGill Queen's University Press, 1999), 63-69; Jennifer Smith, *The Meaning of Provincial Equality in Canadian Federalism,* Working Papers (Kingston: Institute for Intergovernmental Relations, Queen's University, 1998).
20 Watts, *Comparing Federal Systems,* 50-54; Paul E. Peterson, *The Price of Federalism* (Washington: Brookings Institution, 1995); John A. Ferejohn, *The New Federalism: Can the States Be Trusted?* (Stanford, CA: Hoover Institute Press, 1997).

21 Cairns, "The Judicial Committee and Its Critics."
22 G.P. Browne, *The Judicial Committee and the British North America Act: An Analysis of the Interpretive Scheme for the Distribution of Legislative Powers* (Toronto: University of Toronto Press, 1967). Bora Laskin and G.P. Browne, "The Judicial Committee and the British North America Act" (book review), *Canadian Public Administration* 10 (1967): 514.
23 Paul C. Weiler, *In the Last Resort: A Critical Study of the Supreme Court of Canada* (Toronto: Carswell-Methuen, 1974).
24 Ibid., 53.
25 Ibid., 4.
26 An ideology that Monahan argues was almost solely subscribed to prior to 1940 in Canada. Patrick Monahan, *Politics and the Constitution: The Charter, Federalism, and the Supreme Court of Canada* (Toronto: Carswell, 1987), 143.
27 Howard Gillman, "What's Law Got to Do with It? Judicial Behavioralists Test the 'Legal Model' of Judicial Decision Making," *Law and Social Inquiry* 23 (2001): 466.
28 Patrick Monahan, "At Doctrine's Twilight: The Structure of Canadian Federalism," *University of Toronto Law Journal* 34 (1984): 89.
29 Ibid., 99.
30 Ibid., 96.
31 It does not always have the chance. A prominent example is the *Reference Re: Canada Assistance Plan,* [1991] 2 S.C.R. 525, discussed in later chapters. See also Katherine Swinton, "Courting Our Way to Economic Integration: Judicial Review and the Canadian Economic Union," *Canadian Business Law Journal* 25 (1995): 280-304.
32 Monahan, "At Doctrine's Twilight," 98.
33 André Bzdera, "Comparative Analysis of Federal High Courts: A Political Theory of Judicial Review," *Canadian Journal of Political Science* 26, 1 (1993): 28.
34 While procedures vary across federations, most high court judges are appointed by the central government. Bzdera neglects to acknowledge that most federations, including Canada, have either conventions or written constitutional provisions that give constituent units advisory roles in senior court appointments. Watts, *Comparing Federal Systems,* 100-1.
35 Bzdera, "Comparative Analysis," 6.
36 Ibid., 29.
37 Ibid., 7.
38 Barry Cushman, *Rethinking the New Deal Court: The Structure of a Constitutional Revolution* (New York: Oxford University Press, 1998), 33.
39 Lorne Sossin, "The Sounds of Silence: Law Clerks, Policy Making and the Supreme Court of Canada," *University of British Columbia Law Review* 30 (1996): 279-308.
40 Cushman, *Rethinking the New Deal Court,* 41.
41 Ibid., 5.
42 Ibid., 41.
43 Howard Gillman, "The Court as an Idea, Not a Building (or a Game): Interpretive Institutionalism and the Analysis of Supreme Court Decision-Making," in Howard Gillman and Cornell Clayton, eds., *Supreme Court Decision-Making: New Institutionalist Approaches* (Chicago: University of Chicago Press, 1999), 68.
44 Rogers Smith, "Political Jurisprudence, the 'New Institutionalism,' and the Future of Public Law," *American Political Science Review* 82, 1 (1988): 89-108. Quoted in Cornell W. Clayton, "The Supreme Court and Political Jurisprudence: New and Old Institutionalisms," in Howard Gillman and Cornell Clayton, eds., *Supreme Court Decision-Making: New Institutionalist Approaches* (Chicago: University of Chicago Press, 1999), 31.
45 Ibid., 32.
46 Mark J. Richards and Herbert M. Kritzer, "Jurisprudential Regimes in Supreme Court Decision Making," *American Political Science Review* 96, 2 (2002): 306.
47 Ibid., 308.
48 Hogg, *Constitutional Law of Canada,* 121n101.
49 The Canadian practice of allowing governments to place reference questions before the courts without actual conflicts sometimes puts provincial appeal courts or the Supreme

Court in a political spotlight. Courts have no control over the use of this political expedient. They have been criticized for failing to live up to the challenges to their objectivity that references present. See Peter H. Russell, "Bold Statecraft, Questionable Jurisprudence," in Keith Banting and Richard Simeon, eds., *And No One Cheered: Federalism, Democracy and the Constitution Act* (Toronto: Methuen, 1983), 210-38.

Chapter 2: A Brief History of Federalism Doctrine in Practice

1 K.C. Wheare, *Federal Government*, 3rd ed. (New York: Oxford University Press, 1953), 12.
2 Martin Diamond, "The Federalist's View of Federalism," in George C.S. Benson, ed., *Essays in Federalism* (Claremont: Claremont Men's College, 1961), 21-64; Jennifer Smith, "Canadian Confederation and the Influence of American Federalism," *Canadian Journal of Political Science* 21 (1988): 443-63.
3 Specifically, Congress was given the power in Article 1(8) to create taxes, borrow, regulate commerce among the states, create rules of naturalization and bankruptcy, coin money, control counterfeiting, set up a post office, control patents and copyrights, create courts, punish piracy, declare war, create an army and navy, call forth militias, govern the capital district, and make all laws considered necessary and proper to the exercise of the foregoing powers. The states were specifically prevented from engaging in these pursuits by Article 1(10).
4 Dicey argues that the Canadian founders looked much more to the United States as a model for the constitution than the United Kingdom, despite the preamble's protestations that it is a constitution "similar in principle to that of the United Kingdom." A.V. Dicey, *Introduction to the Study of the Law of the Constitution*, 10th ed., ed. E.C.S. Wade (London: Macmillan, 1959), 166. That the founders may have read the American system wrong is discussed in Smith, "Canadian Confederation and the Influence of American Federalism."
5 By section 91(29) of the *Constitution Act, 1867*.
6 Bora Laskin, "Peace, Order, and Good Government Re-Examined," *Canadian Bar Review* 25 (1947): 1054-87; F.R. Scott, "Centralization and Decentralization in Canadian Federalism," *Canadian Bar Review* 29 (1951): 1095-1125.
7 W.R. Lederman suggests that property and civil rights had an established meaning in British North America well before Confederation. "The Fathers of Confederation knew all about this – they lived with it every day – and naturally they took the broad scope of the phrase for granted." W.R. Lederman, "Unity and Diversity in Canadian Federalism," *Canadian Bar Review* 53 (1975): 601.
8 Robert Vipond, *Liberty and Community: Canadian Federalism and the Failure of the Constitution* (Albany: SUNY Press, 1991).
9 Richard Simeon and Ian Robinson, *State, Society, and the Development of Canadian Federalism*, Royal Commission on the Economic Union and Development Prospects for Canada, vol. 71 (Toronto: University of Toronto Press, 1990), especially Chapter 3, "The Confederation Settlement."
10 Leslie Zines, "Federal Theory and Australian Federalism: A Legal Perspective," in Brian Galligan, ed., *Australian Federalism* (Melbourne: Longman Cheshire, 1989), 16.
11 *Commonwealth of Australia Constitution Act*, s. 107.
12 *Constitution of the United States*, Art. 1, s. 8.
13 In *Federalist* 78, Hamilton argued, "whoever attentively considers the different departments of power must perceive, that in a government in which they are separated from each other, the judiciary from the nature of its functions will always be the least dangerous to the political rights of the constitution; because it will be least in a capacity to annoy or injure them ... It may truly be said to have neither force nor will, but merely judgement; and must ultimately depend upon the aid of the executive arm even for the efficacy of its judgements." Jacob E. Cooke, ed. *The Federalist Papers* (Middletown, CT: Wesleyan University Press, 1961), 522-23.
14 Larry Alexander and Fredrick Shauer, "On Extra-Judicial Constitutional Interpretation," *Harvard Law Review* 11 (1997): 1359-87.
15 *Gibbons v. Ogden*, 9 Wheaton 1 (1824).

16 Walter Ehrlich, "Scott v. Sanford," in Kermit L. Hall, ed., *The Oxford Guide to United States Supreme Court Decisions* (New York: Oxford, 1999), 277-79.
17 Felix Frankfurter, *The Commerce Clause under Marshall, Taney, and Waite* (Chicago: Quadrangle, 1964), 50.
18 *The Constitution of the United States,* Amendment XIV, s. 1.
19 Bruce Ackerman, *We the People: Foundations* (Cambridge, MA: Belknap, 1991), 81.
20 *Slaughter-House Cases,* 16 Wallace 36 (1873).
21 Ibid., 81.
22 *The Daniel Ball,* 10 Wallace 557 (1871); *Swift and Co. v. U.S.,* 196 U.S. 375 (1905).
23 Arthur M. Schlesinger, Jr., *The Age of Roosevelt: The Politics of Upheaval,* Vol. 3 (Boston: Houghton Mifflin, 1960), 448.
24 *Panama Refining Co. v. Ryan,* 293 U.S. 388 (1935).
25 *Norman v. Baltimore and Ohio Railroad,* 294 U.S. 240 (1935).
26 *Railroad Retirement Board et al. v. Alton Railroad Co. et al.,* 295 U.S. 330 (1935). For a sympathetic account of the railroaders' predicament, see William E. Leuchtenburg, *The Supreme Court Reborn: The Constitutional Revolution in the Age of Roosevelt* (New York: Oxford University Press, 1995), Chapter 2, "Mr. Justice Roberts and the Railroaders."
27 *Schecter Poultry Corp. v. U.S.,* 295 U.S. 495 (1935).
28 Justices Willis Van Devanter, George Sutherland, Pierce Butler, and James McReynolds made up the foursome. The "liberal" justices were Louis Brandeis, Benjamin Cardozo, and Harlan Fiske Stone. Charles Evans Hughes, the chief justice, and Justice Owen Roberts represented the crucial swing faction on the court.
29 Schlesinger, *The Politics of Upheaval,* 280.
30 Ibid., 284.
31 *Schecter Poultry Corp. v. U.S.,* 550.
32 Schlesinger, *The Politics of Upheaval,* 283.
33 *Carter v. Carter Coal,* 298 U.S. 238 (1936), 309.
34 William Leuchtenburg, "The Origins of FDR's Court Packing Plan," in Phillip Kurland, ed., *Supreme Court Review, 1966* (Chicago: University of Chicago Press, 1966), 348.
35 Barry Cushman, *Rethinking the New Deal Court: The Structure of a Constitutional Revolution* (New York: Oxford University Press, 1998), especially Part 2, "A New Trial for Justice Roberts."
36 Some dispute exists about whether it was the effectiveness of the NLRB's case that determined the positive outcome. If one ascribes greater weight to the influence of the court-packing plan, the skill of the NLRB lawyers in relation to other New Deal lawyers is less relevant. See Barry Cushman, "A Stream of Legal Consciousness: The Current of Commerce Doctrine from *Swift* to *Jones & Laughlin,*" *Fordham Law Review* 61 (1992): 105-60; and Cushman, *Rethinking the New Deal Court.*
37 *Gibbons v. Ogden,* 9 Wheaton 1 (1824).
38 *NLRB v. Jones and Laughlin Steel,* 301 U.S. 1 (1937), 41.
39 Forrest McDonald, *A Constitutional History of the United States* (Malabar, FL: Kreiger Publishing, 1982), 199.
40 *Amalgamated Society of Engineers v. Adelaide Steamship Co. Ltd.* (1920), 28 C.L.R. 129 [Engineers].
41 All appeals to the JCPC were finally abolished in 1968. See Brian Galligan, *The Politics of the High Court* (St. Lucia: University of Queensland Press, 1987), 75-76.
42 Ibid., 80.
43 Wheare, *Federal Government,* 11-12.
44 *D'Emden v. Pedder* (1904), 1 C.L.R. 91.
45 *McCullough v. Maryland,* 4 Wheaton 316 (1819).
46 There are now numerous interstate lines that were completed at great expense to both state and Commonwealth governments. However, even today gaps remain in the system. A complete account of the federal challenges to rail standardization can be found in Garth Stevenson, *Rail Transport and Australian Federalism* (Canberra: Centre for Research on Federal Financial Relations, 1987). Chapter 2, "The Gauge Problem," describes some of the physical challenges presented by differing engineering specifications.

47 Quoted in Robert Menzies, *Central Power in the Australian Commonwealth* (London: Cassell, 1967), 35.
48 Geoffrey Sawer, *Australian Federalism in the Courts* (Carlton, Victoria: Melbourne University Press, 1967), 127.
49 Leslie Zines, *The High Court and the Constitution* (Melbourne: Butterworths, 1991), 5.
50 Barry Strayer argues that the introduction of judicial review in Canada was beneficial for that reason in addition to the restrictive conditions under which disallowance could actually be used. Barry Strayer, *The Canadian Constitution and the Courts: The Function and Scope of Judicial Review* (Toronto: Butterworths, 1988), 21. Jennifer Smith also points to the unruly backlog of provincial legislation scheduled for federal cabinet review as a further incentive to pass some of that work off to a Supreme Court. Jennifer Smith, "The Origins of Judicial Review in Canada," *Canadian Journal of Political Science* 16, 2 (1983): 115-34.
51 *Farey v. Burvett* (1916), 21 C.L.R. 433.
52 Quoted in Galligan, *The Politics of the High Court,* 95.
53 *Amalgamated Workers Union v. The Adelaide Milling Company* (1919), 26 C.L.R. 460, reaffirmed the implied immunity doctrine. The application of immunity required that the activity regulated be shown to be governmental. The generosity of the court allowed many essentially non-governmental activities to be approved for immunity as long as they were controlled by a state. Menzies wittily remarked some years later that, in the above case, "a wheat lumper [employed in the milling of wheat by a state enterprise] ... was unconsciously, but splendidly, performing one of the primary functions of government." Menzies, *Central Power in the Australian Commonwealth,* 36.
54 Ibid., 38.
55 Galligan, *The Politics of the High Court,* 99.
56 Zines, *The High Court and the Constitution,* 10.
57 John Nethercote, "The Engineers' Case: Seventy-Five Years On," in John Stone, ed., *Proceedings: Sixth Conference of the Samuel Griffith Society* (Melbourne: Samuel Griffith Society, 1995), 4.
58 Galligan, *The Politics of the High Court,* 101.
59 *Strickland v. Rocla Concrete Pipes Ltd.* (1971), 124 C.L.R. 468 [*Concrete Pipes*], 487.
60 Galligan, *The Politics of the High Court,* 106, 220. See also Geoffrey Sawer, *Federation under Strain: Australia 1972-1975* (Carlton: Melbourne University Press, 1977), 1-9. Gough Whitlam claims credit for removing the pledge against federalism from the Labor Party's constitution in 1969. See Gough Whitlam, *The Whitlam Government 1972-1975* (Ringwood, Victoria: Penguin, 1985), 712.
61 *Commonwealth v. Tasmania* (1983), 46 A.L.R. 625 [*Tasmanian Dam*]. See the complete discussion in Chapter 5 below.
62 "The Constitution versus Labor," in Gough Whitlam, *On Australia's Constitution* (Camberwell, Victoria: Widescope, 1977), 15-45.
63 Brian Galligan, "Constitutionalism and the High Court," in Scott Prasser, J.R. Nethercote, and John Warhurst, eds., *The Menzies Era* (Sydney: Hale and Iremonger, 1995), 154.
64 Ibid., 156.
65 R.L. Mathews and W.R.C. Jay, *Federal Finance: Intergovernmental Financial Relations in Australia since Federation* (Melbourne: Nelson, 1972), 175.
66 Menzies, *Central Power in the Australian Commonwealth,* 90-91.
67 *South Australia v. Commonwealth* (1942), 65 C.L.R. 373 [*First Uniform Tax*], 429.
68 *A.G. Victoria (ex rel Dale) v. Commonwealth* (1945), 71 C.L.R. 237.
69 *Melbourne Corporation v. Commonwealth* (1947), 74 C.L.R. 31 [*State Banking*].
70 R.P. Meagher and W.M.C. Gummow, "Sir Owen Dixon's Heresy," *Australian Law Journal* 54 (1980): 25.
71 Quoted in Zines, *The High Court and the Constitution,* 278.
72 *Uther v. Federal Commissioner of Taxation* (1947), 74 C.L.R. 508.
73 *Commonwealth v. Cigamatic Pty Ltd.* (1962), 108 C.L.R. 372.
74 *Strickland v. Roda Concrete Pipes Ltd.* (1971), 124 C.L.R. 468 [*Concrete Pipes*].
75 *Huddart, Parker and Co. Pty Ltd. v. Moorhead* (1909), 8 C.L.R. 330.
76 *Concrete Pipes,* 488.
77 Ibid., 489.

78 Ibid., 490.

79 *R. v. Federal Court of Australia; Ex parte WA National Football League* (1979), 143 C.L.R. 190 [*Adamson's*]; and *State Superannuation Board of Victoria v. Trade Practices Commission* (1982), 150 C.L.R. 282.

80 Alan Cairns, "The Judicial Committee and Its Critics," *Canadian Journal of Political Science* 4, 3 (1971): 301-45. The critics included Frank R. Scott, Bora Laskin, Vincent L. Macdonald, W.P.M. Kennedy, and William Lederman. For a more biographical account, see Richard Risk, "The Scholars and the Constitution: P.o.g.g. and the Privy Council," *Manitoba Law Journal* 23 (1995): 496-523. Representative works of the critics include Laskin, "Peace, Order, and Good Government Re-Examined"; F.R. Scott, "The Consequences of the Privy Council Decisions," *Canadian Bar Review* 15 (1937): 485-94; Scott, "Centralization and Decentralization in Canadian Federalism"; and Vincent Macdonald, "The British North America Act: Past and Future," *Canadian Bar Review* 15 (1937): 393-400.

81 Laskin, "Peace, Order, and Good Government Re-Examined," 1054.

82 *Russell v. The Queen* (1882), 7 A.C. 829. Sir Montague Smith, in a fury of negatives, wrote for the committee that, "if the Act does not fall within any of the classes of subjects in sect. 92, no further question will remain, for it cannot be contended ... that, if the Act does not come within one of the classes of subjects assigned to the Provincial legislatures, the Parliament of Canada had not, by its general power 'to make laws for the peace, order and good government of Canada,' full legislative authority to pass it." Ibid., 836.

83 *A.G. Ontario v. A.G. Canada* (1896), A.C. 348 [*Local Prohibition*]. The committee ruled that "the exercise of legislative power by the parliament of Canada, in regard to all manners not enumerated in sect. 91, ought to be strictly confined to such matters as are unquestionably of Canadian interest and importance, and ought not to trench upon provincial legislation with respect to any of the classes of subjects enumerated in sect. 92." Ibid., 360. Determining what qualifies as a matter of Canadian interest and importance continues to occupy the court. The effect of the last part of the quotation above makes POGG a third compartment. There is a prior claim to section 92 – legislation must first be found not to fit a section 92 heading before it can qualify for POGG justification.

84 *In Re: Board of Commerce Act* (1922), 1 A.C. 191.

85 *Fort Frances Pulp & Power Co. v. Manitoba Free Press* (1923), A.C. 695.

86 *Toronto Electric Commissioner v. Snider* (1925), A.C. 396.

87 *Re: Regulation and Control of Aeronautics in Canada* (1932), A.C. 54.

88 *In Re: Regulation and Control of Radio Communication in Canada* (1932), A.C. 304.

89 *A.G. Canada v. A.G. Ontario (Labour Conventions Reference)* (1937), A.C. 326; *Employment and Social Insurance Reference* (1937), A.C. 355; and *A.G. British Columbia v. A.G. Canada (National Products Marketing Act Reference)* (1937), A.C. 377.

90 *Employment and Social Insurance Reference* (1937), A.C. 355.

91 S. 91(2A) added by the *British North America Act,* 1940 3-4 Geo. VI, c. 36 (U.K.).

92 Scott, "Centralization and Decentralization in Canadian Federalism," 1106.

93 *Citizens Insurance Co. v. Parsons* (1881), 7 A.C. 96.

94 Ibid., 112.

95 *Attorney-General for Canada v. Attorney-General for Alberta* (1916), 1 A.C. 589 [*1916 Insurance Reference*], in Peter Russell, *Leading Constitutional Decisions* (Toronto: McClelland and Stewart, 1968), 83.

96 *Toronto Electric Commissioners v. Snider* (1925), A.C. 396 .

97 *Employment and Social Insurance Reference* (1937), A.C. 355.

98 *Johannesson v. West St. Paul,* [1952] S.C.R. 292; *Pronto Uranium Mines, Ltd. v. O.L.R.B.* (1956), 5 D.L.R. (2nd) 342; *Munro v. National Capital Commission*, [1966] S.C.R. 663; and *Reference re: Offshore Mineral Rights of B.C.* [1967] S.C.R. 792.

99 *A.G. Ontario v. A.G. Canada* (1896), A.C. 348, 361. Quoted in Lederman, "Unity and Diversity in Canadian Federalism," 609.

100 The image comes from a poem by poet (and constitutional lawyer) F.R. Scott: "But the judges fidgeted over their digests / And blew me away with the canons of construction." The same poem recognized the "fresh approach of Lord Simon," who was, however, smothered by "the wet blanket of provincial autonomy." F.R. Scott, "Some Privy Counsel," *Canadian Bar Review* 28, 7 (1950): 780.

101 *Attorney General of Nova Scotia v. Attorney General of Canada*, [1951] S.C.R. 31.
102 *PEI Potato Marketing Board v. H.B. Willis*, [1952] 2 S.C.R. 392.
103 Peter Hogg, "Is the Supreme Court of Canada Biased in Constitutional Cases?" *Canadian Bar Review* 57 (1979): 739.
104 See James C. Macpherson, "Justice Jean Beetz: A Rich and Enduring Legacy in Canadian Constitutional Scholarship and Jurisprudence," *Revue juridique themis* 28 (1994): 761.
105 Peter H. Russell, "The Supreme Court and Federal-Provincial Relations: The Political Use of Legal Resources," *Canadian Public Policy* 11, 2 (1985): 161.

Chapter 3: The US Supreme Court

1 Kathleen Sullivan, "Duelling Sovereignties: *U.S. Term Limits, Inc. v. Thornton*," *Harvard Law Review* 109 (1995): 81.
2 See Jeffrey Rosen, "The Agonizer," *New Yorker*, 11 November 1996: 82-90; Linda Greenhouse, "Justices Seem Ready to Tilt More toward States in Federalism," *New York Times*, 1 April 1999; and Robert W. Van Sickel, *Not a Particularly Different Voice: The Jurisprudence of Sandra Day O'Connor* (New York: Peter Lang, 1998).
3 See Alan Cairns, "The Governments and Societies of Canadian Federalism," *Canadian Journal of Political Science* 10, 4 (1977): 695-725; and Donald V. Smiley and Ronald L. Watts, *Intrastate Federalism in Canada*, Research Studies for the Royal Commission on the Economic Union and Development Prospects for Canada, vol. 39 (Toronto: University of Toronto Press, 1985). On the difficulty of applying the concept to other federations, see Herman Bakvis, "Intrastate Federalism in Australia," *Australian Journal of Political Science* 29, 2 (1994): 259-76.
4 *National League of Cities v. Usery*, 426 U.S. 833 (1976). Tony Mauro traces Rehnquist's thinking back to his solitary dissent in *Fry v. United States* in 1975. Former Acting Solicitor General Walter Dellinger III has called *Fry* "the Rosetta Stone for understanding the Rehnquist Court." "Alpha Rehnquist," *Legal Times*, January 2003: 59.
5 *United States v. Darby*, 312 U.S. 100 (1941).
6 *Hammer v. Dagenhart*, 247 U.S. 251 (1918).
7 *Fry v. United States*, 421 U.S. 542 (1975). C. Herman Pritchett, *Constitutional Law of the Federal System* (Englewood Cliffs, NJ: Prentice-Hall, 1984), 234.
8 *National League of Cities v. Usery*, 844.
9 Ibid., 845.
10 Ibid., 846.
11 Ibid., 849.
12 The source of the doctrine is essentially theory, not precedent. Jeff Powell, "The Compleat Jeffersonian: Justice Rehnquist and Federalism," *Yale Law Journal* 91 (1982): 1329.
13 Ibid., 1322.
14 Pritchett, *Constitutional Law of the Federal System*, 537.
15 *Hodel v. Virginia Surface Mining and Reclamation Association*, 452 U.S. 264 (1981); *Equal Employment Opportunity Commission v. Wyoming*, 103 S. Ct. 1054 (1983).
16 *Hodel*, 287.
17 The cases are listed in Pritchett, *Constitutional Law of the Federal System*, 538-39.
18 *Garcia*, 1020.
19 The text of the amendment reads, "the powers not delegated to the United States ... are reserved to the States respectively." Some judges have interpreted this just as a statement of the obvious: what is not left to Congress is not left to Congress.
20 From the dissent in *Hodel*, 307-8. Quoted in *Garcia*, 1347.
21 Antonin Scalia, "American Federalism and the Supreme Court," in Kjell Åke Modéer, ed., *The New Federalism. Structures and Infrastructures, American and European Perspectives* (Stockholm: Forskningsrådsnämnden, 2000), 56-67; Herbert Wechsler, "The Political Safeguards of Federalism: The Role of the States in the Composition and Selection of the National Government," *Columbia Law Review* 53 (1954): 543; Jesse Choper, "The Scope of National Power vis-à-vis the States: The Dispensability of Judicial Review," *Yale Law Journal* 86 (1977): 1552; Jesse Choper, *Judicial Review and the National Political Process: A Functional Reconsideration of the Role of the Supreme Court* (Chicago: University of Chicago Press, 1980).

22 A.E. Dick Howard, "*Garcia:* Of Federalism and Constitutional Values," *Publius: The Journal of Federalism* 16 (1986): 17-32.
23 *New York v. United States,* 505 U.S. 144 (1992).
24 *South Dakota v. Dole,* 483 U.S. 203 (1987).
25 *Davis v. Monroe County School Board,* 526 U.S. 629 (1999).
26 *United States v. Lopez,* 115 S. Ct. 1624 (1995).
27 Ibid., 1634.
28 Such opinions are in character. Mark Graber suggests that lone dissents are the trademark of the Thomas approach. "Clarence Thomas and the Perils of Amateur History," in Earl Maltz, ed., *Rehnquist Justice: Understanding the Court Dynamic* (Lawrence: University Press of Kansas, 2003), 70-102.
29 *Wickard v. Filburn,* 317 U.S. 111 (1942).
30 *Lopez,* 1650.
31 Arkansas passed Amendment 73 by referendum in November 1992. It prohibited the name of otherwise-eligible candidates from appearing on the ballot if they had served three terms in the House of Representatives or two terms in the Senate. There was something of an attempt to bulletproof the provision in the way that it was drafted. By only excluding names from the ballot, the state law played it safe in that Congress is to be the sole judge of qualifications (and disqualifications) of its members. This way the states were merely fine-tuning the electoral process as they are entitled under Article 1, section 4, of the constitution. Candidates were not truly excluded – they could mount a write-in campaign and serve if elected, but a ballot exclusion effectively barred most if not all candidates from achieving electoral success.
32 *U.S. Term Limits, Inc., v. Thornton,* 115 S. Ct. 1842 (1995), 1854. Quoting from Joseph Story, *Commentaries on the Constitution of the United States,* 3rd ed. (1858, repr. Boston: Little Brown, 2001), 627.
33 *Term Limits,* 1855.
34 The section reads, "the Times, Places and Manner of holding Elections for Senators and Representatives, shall be prescribed in each state by the Legislature thereof; but the Congress may at any time by Law make or alter such Regulations."
35 *Term Limits,* 1869.
36 Ibid., 1857.
37 Ibid., 1875.
38 Ibid., 1878.
39 Sullivan, "Duelling Sovereignties," 81.
40 *Term Limits,* 1872.
41 *Printz v. U.S.,* 517 U.S. 44 (1997).
42 Ibid., 2370.
43 Ibid., 2396.
44 *Seminole Tribe of Florida v. Florida,* 116 S. Ct. 1114 (1996).
45 The amendment grants the states immunity from suits "commenced or prosecuted against one of the United States by Citizens of another State, or by Citizens or Subjects of any Foreign State."
46 *Pennsylvania v. Union Gas,* 491 U.S. 1 (1989).
47 *Seminole Tribe,* 72.
48 *Idaho v. Coeur d'Alene Tribe,* 521 U.S. 261 (1997).
49 *Alden v. Maine,* 527 U.S. 706 (1999), 707.
50 Ibid., 754.
51 Linda Greenhouse, "States Are Given New Legal Shield by Supreme Court," *New York Times,* 24 June 1999.
52 *Alden v. Maine,* 814, para. 41.
53 *Kimel v. Florida Board of Regents,* 528 U.S. 62 (2000) [*Kimel*].
54 *City of Boerne v. Flores,* U.S. 527 (1997).
55 *Kimel,* 181.
56 *Alabama v. Garrett,* 531 U.S. 356 (2001).
57 *Federal Maritime Commission v. South Carolina State Ports Authority et al.,* 535 U.S. 743 (2002).

58 H. Jefferson Powell and Benjamin J. Preister, "Convenient Shorthand: The Supreme Court and the Language of State Sovereignty," *University of Colorado Law Review* 71 (2000): 668.
59 Ibid.
60 *U.S. v. Morrison,* 529 U.S. 598 (2000) 611.
61 Ibid, 613.
62 Ibid.
63 Ibid., 656.
64 Ibid., 663.
65 *Federal Maritime Commission,* 535 U.S. 743 (2002), 788, last paragraph of Breyer's dissent.
66 Linda Greenhouse, "At the Court, Dissent over States' Rights Is Now War," *New York Times,* 9 June 2002.
67 Linda Greenhouse, "A Conservative Voice, but Clearly a Woman's," *New York Times,* 26 May 1999.
68 *Raich v. Gonzales,* 545 U.S. (2005).
69 *Kimel,* 109.
70 Hillary Rodham Clinton, "Separation Anxiety: The Intersection of Congress, the Courts, and the Constitution," remarks delivered to the American Constitution Society, Georgetown Law Center Chapter, Washington, DC, 12 March 2002.
71 Keith E. Whittington, "Commentary: Taking What They Give Us: Explaining the Court's Federalism Offensive," *Duke Law Journal* 51 (2001): 519.
72 Ibid., 480.
73 Ibid., 484.
74 Richard A. Brisbin, Jr., "The Reconstitution of American Federalism? The Rehnquist Court and Federal-State Relations, 1991-1997," *Publius: The Journal of Federalism* 28, 1 (1998): 190.
75 Ibid., 191.
76 J. Mitchell Pickerill and Cornell W. Clayton, "The Rehnquist Court and the Political Dynamics of Federalism," *Perspectives on Politics* 2, 2 (2004): 233-48. The most recent formulation for this argument can be found in Mark Tushnet, *Taking the Constitution Away from the Courts* (Princeton, NJ: Princeton University Press, 1999).
77 Sullivan, "Duelling Sovereignties," 81.
78 This manoeuvring is evidenced by the court's ruling in *Lopez v. Monterey County,* 525 U.S. 266 (1999). The court upheld the application of the *Voting Rights Act,* which required counties to "pre-clear" changes to their voting rules with federal officials. Only Justice Thomas objected to the substantial "federalism costs" that the practice exacted from the political subdivisions of the states.

Chapter 4: The Australian High Court

1 *Amalgamated Society of Engineers v. Adelaide Steamship Co. Ltd.* (1920), 28 C.L.R. 129 [*Engineers*], 150.
2 Brian Galligan, "Legitimating Judicial Review: The Politics of Legalism," *Journal of Australian Studies* 8 (1981): 39-45; Leslie Zines, *The High Court and the Constitution* (Melbourne: Butterworths, 1991).
3 W.G. McMinn, *A Constitutional History of Australia* (Melbourne: Oxford University Press, 1979), 197.
4 Patrick Weller and Jenny Flemming, "The Commonwealth," in Jeremy Moon and Campbell Sharman, eds., *Australian Politics and Government: The Commonwealth, the States, and the Territories* (Cambridge, UK: Cambridge University Press, 2003), 12; Geoffrey Sawer, *Australian Federalism in the Courts* (Carlton, Victoria: Melbourne University Press, 1967), 208.
5 Zines, *The High Court and the Constitution,* Chapter 13, "Australia as a Nation in External and Internal Affairs."
6 Gough Whitlam, *On Australia's Constitution* (Camberwell, Victoria: Widescope, 1977), 40-41.
7 *R. v. Burgess; Ex parte Henry* (1936), 55 C.L.R. 608.

8 Robert Menzies, *Central Power in the Australian Commonwealth* (London: Cassell, 1967), 134.
9 *Koowarta v. Bjelke-Petersen* (1982), 153 C.L.R. 168. At least one observer was able to state that "it is a tenable view of *Commonwealth v. Tasmania* that as a matter of *ratio decidendi* it added nothing to the judicial construction of the Commonwealth's external affairs powers ... which was not already ... clearly established in *Koowarta v. Bjelke-Petersen.*" Geoffrey Sawer, "The External Affairs Power," *Federal Law Review* 14 (1984): 199.
10 Tony Blackshield, George Williams, and Brian Fitzgerald, *Australian Constitutional Law and Theory: Commentary and Materials* (Sydney: Federation Press, 1996), 458.
11 Coper acknowledges as much when noting that little change had actually taken place in the law as a result of *Tasmanian Dam.* Michael Coper, *The Franklin Dam Case* (Melbourne: Butterworths, 1983), 25.
12 Some doubts have been cast on the ability of federal governments to be effective in the "development versus environmentalism" trade-off. See the example of pulp and paper regulation in Canada in Kathryn Harrison, "Regulation of Pulp Mill Effluents in the Canadian Federal State," *Canadian Journal of Political Science* 29, 3 (1996): 469-96.
13 *Commonwealth v. Tasmania* (1983), 57 A.L.J.R. 450 [*Tasmanian Dam*].
14 Quoted in Mary Crock, "Federalism and the External Affairs Power," *Melbourne University Law Review* 14 (1983): 239.
15 *Tasmanian Dam,* 486.
16 *Koowarta v. Bjelke-Petersen,* 201.
17 *Tasmanian Dam,* 475.
18 *Koowarta,* 200.
19 Coper, *The Franklin Dam Case,* 10.
20 *R. v. Burgess,* 608.
21 *Tasmanian Dam,* 475.
22 Ibid.
23 Zines, *The High Court and the Constitution,* 242. H.P. Lee suggests that the "federal balance" doctrine is relevant today only to the extent that it protects these two principles; H.P. Lee, "The High Court and the External Affairs Power," in H.P. Lee and George Winterton, eds., *Australian Constitutional Perspectives* (Sydney: Law Book Company, 1992), 88. Cheryl Saunders also recognizes the survival of the implications theory as a minor, but possibly crucial, indication that federalism is not entirely dead as a result of the *Tasmanian Dam* decision. Cheryl Saunders, "The Federal System," *Papers on Federalism 6* (Melbourne: Intergovernmental Relations in Victoria Program, University of Melbourne, 1985), 13.
24 Zines, *The High Court and the Constitution,* 76.
25 Ibid., 77, and Coper, *The Franklin Dam Case,* 16.
26 Coper, *The Franklin Dam Case,* 25.
27 Sir Daryl Dawson, "The Constitution: Major Overhaul or Simple Tune-Up?" *Melbourne University Law Review* 14 (1984): 358.
28 Brian Galligan, *A Federal Republic* (Melbourne: Cambridge University Press, 1995), 179.
29 *Richardson v. Forestry Commission* (1988), 164 C.L.R. 261.
30 *Queensland v. Commonwealth* (1989), 167 C.L.R. 232 [*Tropical Rainforests*].
31 *Richardson v. Forestry Commission,* 322.
32 *Polyukhovich v. Commonwealth* (1991), 172 C.L.R. 501, 531 [*War Crimes Act*].
33 *Horta v. Commonwealth* (1994), 181 C.L.R. 183.
34 Chris Ryan, "Biggest Environmental Stoush since Franklin Dam," *Age* (Melbourne) 11 July 1998; Janine MacDonald and Chris Ryan, "UN Says No to Mining at Jabiluka," *Age* (Melbourne) 26 November 1998.
35 See, generally, Richard Marlin, "The External Affairs Power and Environmental Protection in Australia," *Federal Law Review* 24, 2(1996): 71-92.
36 Orietta Guerrera, "No Kyoto Accord Despite Greenhouse Gas Progress," *Age* (Melbourne) 19 September 2003. The Australian government would have considerable ease overcoming federal problems if it chose to implement the accord. This is not the case in Canada. See Gerald Baier, "The Kyoto Accord: Challenges of and for Canadian Federalism," in Van

Lantz and Joe Ruggeri, eds., *The Kyoto Protocol and Environmental Policy in Atlantic Canada* (Fredericton: UNB Centre for Policy Studies, 2003), 125-41.

37 In that case, the High Court upheld changes to the *Industrial Relations Reform Act* on the basis of external affairs. The changes were introduced to implement commitments made in the International Labour Organization (ILO) treaty of which the Commonwealth is a party. The majority refused to grant the state's argument that labour, despite the presence of international treaties on the subject, was not an issue of international concern according to the test in *Koowarta.* The majority argued that, according to the *Tasmanian Dam* test, the ILO treaty was well within international concern. *Victoria v. Commonwealth* (1996), 187 C.L.R. 416 [*Industrial Relations Reform Act*].

38 *New South Wales v. Commonwealth* (1990), 169 C.L.R. 482, 501 [*Incorporation*].

39 Greg Craven, "The Crisis of Constitutional Literalism in Australia," in H.P. Lee and George Winterton, eds., *Australian Constitutional Perspectives* (Sydney: Law Book Company, 1992), 27.

40 Greg Craven, "After Literalism, What?" *Melbourne University Law Review* 1 (1992), 896-97.

41 *Re Dingjan; Ex parte Wagner* (1995), 69 A.L.J.R. 284.

42 Ibid., 286.

43 B.M. Selway, "Hughes Case and the Referral of Powers," *Public Law Review* 12 (2001): 288.

44 *Re: Wakim; Ex Parte McNally* (1999), 198 C.L.R. 511.

45 *R. v. Hughes* (2000), 74 A.L.J.R. 802.

46 Selway, "Hughes Case," 294.

47 Ibid., 295.

48 Michael J. Whincop, "The National Scheme for Corporations and the Referral of Powers: A Sceptical View," *Public Law Review* 12 (2001): 268.

49 Cheryl Saunders, "A New Direction for Intergovernmental Arrangements," *Public Law Review* 12 (2001): 282.

50 Ibid., 285.

51 Ronald L. Watts, *The Spending Power in Federal Systems: A Comparative Study* (Kingston: Institute for Intergovernmental Relations, Queen's University, 1999), 52.

52 R.L. Mathews and W.R.C. Jay, *Federal Finance: Intergovernmental Financial Relations in Australia since Federation* (Melbourne: Nelson, 1972).

53 *Dennis Hotels Pty Ltd. v. Victoria* (1960), 104 C.L.R. 529.

54 *Dickenson's Arcade Pty Ltd. v. Tasmania* (1974), 130 C.L.R. 177.

55 *Phillip Morris Ltd. v. Commissioner of Business Franchises* (1989), 167 C.L.R. 399.

56 *Ngo Ngo Ha and Anor v. New South Wales* (1997), 189 C.L.R. 465.

57 Deborah Z. Cass, "Lionel Murphy and Section 90 of the Australian Constitution," in Michael Coper and George Williams, eds., *Justice Lionel Murphy: Influential or Merely Prescient?* (Sydney: Federation Press, 1997), 21.

58 *Ha,* 488.

59 Bhajan Grewal, "Economic Integration and Federalism: Two Views from the High Court of Australia," in John Stone, ed., *Upholding the Constitution* (Melbourne: Samuel Griffith Society, 1998), 76-87.

60 Douglas M. Brown, *Market Rules: Economic Union Reform and Intergovernmental Policy Making in Australia and Canada* (Kingston and Montreal: McGill-Queen's University Press, 2002), 218-22.

61 *Commonwealth v. Cigamatic Pty Ltd.* (1962), 108 C.L.R. 372.

62 *Queensland Electricity Commission v. Commonwealth* (1985), 61 A.L.R. 1.

63 *Re: Residential Tenancies Tribunal (NSW); Ex parte Defense Housing Authority* (1997), 190 C.L.R. 410.

64 Craven, "After Literalism, What?"; Craven, "The Crisis of Constitutional Literalism in Australia."

65 Greg Craven, "Cracks in the Facade of Literalism: Is There an Engineer in the House?" *Melbourne University Law Review* 18 (1992): 563.

66 Ibid., 545.

67 Galligan, *A Federal Republic,* 187.

68 Ibid., 187-88.

69 Craven,"Cracks in the Facade of Literalism," 563.

Chapter 5: The Canadian Supreme Court

1 The legislation abolishing appeals to the Privy Council came into effect on 23 December 1949 – any actions begun before that point retained a right of appeal to the JCPC. All actions following that date were determined in the final instance by the Supreme Court of Canada. See Peter Hogg, *Constitutional Law of Canada*, 4th ed. (Scarborough: Carswell, 1996), 200. On Australia, see Chapter 2, n39.

2 Peter H. Russell, "The Supreme Court and Federal-Provincial Relations: The Political Use of Legal Resources," *Canadian Public Policy* 11, 2 (1985): 326-37; Peter Hogg, "Is the Supreme Court of Canada Biased in Constitutional Cases?" *Canadian Bar Review* 57 (1979): 721-39; Donna Greschner, "The Supreme Court, Federalism, and Metaphors of Moderation," *Canadian Bar Review* 79 (2000): 47-76; for a dissenting view, see André Bzdera, "Comparative Analysis of Federal High Courts: A Political Theory of Judicial Review," *Canadian Journal of Political Science* 26, 1 (1993): 3-29.

3 John Saywell, *The Lawmakers: Judicial Power and the Shaping of Canadian Federalism* (Toronto: University of Toronto Press, 2002), 302.

4 Chief Justice Laskin was joined in the plurality decision by Spence, Dickson, and Judson. The three partial concurrers were led by Ritchie, with Pigeon and Martland. Justice Beetz wrote the dissent for himself and de Grandpré.

5 W.R. Lederman, "Unity and Diversity in Canadian Federalism," *Canadian Bar Review* 53 (1975): 606.

6 Lederman's argument to the court is summarized in Peter H. Russell, "The *Anti-Inflation* Case: The Anatomy of a Constitutional Decision," *Canadian Public Administration* 20, 4 (1977): 651.

7 *Reference Re: Anti-Inflation Act* (1976), 68 D.L.R. (3rd) 524.

8 Russell, "The *Anti-Inflation* Case," 656.

9 Russell, "The Supreme Court and Federal-Provincial Relations."

10 Richard Simeon, *Federal-Provincial Diplomacy* (Toronto: University of Toronto Press, 1971).

11 Russell, "The *Anti-Inflation* Case," 665.

12 The development of this concept is explained more fully in Gerald Baier, "Tempering Peace, Order, and Good Government: Provincial Inability and Canadian Federalism," *National Journal of Constitutional Law* 9, 3 (1998): 1-29. The following draws directly from the discussion therein.

13 Dale Gibson, "Measuring National Dimensions," *Manitoba Law Journal* 7 (1976): 13-37.

14 Ibid., 33.

15 Ibid.

16 Ibid., 34.

17 Peter Hogg, *Constitutional Law of Canada,* 1st ed. (Toronto: Carswell, 1977), 260.

18 Ibid., 261.

19 *Labatt Breweries of Canada v. A.-G. Canada* (1980), 110 D.L.R. (3rd) 594.

20 Ibid., 627.

21 *Schneider v. The Queen,* [1982] 2 S.C.R. 112.

22 Established by its power in criminal law as well as the court's own awarding of authority under POGG in *R. v. Hauser* (1979), 98 D.L.R. (3rd) 193.

23 Gibson, "Measuring National Dimensions," 35.

24 *R. v. Wetmore* (1983), 2 D.L.R. (4th) 577, 587.

25 The court has revisited the control of narcotics as a matter for the POGG power in *R. v. Malmo-Levine,* 2003 SCC 74, which is discussed on page 142.

26 *The Queen v. Crown Zellerbach Canada Ltd.* (1988), 49 D.L.R. (4th) 161, 173 [*Crown Zellerbach*].

27 Ibid., 184.

28 Ibid., 185.

29 The classical notion is embodied in K.C. Wheare's definition of the federal principle: namely, "the method of dividing powers so that the general and regional governments are each, within a sphere, co-ordinate and independent." *Federal Government*, 3rd ed. (New York: Oxford University Press, 1953), 10.

30 *Crown Zellerbach,* 185.

31 Ibid.

32 Ibid., 187.

33 Ibid., 195.
34 Ibid., 188.
35 Ibid., 199.
36 Ibid.
37 *Friends of the Oldman River Society v. Canada (Minister of Transport)* (1992), 88 D.L.R. (4th) 1.
38 Ibid., 42.
39 Ibid., 47.
40 *Ontario Hydro v. Ontario (Labour Relations Board)* (1993), 107 D.L.R. (4th) 457.
41 *Toronto Electric Commissioners v. Snider* (1925), A.C. 396.
42 Section 92(10)(c) of the *Constitution Act, 1867,* omits from provincial jurisdiction "such Works as, although wholly situated within the Province, are before or after their Execution declared by the Parliament of Canada to be for the general Advantage of Canada or for the Advantage of Two or more of the Provinces."
43 *Pronto Uranium Mines v. Ontario Labour Relations Board* (1956), 5 D.L.R. (2nd) 342.
44 *Ontario Hydro,* 478.
45 Ibid., 486.
46 Ibid., 523.
47 *RJR-MacDonald Inc. v. Canada (A.G.)* (1995), 127 D.L.R. (4th) 1.
48 David Schneiderman, "A Comment on *RJR-MacDonald v. Canada (A.G.),*" *University of British Columbia Law Review* 30 (1996): 165-80; Michael D. Parrish, "On Smokes and *Oakes:* A Comment on *RJR-MacDonald v. Canada (A.G.),*" *Manitoba Law Journal* 24 (1997): 665-98.
49 *RJR-MacDonald Inc. v. Canada (A.G.)* (1993), 102 D.L.R. (4th) 307 (Q.C.C.A.); *RJR-MacDonald Inc. v. Canada (A.G.)* (1995) 1.
50 *RJR-MacDonald* (1993), 307.
51 Ibid., 303.
52 *R. v. Hydro-Québec* (1997), 151 D.L.R. (4th) 95.
53 Ibid., 94.
54 Ibid., 93.
55 Ibid., 102.
56 Which was led by La Forest himself. Ibid., 95.
57 The dissent is noted by Vicki Jackson in "Holistic Interpretation: *Fitzpatrick v. Bitzer* and our Bifurcated Constituion," *Stanford Law Review* 53, 5 (May 2001): 1300.
58 The "double aspect" doctrine is used when a general subject matter can fit more than one jurisdictional heading. One aspect of firearms regulation is the control of criminal activity; another aspect is the regulation of property. Both are permissible and are competent to both Parliament and provincial legislatures according to the Alberta Court of Appeal. For a general discussion of the doctrine, see Hogg, *Constitutional Law of Canada,* 333-34.
59 Kirk Makin, "The Duel to Decide Gun Control," *Globe and Mail,* 19 February 2000, A13.
60 *Reference Re: Firearms Act (Canada)* (1998), 164 D.L.R. (4th) 513.
61 *R. v. Malmo-Levine,* 2003 SCC 74.
62 *R. v. Hauser* (1979), 98 D.L.R. (3rd) 193.
63 Paragraph 72.
64 The most important cases include *Citizens Insurance Co. v. Parsons, In Re: Board of Commerce Act,* and *1916 Insurance Reference.*
65 Bruce L. McDonald, "Constitutional Aspects of Canadian Anti-Combines Law Enforcement," *Canadian Bar Review* 47 (1969): 189. Quoted in *General Motors of Canada Ltd. v. City National Leasing* (1989), 58 D.L.R. (4th) 255, 266.
66 *MacDonald v. Vapour Canada Ltd.* (1976), 66 D.L.R. (3rd) 1.
67 *Trade Marks Act,* R.S.C. 1970, c. T-10.
68 Ibid., s. 7(e).
69 A legitimate exercise of the federal power had to be patrolled by a regulator; if enforcement was left to the initiative of affected individuals alone, it risked interfering with the provincial power to oversee the conduct of civil actions. *MacDonald,* 25.
70 *A.G. Canada v. Canadian National Transportation Ltd.* (1983), 3 D.L.R. (4th) 16.
71 Under the auspices of their power over the administration of justice in s. 92(14).
72 *A.G. Canada v. Canadian National,* 62.

73 Ibid., 70. Despite the potential expansion of federal power over trade and commerce that the decision seemingly invited, in their biography of Chief Justice Dickson, Robert Sharpe and Kent Roach note that the *Canadian National Transportation* decision "dealt the final blow to Dickson's 'pro-province' administration of justice theory." That Justice Dickson was on one hand advancing a case for provincial power in the prosecution of crimes and on the other advancing a broader scope for federal regulation of trade make him the embodiment of a balanced approach to federalism. *Brian Dickson: A Judge's Journey* (Toronto: University of Toronto Press, 2003), 254-55.

74 *Combines Investigation Act,* R.S.C. 1970, c. C-23.

75 Peter Hogg and Warren Grover, "The Constitutionality of the Competition Bill," *Canadian Business Law Journal* 1 (1976): 197-228. Quoted in *General Motors,* 273.

76 Ibid., 274.

77 The Liberal government elected in 1993 altered the arrangements for fiscal transfers to the provinces by placing EPF and CAP entitlements under a single umbrella known as the Canada Health and Social Transfer (CHST). At the same time, the federal government cut the total amount of transfers by something close to 33 percent. The CHST, by operating as a single, "super block fund" from the federal government to the provinces, superficially masked any variations in the amounts that fiscally strong or weak provinces received.

78 In the most extreme example, at the end of the five years that the "cap on CAP" existed, the level of funding by the federal government for CAP programs in Ontario had dropped from 50 to 29 percent. See Allan M. Maslove, "The Canada Health and Social Transfer: Forcing Issues," in Gene Swimmer, ed., *How Ottawa Spends 1996-97: Life under the Knife* (Ottawa: Carleton University Press, 1996), 288.

79 See Trudeau's "Federal Grants to Universities," in *Federalism and the French Canadians* (Toronto: Macmillàn, 1968), 79-102.

80 Peter Hogg seems to agree but fails to recognize exclusivity. Rather, he claims that, "by virtue" of section 93, "the establishment and administration of schools and universities is a provincial responsibility." *Constitutional Law of Canada,* looseleaf ed. (Scarborough: Carswell, 1997), 54–1.

81 Trudeau, *Federalism and the French Canadians,* 90. Similar objections were raised to the federal government's Millennium Scholarships, administered by a foundation endowed with $2.5 billion to award directly to students across the country. A comprehensive account of the foundation's activities can be found in Institute of Intergovernmental Relations, *Canadian Millennium Scholarship Foundation: Evaluation of the Foundation's Performance 1998-2002* (Kingston: Institute of Intergovernmental Relations, Queen's University, 30 May 2003).

82 Rand Dyck, "The Canada Assistance Plan: The Ultimate in Co-Operative Federalism," *Canadian Public Administration* 19, 4 (1976): 587-602.

83 *Reference Re: Canada Assistance Plan (B.C.)* (1991), 83 D.L.R. (4th) 297, 326.

84 Ibid.

85 Trudeau's turnaround was defended in Pierre Trudeau, *Federal-Provincial Grants and the Federal Spending Power* (Ottawa: Queen's Printer, 1969).

86 Alain Noël, France St-Hilaire, and Sarah Fortin, "Learning from the SUFA Experience," in Sarah Fortin, Alain Noël, and France St-Hilaire, eds., *Forging the Canadian Social Union: SUFA and Beyond* (Montreal: IRPP, 2003), 1-30.

87 Lorne Sossin, "Salvaging the Welfare State? The Prospects for Judicial Review of the Canada Health and Social Transfer," *Dalhousie Law Journal* 21, 1 (1998): 141-98.

88 Katherine Swinton, "Federalism under Fire: The Role of the Supreme Court of Canada," *Law and Contemporary Problems* 55, 1 (1992): 140.

89 Paul Barker, "Acceptable Law, Questionable Politics: The Canada Assistance Plan Reference," in Hugh Mellon and Martin Westmacott, eds., *Political Dispute and Judicial Review: Assessing the Work of the Supreme Court of Canada* (Scarborough: Nelson, 2000), 165-82; Gerald Baier, "Judicial Review and Federalism," in Herman Bakvis and Grace Skogstad, eds., *Canadian Federalism: Performance, Effectiveness, and Legitimacy* (Toronto: Oxford University Press, 2002), 24-39.

90 *Finlay No. 1,* [1986] 2 S.C.R. 633; *Finlay v. Canada,* [1993] 1 S.C.R. 1080.

91 Swinton, "Federalism under Fire," 145.
92 Ibid.
93 Canada, *Agreement on Internal Trade* (Ottawa: Industry Canada, 1994).
94 G. Bruce Doern and Mark MacDonald, *Free-Trade Federalism: Negotiating the Agreement on Internal Trade* (Toronto: University of Toronto Press, 1999), 142.
95 Ibid., 140.
96 Ibid., 141.
97 Internal Trade Secretariat, "Status of AIT Disputes: November 2005." http://www.intrasec.mb.ca/index_en/dispute.htm.
98 Patrick Monahan, "'To the Extent Possible': A Comment on Dispute Settlement in the Agreement on Internal Trade," in Michael Trebilcock and Daniel Schwanen, eds., *Getting There: An Assessment of the Agreement on Internal Trade* (Toronto: C.D. Howe Institute, 1995), 211-17.
99 Andrew Wahl, "Trade Secrets: Why Is Nothing Being Done about Interprovincial Barriers?" *Canadian Business* 29 May 2000: 62. Opinions do differ; Douglas Brown argues that the dispute resolution mechanisms have proven their worth in the dispute over the fuel additive MMT. Douglas M. Brown, *Market Rules: Economic Union Reform and Intergovernmental Policy Making in Australia and Canada* (Kingston and Montreal: McGill-Queen's University Press, 2002), 173.
100 Katherine Swinton, "Law, Politics, and the Enforcement of the Agreement on Internal Trade," in Michael Trebilcock and Daniel Schwanen, eds., *Getting There: An Assessment of the Agreement on Internal Trade* (Toronto: C.D. Howe Institute, 1995), 196-209.
101 Sujit Choudry, "Strengthening the Economic Union: The *Charter* and the *Agreement on Internal Trade*," *Constitutional Forum* 12, 2 (2002): 57.
102 David M. Beatty, "Polluting the Law to Protect the Environment," *Constitutional Forum* 9, 2 (1998): 57.
103 Ibid., 55.
104 Ibid., 57.
105 Ibid.
106 Patrick Monahan, *Politics and the Constitution: The Charter, Federalism, and the Supreme Court of Canada* (Toronto: Carswell, 1987), 142.

Conclusion

1 Cass Sunstein, *Legal Reasoning and Political Conflict* (New York: Oxford University Press, 1996).
2 Gerald Baier, "Judicial Review and Canadian Federalism," in Herman Bakvis and Grace Skogstad, eds., *Canadian Federalism: Performance, Effectiveness, and Legitimacy* (Toronto: Oxford University Press, 2002).
3 Patrick Monahan, *Politics and the Constitution: The Charter, Federalism, and the Supreme Court of Canada* (Toronto: Carswell, 1987), 224.
4 Hon. Beverly McLachlin, "Courts, Legislatures, and Executives in the Post-Charter Era," *Policy Options* June 1999: 46.
5 Gerald Baier, "New Judicial Thinking on Sovereignty and Federalism: American and Canadian Comparisons," *Justice System Journal* 23, 1 (2002): 1-24.
6 Henri Brun and Guy Tremblay, *Droit constitutionnel,* 2nd ed. (Cowansville: Les Éditions Yvon Blais, 1990); John Saywell, *The Lawmakers: Judicial Power and the Shaping of Canadian Federalism* (Toronto: University of Toronto Press, 2002).
7 Saywell, *The Lawmakers,* 308.
8 Sujit Choudry, "Beyond the Flight from Constitutional Legalism: Rethinking the Politics of Social Policy Post-Charlottetown," *Constitutional Forum* 12, 3 (2003): 77-83.

Bibliography

Primary Sources

Cases

Canada

A.G. British Columbia v. A.G. Canada (National Products Marketing Act Reference) (1937), A.C. 377.

A.G. Canada v. A.G. Ontario (1937), A.C. 355 [*Employment and Social Insurance Act References*]

A.G. Canada v. A.G. Ontario (Labour Conventions Reference) (1937), A.C. 326.

A.G. Canada v. Canadian National Transportation Ltd. (1983), 3 D.L.R. (4th) 16.

A.G. Manitoba v. Manitoba Egg and Poultry Association (1971), 19 D.L.R. (3rd) 169.

A.G. Ontario v. A.G. Canada (1896), A.C. 348 [*The Local Prohibition*].

A.G. Ontario v. Canada Temperance Federation (1946), A.C. 193.

Attorney-General for Canada v. Attorney-General for Alberta (1916), 1 A.C. 589 [*1916 Insurance Reference*].

Attorney General of Nova Scotia v. Attorney General of Canada, [1951] S.C.R. 31.

Citizens Insurance Co. v. Parsons (1881), 7 A.C. 96.

Finlay No. 1, [1986] 2 S.C.R. 633.

Finlay v. Canada, [1993] 1 S.C.R. 1080.

Fort Frances Pulp & Power Co. v. Manitoba Free Press (1923), A.C. 695.

Friends of the Oldman River Society v. Canada (Minister of Transport) (1992), 88 D.L.R. (4th) 1.

General Motors of Canada Ltd. v. City National Leasing, [1989] 1 S.C.R. 641.

In Re: Board of Commerce Act (1922), 1 A.C. 191.

In Re: Regulation and Control of Aeronautics in Canada (1932), A.C. 54.

In Re: Regulation and Control of Radio Communication in Canada (1932), A.C. 304.

Johannesson v. West St. Paul, [1952] 1 S.C.R. 292.

Labatt Breweries of Canada v. A.-G. Canada (1980), 110 D.L.R. (3rd) 594.

MacDonald v. Vapour Canada Ltd. (1976), 66 D.L.R. (3rd) 1.

Munro v. National Capital Commission, [1966] S.C.R. 663.

Ontario Hydro v. Ontario (Labour Relations Board) (1993), 107 D.L.R. (4th) 457.

PEI Potato Marketing Board v. H.B. Willis, [1952] 2 S.C.R. 392.

Pronto Uranium Mines, Ltd. v. Ontario Labour Relations Board (1956), 5 D.L.R. (2nd) 342.

The Queen v. Crown Zellerbach Canada Ltd. (1988), 49 D.L.R. (4th) 161.

R. v. Hauser (1979), 98 D.L.R. (3rd) 193.

R. v. Hydro-Québec (1997), 151 D.L.R. (4th) 95.

R. v. Malmo-Levine, 2003 SCC 74.

R. v. Wetmore (1983), 2 D.L.R. (4th) 577.

Reference Re: Anti-Inflation Act (1976), 68 D.L.R. (3rd) 524.

Reference Re: Canada Assistance Plan (B.C.), [1991] 2 S.C.R. 525, 83 D.L.R. (4th) 297.

Reference Re: Firearms Act (Canada) (1998), 164 D.L.R. (4th) 513.

Reference Re: Offshore Mineral Rights of B.C., [1967] S.C.R. 792.
Reference Re: The Secession of Quebec (1998), 161 D.L.R. (4th) 385.
RJR-MacDonald Inc. v. Canada (A.G.) (1993), 102 D.L.R. (4th) 289 (Q.C.C.A.).
RJR-MacDonald Inc. v. Canada (A.G.) (1995), 127 D.L.R. (4th) 1 (SCC).
Russell v. The Queen (1882), 7 A.C. 829.
Schneider v. The Queen, [1982] 2 S.C.R. 112.
Toronto Electric Commissioners v. Snider (1925), A.C. 396.

United States
Alabama v. Garrett, 531 U.S. 356 (2001).
Alden v. Maine, 527 U.S. 706 (1999).
Carter v. Carter Coal, 298 U.S. 238 (1936).
City of Boerne v. Flores, 521 U.S. 507 (1997).
Collector v. Day, 78 U.S. 113 (1870).
College Savings Bank v. Florida Prepaid Postsecondary Education Expense Board (98-149).
The Daniel Ball, 10 Wallace 557 (1871).
Davis v. Monroe County School Board, 526 U.S. 629 (1999).
Equal Employment Opportunity Commission (EEOC) v. Wyoming, 460 U.S. 226 (1983).
Ex parte Young, 209 U.S. 123 (1980).
Federal Maritime Commission v. South Carolina State Ports Authority, 535 U.S. 743 (2002).
Florida Prepaid Postsecondary Education Expense Board v. College Savings Bank (98-531).
Fry v. United States, 421 U.S. 542 (1975).
Garcia v. San Antonio Metropolitan Transit Authority, 469 U.S. 528 (1985).
Gibbons v. Ogden, 9 Wheaton 1 (1824).
Hammer v. Dagenhart, 247 U.S. 251 (1918).
Heart of Atlanta Motel v. United States, 379 U.S. 241 (1964).
Hodel v. Virginia Surface Mining and Reclamation Association, 452 U.S. 264 (1981).
Idaho v. Coeur d'Alene Tribe, 521 U.S. 261 (1997).
Kimel v. Florida Board of Regents, 528 U.S. 62 (2000).
Lopez v. Monterey County, 525 U.S. 266 (1999).
Marbury v. Madison, 1 Cranch 137 (1803).
McCulloch v. Maryland, 4 Wheaton 316 (1819).
National League of Cities v. Usery, 426 U.S. 833 (1976).
New York v. United States, 505 U.S. 144 (1992).
NLRB v. Jones and Laughlin Steel, 301 U.S. 1 (1937).
Norman v. Baltimore and Ohio Railroad, 294 U.S. 240 (1935).
Panama Refining Co. v. Ryan, 293 U.S. 388 (1935).
Pennsylvania v. Union Gas, 491 U.S. 1 (1989).
Printz v. U.S., 517 U.S. 44 (1997).
Raich v. Gonzales, 545 U.S. ___ (2005).
Railroad Retirement Board et al. v. Alton Railroad Co. et al., 295 U.S. 330 (1935).
Schecter Poultry Corp. v. U.S., 295 U.S. 495 (1935).
Seminole Tribe of Florida v. Florida, 116 S. Ct. 1114 (1996).
Slaughter-House Cases, 16 Wallace 36 (1873).
South Dakota v. Dole, 483 U.S. 203 (1987).
Swift and Co. v. U.S., 196 U.S. 375 (1905).
U.S. Term Limits, Inc. v. Thornton, 115 S. Ct. 1842 (1995).
U.S. v. Morrison, 529 U.S. 598 (2000).
United States v. Darby, 312 U.S. 100 (1941).
United States v. Lopez, 115 S. Ct. 1624 (1995).
West Coast Hotel v. Parrish, 300 U.S. 379 (1937).
Wickard v. Filburn, 317 U.S. 111 (1942).

Australia
A.G. Victoria (ex rel Dale) v. Commonwealth (1945), 71 C.L.R. 237.

Amalgamated Society of Engineers v. Adelaide Steamship Co. Ltd. (1920), 28 C.L.R. 129 [*Engineers*].
Amalgamated Workers Union v. The Adelaide Milling Company (1919), 26 C.L.R. 460.
Commonwealth v. Cigamatic Pty Ltd. (1962), 108 C.L.R. 372.
Commonwealth v. Tasmania (1983), 57 A.J.L.R. 450 [*Tasmanian Dam*].
D'Emden v. Pedder (1904), 1 C.L.R. 91.
Dennis Hotels Pty Ltd. v. Victoria (1960), 104 C.L.R. 529.
Dickenson's Arcade Pty Ltd. v. Tasmania (1974), 130 C.L.R. 177.
Farey v. Burvett (1916), 21 C.L.R. 433.
Federated Amalgamated Government Railway and Tramway Service Association v. New South Wales Railway Traffic Employees Association (1904), 4 C.L.R. 488 [Railway Servants].
Horta v. Commonwealth (1994), 181 C.L.R. 183.
Huddart, Parker, and Co. Pty Ltd. v. Moorhead (1909), 8 C.L.R. 330.
Koowarta v. Bjelke-Petersen (1982), 153 C.L.R. 168.
Melbourne Corporation v. Commonwealth (1947), 74 C.L.R. 31 [*State Banking*].
New South Wales v. Commonwealth (1990), 169 C.L.R. 482 [*Incorporation*].
Ngo Ngo Ha and Anor v. New South Wales (1997), 189 C.L.R. 465.
Phillip Morris Ltd. v. Commissioner of Business Franchises (1989), 167 C.L.R. 399.
Polyukhovich v. Commonwealth (1991), 172 C.L.R. 501 [*War Crimes Act*].
Queensland v. Commonwealth (1989), 167 C.L.R. 232 [*Tropical Rainforests*].
Queensland Electricity Commission v. Commonwealth (1985), 61 A.L.R. 1.
R. v. Burgess; Ex parte Henry (1936), 55 C.L.R. 608.
R. v. Federal Court of Australia; Ex parte WA National Football League (Adamson's Case) (1979), 143 C.L.R. 190.
R. v. Hughes (2000), 171 A.L.R. 155.
Re: Dingjan; Ex parte Wagner (1995), 69 A.L.J.R. 284 [Dingjan's Case].
Re: Residential Tenancies Tribunal (NSW); Ex parte Defense Housing Authority (1997), 190 C.L.R. 410.
Re: Wakim; Ex parte McNally (1999), 198 C.L.R. 511.
Richardson v. Forestry Commission (1988), 164 C.L.R. 261.
South Australia v. Commonwealth (1942), 65 C.L.R. 373 [*First Uniform Tax*].
State Superannuation Board of Victoria v. Trade Practices Commission (1982), 150 C.L.R. 282.
Strickland v. Rocla Concrete Pipes Ltd. (1971), 124 C.L.R. 468 [*Concrete Pipes*].
Victoria v. Commonwealth (1996), 187 C.L.R. 416 [*Industrial Relations Reform Act*].
Uther v. Federal Commissioner of Taxation (1947), 74 C.L.R. 508.

Constitutions and Statutes

Canada. *Agreement on Internal Trade.* Ottawa: Industry Canada, 1994.
Combines Investigation Act, R.S.C. 1970, c. C-23.
The Commonwealth of Australia Constitution Act, 1900.
Constitution Act, 1867 (Canada), U.K. 30 and 31 Victoria, c.3.
Constitution of the United States, Stats at Large of USA, 1787.
Trade Marks Act, R.S.C. 1970, c. T-10.

Reports, Speeches, etc.

Clinton, Hillary Rodham. "Separation Anxiety: The Intersection of Congress, the Courts, and the Constitution." Remarks delivered to the American Constitution Society, Georgetown Law Center Chapter, Washington, DC, 12 March 2002.
Institute of Intergovernmental Relations. *Canadian Millennium Scholarship Foundation: Evaluation of the Foundation's Performance 1998-2002.* Kingston: Institute of Intergovernmental Relations, 30 May 2003.
Internal Trade Secretariat. "Status of AIT Disputes: November 2005." http://www.intrasec.mb.ca/index_en/dispute.htm.

Secondary Sources

Ackerman, Bruce. *We the People: Foundations*. Cambridge, MA: Belknap, 1991.

Alexander, Larry, and Fredrick Shauer. "On Extrajudicial Constitutional Interpretation." *Harvard Law Review* 11, 7 (1997): 1359-87.

Baier, Gerald. "Judicial Review and Federalism." In *Canadian Federalism: Performance, Effectiveness, and Legitimacy*, ed. Herman Bakvis and Grace Skogstad, 24-39. Toronto: Oxford, 2002.

–. "The Kyoto Accord: Challenges of and for Canadian Federalism." In *The Kyoto Protocol and Environmental Policy in Atlantic Canada*, ed. Van Lantz and Joe Ruggeri, 125-41. Fredericton: UNB Centre for Policy Studies, 2003.

–. "New Judicial Thinking on Sovereignty and Federalism: American and Canadian Comparisons." *Justice System Journal* 23, 1 (2002): 1-24.

–. "Tempering Peace, Order, and Good Government: Provincial Inability and Canadian Federalism." *National Journal of Constitutional Law* 9, 3 (1998): 1-29.

Bakvis, Herman. "Intrastate Federalism in Australia." *Australian Journal of Political Science* 29, 2 (1994): 259-76.

Banting, Keith, and Richard Simeon, eds. *And No One Cheered: Federalism, Democracy and the Constitution Act*. Toronto: Methuen, 1983.

Barker, Paul. "Acceptable Law, Questionable Politics: The Canada Assistance Plan Reference." In *Political Dispute and Judicial Review: Assessing the Work of the Supreme Court of Canada*, ed. Hugh Mellon and Martin Westmacott, 165-82. Scarborough: Nelson, 2000.

Beatty, David M. "A Conservative's Court: The Politicization of Law." *University of Toronto Law Journal* 41 (1991): 147-67.

–. *Constitutional Law in Theory and in Practice*. Toronto: University of Toronto Press, 1995.

–. "Law and Politics." *American Journal of Comparative Law* 44 (1996): 131-50.

–. "Polluting the Law to Protect the Environment." *Constitutional Forum* 9, 2 (1998): 55-58.

–. *Talking Heads and the Supremes: The Canadian Production of Constitutional Review*. Toronto: Carswell, 1990.

Bermann, George A. "The Role of Law in the Functioning of Federal Systems." In *The Federal Vision: Legitimacy and Levels of Governance in the United States and the European Union*, ed. Kalypso Nicolaidis and Robert Howse, 191-212. Oxford: Oxford University Press, 2001.

Blackshield, Tony, George Williams, and Brian Fitzgerald. *Australian Constitutional Law: Commentary and Materials*. Sydney: Federation Press, 1996.

Brisbin, Jr., Richard A. "The Reconstitution of American Federalism? The Rehnquist Court and Federal-State Relations, 1991-1997." *Publius: The Journal of Federalism* 28, 1 (1998): 189-215.

Brown, Douglas M. *Market Rules: Economic Union Reform and Intergovernmental Policy Making in Australia and Canada*. Kingston and Montreal: McGill-Queen's University Press, 2002.

Browne, G.P. *The Judicial Committee and the British North America Act: An Analysis of the Interpretive Scheme for the Distribution of Legislative Powers*. Toronto: University of Toronto Press, 1967.

Brun, Henri, and Guy Tremblay. *Droit constitutionnel*. 2nd ed. Cowansville: Les Éditions Yvon Blais, 1990.

Burgess, Michael. *The British Tradition of Federalism*. London: Leicester University Press, 1995.

Bzdera, André. "Comparative Analysis of Federal High Courts: A Political Theory of Judicial Review." *Canadian Journal of Political Science* 26, 1 (1993): 3-29.

Cairns, Alan C. "Alternative Styles in the Study of Canadian Politics." *Canadian Journal of Political Science* 7, 1 (1974): 100-28.

–. *Charter versus Federalism: The Dilemmas of Constitutional Reform*. Montreal and Kingston: McGill-Queen's University Press, 1992.

–. "The Governments and Societies of Canadian Federalism." *Canadian Journal of Political Science* 10, 4 (1977): 695-725.

–. "The Judicial Committee and Its Critics." *Canadian Journal of Political Science* 4, 3 (1971): 301-45.

Cass, Deborah Z. "Lionel Murphy and Section 90 of the Australian Constitution." In *Justice Lionel Murphy: Influential of Merely Prescient?* ed. Michael Coper and George Williams,19-49. Sydney: Federation Press, 1997.

Choper, Jesse. *Judicial Review and the National Political Process: A Functional Reconsideration of the Role of the Supreme Court.* Chicago: University of Chicago Press, 1980.

–. "The Scope of National Power vis-à-vis the States: The Dispensability of Judicial Review." *Yale Law Journal* 86 (1977): 1552-1621.

Choudry, Sujit. "Beyond the Flight from Constitutional Legalism: Rethinking the Politics of Social Policy Post-Charlottetown." *Constitutional Forum* 12, 3 (2003): 77-83.

–. "Strengthening the Economic Union: The *Charter* and the *Agreement on Internal Trade.*" *Constitutional Forum* 12, 2 (2002): 52-59.

Clayton, Cornell W. "The Supreme Court and Political Jurisprudence: New and Old Institutionalisms." In *Supreme Court Decision-Making: New Institutionalist Approaches*, ed. Howard Gillman and Cornell Clayton, 15-41. Chicago: University of Chicago Press, 1999.

Cooke, Jacob E., ed. *The Federalist Papers*. Middletown, CT: Wesleyan University Press, 1961.

Coper, Michael. *The Franklin Dam Case*. Melbourne: Butterworths, 1983.

Corwin, E.S. "The Progress of Constitutional Theory between the Declaration of Independence and the Meeting of the Philadelphia Convention." *American Historical Review* 30 (1925): 511-36.

Craven, Greg. "After Literalism, What?" *Melbourne University Law Review* 1 (1992): 874-98.

–. "Cracks in the Facade of Literalism: Is There an Engineer in the House?" *Melbourne University Law Review* 18 (1992): 540-64.

–. "The Crisis of Constitutional Literalism in Australia." In *Australian Constitutional Perspectives*, ed. H.P. Lee and George Winterton, 1-28. Sydney: Law Book Company, 1992.

–. "Original Intent and the Australian Constitution: Coming Soon to a Court Near You?" *Public Law Review* 1 (1990): 167-85.

–. "The States: Decline, Fall, or What?" In *Australian Federalism: Towards the Second Century*, ed. Greg Craven, 49-69. Melbourne: Melbourne University Press, 1993.

Crock, Mary. "Federalism and the External Affairs Power." *Melbourne University Law Review* 14 (1983): 238-64.

Cushman, Barry. *Rethinking the New Deal Court: The Structure of a Constitutional Revolution*. New York: Oxford University Press, 1998.

–. "A Stream of Legal Conciousness: The Current of Commerce Doctrine from *Swift* to *Jones & Laughlin.*" *Fordham Law Review* 61 (1992): 105-60.

Dawson, Sir Daryl. "The Constitution: Major Overhaul or Simple Tune-Up." *Melbourne University Law Review* 14 (1984): 353-68.

Diamond, Martin. "The Federalist's View of Federalism." In *Essays in Federalism*, ed. George C.S. Benson, 21-64. Claremont: Claremont Men's College, 1961.

Dicey, A.V. *Introduction to the Study of the Law of the Constitution*. 10th ed. Ed. E.C.S. Wade. London: Macmillan, 1959.

Doern, G. Bruce, and Mark MacDonald. *Free-Trade Federalism: Negotiating the Agreement on Internal Trade*. Toronto: University of Toronto Press, 1999.

Dyck, Rand. "The Canada Assistance Plan: The Ultimate in Co-Operative Federalism." *Canadian Public Administration* 19, 4 (1976): 587-602.

Ehrlich, Walter. "Scott v. Sanford." In *The Oxford Guide to United States Supreme Court Decisions*, ed. Kermit L. Hall, 277-79. New York: Oxford University Press, 1999.

Ferejohn, John A. *The New Federalism: Can the States Be Trusted?* Stanford: Hoover Institute Press, 1997.

Finifter, A., ed. *Political Science: The State of the Discipline II*. Washington, DC: American Political Science Association, 1993.

Fletcher, Martha. "Judicial Review and the Division of Powers in Canada." In *Canadian Federalism: Myth or Reality*, ed. J. Peter Meekison, 100-22. Toronto: Methuen, 1977.

Frankfurter, Felix. *The Commerce Clause Under Marshall, Taney and Waite*. Chicago: Quadrangle, 1964.

Fried, Charles. "Constitutional Doctrine." *Harvard Law Review* 107 (1993-94): 1140-57.

–. *Saying What the Law Is: The Constitution in the Supreme Court.* Cambridge: Harvard University Press, 2004.

Galligan, Brian. "Constitutionalism and the High Court." In *The Menzies Era,* ed. Scott Prasser, J.R. Nethercote, and John Warhurst, 151-65. Sydney: Hale and Iremonger, 1995.

–. *A Federal Republic: Australia's Constitutional System of Government.* Melbourne: Cambridge University Press, 1995.

–. "Legitimating Judicial Review: The Politics of Legalism." *Journal of Australian Studies* 8 (1981): 33-53.

–. *The Politics of the High Court.* St. Lucia: University of Queensland Press, 1987.

Gibson, Dale. "Constitutional Jurisdiction over Environmental Management in Canada." *University of Toronto Law Journal* 23 (1973): 43-87.

–. "Measuring National Dimensions." *Manitoba Law Journal* 7 (1976): 13-37.

Gillman, Howard. "The Court as an Idea, Not a Building (or a Game): Interpretive Institutionalism and the Analysis of Supreme Court Decision-Making." In *Supreme Court Decision-Making: New Institutionalist Approaches,* ed. Howard Gillman and Cornell Clayton, 65-87. Chicago: University of Chicago Press, 1999.

–. "Martin Shapiro and the Movement from 'Old' to 'New' Institutionalist Studies in Public Law Scholarship." *Annual Review of Political Science* 7, 1 (2004): 363-82.

–. "What's Law Got to Do with It? Judicial Behavioralists Test the 'Legal Model' of Judicial Decision Making." *Law and Social Inquiry* 23 (2001): 465-98.

Gillman, Howard, and Cornell Clayton, eds. *Supreme Court Decision-Making: New Institutionalist Approaches.* Chicago: University of Chicago Press, 1999.

Graber, Mark. "Clarence Thomas and the Perils of Amateur History." In *Rehnquist Justice: Understanding the Court Dynamic,* ed. Earl Maltz, 70-102. Lawrence: University Press of Kansas, 2003.

Greenhouse, Linda. "At the Court, Dissent over States' Rights Is Now War." *New York Times,* 9 June 2002.

–. "A Conservative Voice, but Clearly a Woman's." *New York Times,* 26 May 1999.

–. "High Court Faces Moment of Truth in Federalism Cases." *New York Times,* 28 March 1999.

–. "Justices Seem Ready to Tilt More toward States in Federalism." *New York Times,* 1 April 1999.

–. "States Are Given New Legal Shield by Supreme Court." *New York Times,* 24 June 1999.

–. "2 Cases Test Immunity of States from Lawsuits." *New York Times,* 21 April 1999.

Greschner, Donna. "The Supreme Court, Federalism, and Metaphors of Moderation." *Canadian Bar Review* 79, 2 (2000): 47-76.

Grewal, Bhajan. "Economic Integration and Federalism: Two Views from the High Court of Australia." In *Upholding the Constitution,* vol. 9, ed. John Stone, 76-87. Melbourne: Samuel Griffith Society, 1998.

Guerrera, Orietta. "No Kyoto Accord Despite Greenhouse Gas Progress." *Age* (Melbourne), 19 September 2003.

Hall, Kermit L. *The Oxford Guide to United States Supreme Court Decisions.* New York: Oxford, 1999.

Harrison, Kathryn. "Federalism, Environmental Protection and Blame Avoidance." In *New Trends in Canadian Federalism,* ed. François Rocher and Miriam Smith, 414-38. Peterborough: Broadview, 1995.

–. *Passing the Buck: Federalism and Canadian Environmental Policy.* Vancouver: UBC Press, 1996.

–. "Regulation of Pulp Mill Effluents in the Canadian Federal State." *Canadian Journal of Political Science* 29, 3 (1996): 469-96.

Heard, Andrew. *Canadian Constitutional Conventions: The Marriage of Law and Politics.* Toronto: Oxford University Press, 1991.

Hogg, Peter. *Constitutional Law of Canada.* 1st ed. Toronto: Carswell, 1977.

–. *Constitutional Law of Canada.* 4th ed. Scarborough: Carswell, 1996.

–. *Constitutional Law of Canada.* Looseleaf ed. Scarborough: Carswell, 1997.

–. "Is the Supreme Court of Canada Biased in Constitutional Cases?" *Canadian Bar Review* 57, 4 (1979): 721-39.

–. "Subsidiarity and the Division of Powers in Canada." *National Journal of Constitutional Law* 3 (1993): 341-55.

Hogg, Peter, and Warren Grover. "The Constitutionality of the Competition Bill." *Canadian Business Law Journal* 1 (1976): 197-228.

Howard, A.E. Dick. "*Garcia:* Of Federalism and Constitutional Values." *Publius: The Journal of Federalism* 16 (1986): 17-31.

Hudson, Phillip. "Senate Passes the New Tax Deal." *Age* (Melbourne), 29 June 1999.

Jackson, Vicki C. "Holistic Interpretation: *Fitzpatrick v. Bitzer* and our Bifurcated Constitution." *Stanford Law Review* 53, 5 (2001): 1259-1310.

Jhappan, Rhada. "The Federal-Provincial Power-grid and Aboriginal Self-Government." In *New Trends in Canadian Federalism,* ed. François Rocher and Miriam Smith, 155-86. Peterborough: Broadview, 1995.

Laskin, Bora. "Peace, Order, and Good Government Re-Examined." *Canadian Bar Review* 25, 10 (1947): 1054-87.

Laskin, Bora, and G.P. Browne. "The Judicial Committee and the British North America Act" (book review). *Canadian Public Administration* 10 (1967): 514.

Lederman, W.R. "Unity and Diversity in Canadian Federalism." *Canadian Bar Review* 53, 3 (1975): 595-620.

Lee, H.P. "The High Court and the External Affairs Power." In *Australian Constitutional Perspectives,* ed. H.P. Lee and George Winterton, 60-90. Sydney: Law Book Company, 1992.

Leuchtenburg, William E. "The Origins of FDR's Court Packing Plan." In *Supreme Court Review 1966,* ed. Phillip Kurland, 347-400. Chicago: University of Chicago Press, 1966.

–. *The Supreme Court Reborn: The Constitutional Revolution in the Age of Roosevelt.* New York: Oxford University Press, 1995.

Lindell, Geoffrey. "Recent Developments in the Judicial Interpretation of the Australian Constitution." In *Future Directions in Australian Constitutional Law: Essays in Honour of Professor Leslie Zines,* ed. Geoffrey Lindell, 1-46. Sydney: Federation Press, 1994.

Livingston, William. *Federalism and Constitutional Change.* Oxford: Clarendon, 1956.

MacDonald, Janine. "Senate Set to OK Green Shake-Up." *Age* (Melbourne), 23 June 1999.

MacDonald, Janine, and Chris Ryan. "UN Says No to Mining at Jabiluka." *Age* (Melbourne), 26 November 1998.

Macdonald, Vincent. "The British North America Act: Past and Future." *Canadian Bar Review* 15, 6 (1937): 393-400.

MacKay, A. Wayne. "The Supreme Court of Canada and Federalism: Does/Should Anyone Care Anymore?" *Canadian Bar Review* 80 (2001): 241-81.

Macpherson, James C. "Justice Jean Beetz: A Rich and Enduring Legacy in Canadian Constitutional Scholarship and Jurisprudence." *Revue Juridique Themis* 28 (1994): 761-70.

Makin, Kirk. "The Duel to Decide Gun Control." *Globe and Mail,* 19 February 2000, A13.

Mallory, J.R. *Social Credit and the Federal Power in Canada.* Toronto: University of Toronto Press, 1954.

Marlin, Richard. "The External Affairs Power and Environmental Protection in Australia." *Federal Law Review* 24, 1 (1996): 71-92.

Maslove, Allan M. "The Canada Health and Social Transfer: Forcing Issues." In *How Ottawa Spends 1996-97: Life under the Knife,* ed. Gene Swimmer, 283-301. Ottawa: Carleton University Press, 1996.

Mathews, R.L., and W.R.C. Jay. *Federal Finance: Intergovernmental Financial Relations in Australia since Federation.* Melbourne: Nelson, 1972.

Mauro, Tony. "Alpha Rehnquist." *The American Lawyer,* 8 January 2003, n.p.

McCormick, Peter. "Birds of a Feather: Voting Patterns on the Lamer Court 1991-7." *Osgoode Hall Law Journal* 36 (1998): 339-68.

–. "Judges, Journals, and Exegesis: Judicial Leadership and Academic Scholarship." *University of New Brunswick Law Journal* 45 (1996): 139-48.

–. "Judicial Career Patterns and the Delivery of Reasons for Judgement on the Supreme Court of Canada, 1949-1993." *Supreme Court Law Review* 5 (1994): 499-21.

–. "Party Capability Theory and Appellate Success in the Supreme Court of Canada, 1949-1992." *Canadian Journal of Political Science* 26 (1993): 523-40.

McCormick, Peter, and Tammy Praskach. "Judicial Citation, the Supreme Court of Canada, and the Lower Courts: A Statistical Overview and the Influence of Manitoba." *Manitoba Law Journal* 24, 2 (1994): 335-64.

McDonald, Bruce L. "Constitutional Aspects of Canadian Anti-Combines Law Enforcement." *Canadian Bar Review* 47, 2 (1969): 161-240.

McDonald, Forrest. *A Constitutional History of the United States*. Malabar, FL: Krieger Publishing, 1982.

McLachlin, Hon. Beverly. "Courts, Legislatures, and Executives in the Post-Charter Era." *Policy Options* 20, 5 (1999): 41-47.

McMinn, W.G. *A Constitutional History of Australia*. Melbourne: Oxford University Press, 1979.

Meagher, R.P., and W.M.C. Gummow. "Sir Owen Dixon's Heresy." *Australian Law Journal* 54 (1980): 25-29.

Menzies, Robert. *Central Power in the Australian Commonwealth*. London: Cassell, 1967.

Monahan, Patrick. "At Doctrine's Twilight: The Structure of Canadian Federalism." *University of Toronto Law Journal* 34 (1984): 47-99.

–. *Politics and the Constitution: The Charter, Federalism, and the Supreme Court of Canada*. Toronto: Carswell, 1987.

–. "'To the Extent Possible': A Comment on Dispute Settlement in the Agreement on Internal Trade." In *Getting There: An Assessment of the Agreement on Internal Trade*, ed. Michael Trebilcock and Daniel Schwanen, 211-17. Toronto: CD Howe Institute, 1995.

Nethercote, John. "The Engineers' Case: Seventy-Five Years On." In *Proceedings: Sixth Conference of the Samuel Griffith Society*, ed. John Stone, 116-24. Melbourne: Samuel Griffith Society, 1995.

Newman, Jon O. "Between Legal Realism and Neutral Principles: The Legitimacy of Institutional Values." *California Law Review* 72 (1984): 200-16.

Nicholson, Brendan. "Hand-Over Redresses Imbalance." *Age* (Melbourne), 14 August 1998.

Noël, Alain, France St-Hilaire, and Sarah Fortin. "Learning from the SUFA Experience." In *Forging the Canadian Social Union: SUFA and Beyond*, ed. Sarah Fortin, Alain Noël, and France St-Hilaire, 1-30. Montreal: IRPP, 2003.

O'Brien, David M. *Constitutional Law and Politics*. Vol. 1. New York: Norton, 1991.

–. "The Rehnquist Court and Federal Preemption: In Search of a Theory." *Publius: The Journal of Federalism* 23 (1993): 15-31.

Parrish, Michael D. "On Smokes and *Oakes:* A Comment on *RJR-MacDonald v. Canada (A.G.)*." *Manitoba Law Journal* 24 (1997): 665-98.

Peterson, Paul E. *The Price of Federalism*. Washington: Brookings Institution, 1995.

Pickerill, J. Mitchell, and Cornell W. Clayton. "The Rehnquist Court and the Political Dynamics of Federalism." *Perspectives on Politics* 2, 2 (2004): 233-48.

Powell, H. Jefferson. "The Compleat Jeffersonian: Justice Rehnquist and Federalism." *Yale Law Journal* 91 (1982): 1317-70.

Powell, H. Jefferson, and Benjamin J. Preister. "Convenient Shorthand: The Supreme Court and the Language of State Sovereignty." *University of Colorado Law Review* 71 (2000): 645-714.

Pritchett, C. Herman. *Constitutional Law of the Federal System*. Englewood Cliffs, NJ: Prentice-Hall, 1984.

–. *The Roosevelt Court*. New York: Macmillan, 1948.

Richards, Mark J., and Herbert M. Kritzer. "Jurisprudential Regimes in Supreme Court Decision Making." *American Political Science Review* 96, 2 (2002): 305-20.

Risk, Richard. "The Scholars and the Constitution: P.O.G.G. and the Privy Council." *Manitoba Law Journal* 23 (1995): 496-523.

Rocher, François, and Miriam Smith, eds. *New Trends in Canadian Federalism*. Peterborough: Broadview, 1995.

Rosen, Jeffrey. "The Agonizer." *New Yorker*, 11 November 1996: 82-90.

Russell, Peter H. "The *Anti-Inflation* Case: The Anatomy of a Constitutional Decision." *Canadian Public Administration* 20, 4 (1977): 632-65.

–. *Constitutional Odyssey: Can Canadians Become a Sovereign People?* 2nd ed. Toronto: University of Toronto Press, 1993.

–. *The Judiciary in Canada: The Third Branch of Government*. Toronto: McGraw-Hill Ryerson, 1987.

–. *Leading Constitutional Decisions*. Toronto: McClelland and Stewart, 1968.

–. "Overcoming Legal Formalism: The Treatment of the Constitution, the Courts, and Judicial Behaviour in Canadian Political Science." *Canadian Journal of Law and Society* 1 (1986): 5-33.

–. "The Supreme Court and Federal Provincial Relations: The Political Use of Legal Resources." *Canadian Public Policy* 11, 2 (1985): 161-70.

Ryan, Chris. "Biggest Environmental Stoush since Franklin Dam." *Age* (Melbourne), 11 July 1998.

Ryder, Bruce. "The Demise and Rise of the Classical Paradigm in Canadian Federalism: Promoting Autonomy for the Provinces and First Nations," *McGill Law Journal* 36 (1991): 308-81.

Saunders, Cheryl. "Constitutional Arrangements of Federal Systems." *Publius: The Journal of Federalism* 25, 2 (1995): 61-79.

–. *The Federal System*. Papers on Federalism 6. Melbourne: Intergovernmental Relations in Victoria Program, University of Melbourne, 1985.

–. "Fiscal Federalism: A General and Unholy Scramble." In *Australian Federalism: Towards the Second Century*, ed. Greg Craven, 101-30. Melbourne: Melbourne University Press, 1993.

–. "The Mason Court in Context." In *Courts of Final Jurisdiction: The Mason Court in Australia*, ed. Cheryl Saunders, 2-14. Sydney: Federation Press, 1996.

–. "A New Direction for Intergovernmental Arrangements." *Public Law Review* 12 (2001): 274-87.

Sawer, Geoffrey. *Australian Federalism in the Courts*. Carlton, Victoria: Melbourne University Press, 1967.

–. "The External Affairs Power." *Federal Law Review* 14 (1984): 199-207.

–. *Federation under Strain: Australia 1972-1975*. Carlton, Victoria: Melbourne University Press, 1977.

Saywell, John T. *The Lawmakers: Judicial Power and the Shaping of Canadian Federalism*. Toronto: University of Toronto Press, 2002.

Scalia, Antonin. "American Federalism and the Supreme Court." In *The New Federalism: Structures and Infrastructures, American and European Perspectives*, ed. Kjell Åke Modéer, 56-67. Stockholm: Forskningsrådsnämnden, 2000.

Schlesinger, Jr., Arthur M. *The Age of Roosevelt: The Politics of Upheaval*. Vol. 3. Boston: Houghton Mifflin, 1960.

Schneiderman, David. "A Comment on *RJR-MacDonald v. Canada (A.G.)*." *University of British Columbia Law Review* 30 (1996): 165-80.

Schoff, Paul. "The High Court and History: It Still Hasn't Found(ed) What It's Looking For." *Public Law Review* 5 (1994): 253-73.

Schubert, Glendon. *The Judicial Mind: The Attitudes and Ideologies of Supreme Court Justices, 1946-63*. Evanston, IL: Northwestern University Press, 1965.

Scott, F.R. "Centralization and Decentralization in Canadian Federalism." *Canadian Bar Review* 29, 10 (1951): 1095-1125.

–. "The Consequences of the Privy Council Decisions." *Canadian Bar Review* 15, 6 (1937): 485-94.

–. "Some Privy Counsel." *Canadian Bar Review* 28, 7 (1950): 780.

Segal, Jeffrey A., and Harold J. Spaeth. *The Supreme Court and the Attitudinal Model*. New York: Cambridge University Press, 1993.

Selway, B.M. "Hughes Case and the Referral of Powers." *Public Law Review* 12 (2001): 288-300.

Shapiro, Martin. "Public Law and Judicial Politics." In *Political Science: The State of the Discipline II*, ed. A. Finifter, 365-81. Washington, DC: American Political Science Association, 1993.

Sharpe, Robert, and Kent Roach. *Brian Dickson: A Judge's Journey*. Toronto: University of Toronto Press, 2003.

Simeon, Richard. "Criteria for Choice in Federal Systems." *Queen's Law Journal* 8: 131-57.

–. *Federal-Provincial Diplomacy*. Toronto: University of Toronto Press, 1971.

Simeon, Richard, and Ian Robinson. *State, Society, and the Development of Canadian Federalism*. Royal Commission on the Economic Union and Development Prospects for Canada 71. Toronto: University of Toronto Press, 1990.

Smiley, Donald. *Canada in Question: Federalism in the Eighties*. 3rd ed. Toronto: McGraw-Hill, 1980.

Smiley, Donald, and Ronald L. Watts. *Intrastate Federalism in Canada*. Research Studies for the Royal Commission on the Economic Union and Development Prospects for Canada 39. Toronto: University of Toronto Press, 1985.

Smith, Jennifer. "Canadian Confederation and the Influence of American Federalism." *Canadian Journal of Political Science* 21, 3 (1988): 444-63.

–. *The Meaning of Provincial Equality in Canadian Federalism*. Working Papers 1. Kingston: Institute of Intergovernmental Relations, Queen's University, 1998.

–. "The Origins of Judicial Review in Canada." *Canadian Journal of Political Science* 16, 2 (1983): 115-34.

Smith, Rogers. "Political Jurisprudence, the 'New Institutionalism,' and the Future of Public Law." *American Political Science Review* 82, 1 (1988): 89-108.

Sossin, Lorne. "Salvaging the Welfare State: The Prospects for Judicial Review of the Canadian Health and Social Transfer." *Dalhousie Law Journal* 21, 1 (1998): 141-98.

–. "The Sounds of Silence: Law Clerks, Policy Making, and the Supreme Court of Canada." *UBC Law Review* 30, 2 (1996): 279-308.

Stevenson, Garth. *Rail Transport and Australian Federalism*. Canberra: Centre for Research on Federal Financial Relations, 1987.

Story, Joseph. *Commentaries on the Constitution of the United States*. 3rd ed. Boston: Little Brown, 2001 [1858].

Strayer, Barry. *The Canadian Constitution and the Courts: The Function and Scope of Judicial Review*. Toronto: Butterworths, 1988.

Sullivan, Kathleen. "Duelling Sovereignties: *U.S. Term Limits, Inc. v. Thornton*." *Harvard Law Review* 109 (1995): 78-109.

Sunstein, Cass. *Legal Reasoning and Political Conflict*. New York: Oxford University Press, 1996.

Swinton, Katherine. "Courting Our Way to Economic Integration: Judicial Review and the Canadian Economic Union." *Canadian Business Law Journal* 25 (1995): 280-304.

–. "Federalism under Fire: The Role of the Supreme Court of Canada." *Law and Contemporary Problems* 55, 1 (1992): 121-46.

–. "Law, Politics, and the Enforcement of the Agreement on Internal Trade." In *Getting There: An Assessment of the Agreement on Internal Trade*, ed. Michael Trebilcock and Daniel Schwanen, 196-209. Toronto: C.D. Howe Institute, 1995.

–. *The Supreme Court and Canadian Federalism: The Laskin-Dickson Years*. Toronto: Carswell, 1990.

Tremblay, Guy. "The Supreme Court of Canada: Final Arbiter of Political Conflicts." In *The Supreme Court of Canada as an Instrument of Political Change*. Research Studies for the Royal Commission on the Economic Union and Development Prospects for Canada, 47, ed. Ivan Bernier and Andrée Lajoie, 179-201. Toronto: University of Toronto Press, 1986.

Tribe, Lawrence H. "Unraveling *National League of Cities*: The New Federalism and Affirmative Rights to Essential Government Services." *Harvard Law Review* 90, 6 (1977): 1065-1104.

Trudeau, Pierre. *Federalism and the French Canadians*. Toronto: Macmillan, 1968.

–. *Federal-Provincial Grants and the Federal Spending Power*. Ottawa: Queen's Printer, 1969.

–. "The Practice and Theory of Federalism." In *Social Purpose for Canada,* ed. Michael Oliver, 371-93. Toronto: University of Toronto Press, 1961.

Tushnet, Mark. *Taking the Constitution Away from the Courts*. Princeton, NJ: Princeton University Press, 1999.

Van Sickel, Robert W. *Not a Particularly Different Voice: The Jurisprudence of Sandra Day O'Connor.* New York: Peter Lang, 1998.

Vipond, Robert. *Liberty and Community: Canadian Federalism and the Failure of the Constitution*. Albany: SUNY Press, 1991.

–. "1787 and 1867: The Federal Principle and Canadian Confederation Reconsidered." *Canadian Journal of Political Science* 22, 1 (1989): 3-26.

Wahl, Andrew. "Trade Secrets: Why Is Nothing Being Done about Interprovincial Barriers?" *Canadian Business* 29 May 2000: 62.

Watts, Ronald L. *Comparing Federal Systems*. 2nd ed. Montreal and Kingston: McGill-Queen's University Press, 1999.

–. *The Spending Power in Federal Systems: A Comparative Study.* Kingston: Institute for Intergovernmental Relations, 1999.

Wechsler, Herbert. "The Political Safeguards of Federalism: The Role of the States in the Composition and Selection of the National Government." *Columbia Law Review* 53 (1954): 543-60.

–. "Toward Neutral Principles of Constitutional Law." *Harvard Law Review* 73, 1 (1959): 1-35.

Weiler, Paul C. *In the Last Resort: A Critical Study of the Supreme Court of Canada*. Toronto: Carswell-Methuen, 1974.

Weller, Patrick, and Jenny Flemming. "The Commonwealth." In *Australian Politics and Government: The Commonwealth, the States, and the Territories*, ed. Jeremy Moon and Campbell Sharman, 12-40. Cambridge, UK: Cambridge University Press, 2003.

Wheare, K.C. *Federal Government.* 4th ed. New York: Oxford University Press, 1964.

Whincop, Michael J. "The National Scheme for Corporations and the Referral of Powers: A Sceptical View." *Public Law Review* 12 (2001): 263-73.

Whitlam, Gough. *On Australia's Constitution*. Camberwell, Victoria: Widescope, 1977.

–. *The Whitlam Government 1972-1975*. Ringwood, Victoria: Penguin, 1985.

Whittington, Keith E. "Commentary: Taking What They Give Us: Explaining the Court's Federalism Offensive." *Duke Law Journal* 51 (2001): 477-520.

Zines, Leslie. "The Commonwealth." In *Australian Federation: Towards the Second Century*, ed. Greg Craven, 70-101. Melbourne: Melbourne University Press, 1993.

–. "Federal Theory and Australian Federalism: A Legal Perspective." In *Australian Federalism*, ed. Brian Galligan, 16-44. Melbourne: Longman Cheshire, 1989.

–. *The High Court and the Constitution*. Melbourne: Butterworths, 1991.

Index

Avigail Eisenberg (ed.)
Diversity and Equality: The Changing Framework of Freedom in Canada (2006)

Randy K. Lippert
Sanctuary, Sovereignty, Sacrifice: Canadian Sanctuary Incidents, Power, and Law (2005)

James B. Kelly
Governing with the Charter: Legislative and Judicial Activism and Framers' Intent (2005)

Dianne Pothier and Richard Devlin (eds.)
Critical Disability Theory: Essays in Philosophy, Politics, Policy, and Law (2005)

Susan G. Drummond
Mapping Marriage Law in Spanish Gitano Communities (2005)

Louis A. Knafla and Jonathan Swainger (eds.)
Laws and Societies in the Canadian Prairie West, 1670-1940 (2005)

Ikechi Mgbeoji
Global Biopiracy: Patents, Plants, and Indigenous Knowledge (2005)

Florian Sauvageau, David Schneiderman, and David Taras, with Ruth Klinkhammer and Pierre Trudel
The Last Word: Media Coverage of the Supreme Court of Canada (2005)

Gerald Kernerman
Multicultural Nationalism: Civilizing Difference, Constituting Community (2005)

Pamela A. Jordan
Defending Rights in Russia: Lawyers, the State, and Legal Reform in the Post-Soviet Era (2005)

Anna Pratt
Securing Borders: Detention and Deportation in Canada (2005)

Kirsten Johnson Kramar
Unwilling Mothers, Unwanted Babies: Infanticide in Canada (2005)

W.A. Bogart
Good Government? Good Citizens? Courts, Politics, and Markets in a Changing Canada (2005)

Catherine Dauvergne
Humanitarianism, Identity, and Nation: Migration Laws in Canada and Australia (2005)

Michael Lee Ross
First Nations Sacred Sites in Canada's Courts (2005)

Andrew Woolford
Between Justice and Certainty: Treaty Making in British Columbia (2005)

John McLaren, Andrew Buck, and Nancy Wright (eds.)
Despotic Dominion: Property Rights in British Settler Societies (2004)

Georges Campeau
From UI to EI: Waging War on the Welfare State (2004)

Alvin J. Esau
The Courts and the Colonies: The Litigation of Hutterite Church Disputes (2004)

Christopher N. Kendall
Gay Male Pornography: An Issue of Sex Discrimination (2004)

Roy B. Flemming
Tournament of Appeals: Granting Judicial Review in Canada (2004)

Constance Backhouse and Nancy L. Backhouse
The Heiress vs the Establishment: Mrs. Campbell's Campaign for Legal Justice (2004)

Christopher P. Manfredi
Feminist Activism in the Supreme Court: Legal Mobilization and the Women's Legal Education and Action Fund (2004)

Annalise Acorn
Compulsory Compassion: A Critique of Restorative Justice (2004)

Jonathan Swainger and Constance Backhouse (eds.)
People and Place: Historical Influences on Legal Culture (2003)

Jim Phillips and Rosemary Gartner
Murdering Holiness: The Trials of Franz Creffield and George Mitchell (2003)

David R. Boyd
Unnatural Law: Rethinking Canadian Environmental Law and Policy (2003)

Ikechi Mgbeoji
Collective Insecurity: The Liberian Crisis, Unilateralism, and Global Order (2003)

Rebecca Johnson
Taxing Choices: The Intersection of Class, Gender, Parenthood, and the Law (2002)

John McLaren, Robert Menzies, and Dorothy E. Chunn (eds.)
Regulating Lives: Historical Essays on the State, Society, the Individual, and the Law (2002)

Joan Brockman
Gender in the Legal Profession: Fitting or Breaking the Mould (2001)

Printed and bound in Canada by Friesens
Set in Stone by Artegraphica Design Co. Ltd.
Copy editor: Dallas Harrison
Proofreader: Sarah Munro
Indexer: Lillian Ashworth